61890

W9-AAF-099

GV
1002.95
.U5
S39
1998

Schwartz, Brett C.,
1965-

Competitive tennis.

$17.95

DATE

WITHDRAWN

BAKER & TAYLOR

61890

Competitive Tennis

BRETT C. SCHWARTZ
Assistant Men's Tennis Coach
Louisiana State University

CHRIS A. DAZET
Director of Tennis
Bocage Racquet Club

Human Kinetics

Library of Congress Cataloging-In-Publication Data

Schwartz, Brett C., 1965–
Competitive tennis / Brett C. Schwartz and Chris A. Dazet.
p. cm.
ISBN 0-88011-755-9
1. Tennis--United States. I. Dazet, Chris A., 1964-
II. Title.
GV1002.95.U5S39 1998 97-38949
796.342'0973--dc21 CIP

ISBN: 0-88011-755-9

Copyright © 1998 by Brett C. Schwartz and Chris A. Dazet

All rights reserved. Except for use in a review, the reproduction or utilization of this work in any form or by any electronic, mechanical, or other means, now known or hereafter invented, including xerography, photocopying, and recording, and in any information storage and retrieval system, is forbidden without the written permission of the publisher.

Acquisitions Editor: Martin Barnard; **Developmental Editor:** Marni Basic; **Assistant Editor:** Henry V. Woolsey; **Copyeditor:** Barbara Field; **Proofreader:** Erin Cler; **Graphic Designer:** Robert Reuther; **Graphic Artist:** Joe Bellis; **Photo Editor:** Boyd LaFoon; **Cover Designer:** Jack Davis; **Photographer (cover):** © David Stoecklein; **Photographer (interior):** Jennifer Abelson, except where otherwise noted. Photos on pages 1, 3, 167, and 225 by Tom Roberts; **Illustrators:** Joe Bellis and Keith Blomberg; **Printer:** United Graphics

Human Kinetics books are available at special discounts for bulk purchase. Special editions or book excerpts can also be created to specification. For details, contact the Special Sales Manager at Human Kinetics.

Printed in the United States of America

10 9 8 7 6 5 4 3 2 1

Human Kinetics
Web site: http://www.humankinetics.com/

United States: Human Kinetics, P.O. Box 5076, Champaign, IL 61825-5076
1-800-747-4457
e-mail: humank@hkusa.com

Canada: Human Kinetics, Box 24040, Windsor, ON N8Y 4Y9
1-800-465-7301 (in Canada only)
e-mail: humank@hkcanada.com

Europe: Human Kinetics, P.O. Box IW14, Leeds LS16 6TR, United Kingdom
(44) 1132 781708
e-mail: humank@hkeurope.com

Australia: Human Kinetics, 57A Price Avenue, Lower Mitcham, South Australia 5062
(088) 277 1555
e-mail: humank@hkaustralia.com

New Zealand: Human Kinetics, P.O. Box 105-231, Auckland 1
(09) 523 3462
e-mail: humank@hknewz.com

To Loren
For all of your love, support, and understanding through the trials of such a tedious undertaking. Thank you.

Brett C. Schwartz

To Mom and Dad
Thank you for your love, support, encouragement, generosity, and belief in me.

Chris A. Dazet

Contents

Foreword

Competitive Tennis is the most comprehensive book ever written about the National Tennis Rating Program (NTRP) and how to play better tennis as you move up the NTRP ladder. Whether you're new to tournament tennis or trying to win a city or club championship, you will find that this book covers all the skills and drills you need to improve your game.

The book is organized according to the NTRP levels. If you're a player, it will help you develop your game in a meaningful way by showing you the skills you need to master, both at your current level and at the next level. If you're a coach, the drills will help you plan lessons and drill sessions to help your players develop.

The NTRP provides every player the opportunity to compete at his or her own skill level. *Competitive Tennis* shows you how to continue to improve. It will add to the fun you'll have playing a game that offers so many benefits—sociability, creativity, competitiveness, mental focus, and fitness.

The NTRP continues to grow and develop in the tennis community. I encourage you to find out more about the opportunities to participate with players at your skill level and to seek out programs and events that allow for your development.

Good luck as you become a more skilled player.

David E. Schobel
Director of Adult Tennis, United States Tennis Association

Preface

With the advent of the National Tennis Rating Program (NTRP) Classification System and the United States Tennis Association (USTA) League, tennis levels in the 1990s have become more specific and more competitive. As an intermediate player in the early 1980s, for example, you might have been generically designated a B player, a broad classification of limited value. With the NTRP system, you are now specifically rated as either a 3.0 player or a 3.5 player, depending on your skill, and you only compete against players of the same rating. Because the characteristics of players at each level are specifically defined in the NTRP Classification System, strengths and weaknesses can be more readily identified and improved.

Competitive Tennis does what no other book does. It specifically explains the various levels of the USTA League and how to be successful and advance through each level. No matter what your current level, we provide you with a specific blueprint for improving your game, whether or not you are a USTA League participant. We use the NTRP Classification System characteristics and our years of coaching experience to show you how to be successful at your level and improve enough to advance to the next level—from the 2.5 league through the 5.0 league. With this book, you can turn to the chapter for your level and immediately begin learning the things you need to know to be successful. You don't have to work through information that may be too advanced for you or that doesn't apply to your situation. And when you've been promoted to the next level, you can turn to the next chapter and continue your success! After using this book, you will have a better understanding of your own game and those of your opponents. This understanding makes you a more informed, more knowledgeable, and better tennis player.

If you are a teaching professional, you can use this book to expand your knowledge of the NTRP and USTA League levels and your knowledge of the drills you can use to teach these levels.

Competitive Tennis provides you with new and stimulating information to pass along to your students.

For the player, we wrote this book to parallel your progression through the levels: stroke by stroke, formation by formation, strategy by strategy, and drill by drill. We show you how to correct the most common stroking errors. We give you executable strategies to use against the most common formations. We tell you how and when to play offense and defense in each situation. We show you how and when to change your strategy based on your limitations. We also give you drills to reinforce what we're showing you, so that it becomes second nature—leaving you free to think about the overall match and not about each individual shot. And all these things are written specifically for your level of play and explained in terms you can understand!

How often have you gone into a match without a specific game plan? How often have you asked yourself, "What should I have done in that situation?" How often have you told yourself, "I know I can play just as well as players at the next highest level"? The truth is, you *can* be successful at your level and beyond, but you need guidance in clarifying your strategy and sifting through the multitude of formations and shots.

We know this is true, because we've witnessed it for years in our everyday lives as teaching professionals. We have a combined 12 years of experience as USTA-certified verifiers. This responsibility requires us to watch men and women whom we've never seen play tennis and assign them an NTRP rating based on the NTRP Classification System characteristics. In addition, we handle appeals made during the league when a player is deemed too strong or too weak to play at a certain level. We work with or coach teams that have played at every level of the USTA League, sending teams to both district and sectional playoffs. All of this is testament to our belief in and commitment to the USTA League.

Competitive Tennis helps you understand the game at your level, so you can grasp its intricacies. It helps you learn how to capitalize on your strengths and improve your stroking and strategic weaknesses. It shows you what it takes to get to the next level and beyond.

Acknowledgments

I was once told that if you have one true friend in the world, you're a lucky man. If that's the case, then I've been truly blessed. I thank my friends who have helped in ways they might never know or understand: Rich and Kris, Dennis and Vickie, Ed and Elsa, Rich and Beth, Jason and TY, John and Adrienne, Helene and Al, Helen and Ralph, David, Mike, Sean, Djuana, La Famille Durand, John, Nancy, Steph, Robert, Danny, James B., Lynn, Timmy, Jeff, Ben, Chris, the Dietz family, the Landry family, the McNamara family, and the Owens family. And I thank the Florida group: Diamond Dave, Sandra, Cissy, Holly, David M., Kelly, R.E.B., Sharon, Leroy, "Doc" Rick, and Lyle.

Thanks to all the people I've taught or taught with, along the way, who have unknowingly helped me write this book. And special thanks to Chris Dazet, who is truly one of the best adult group teachers in America.

And last, but certainly not least, thanks to my wonderful parents, Wilfred and Patricia Schwartz, for all their love and support.

—Brett Schwartz

Through the game of tennis, I have turned my favorite sport into a long, fulfilling career. Three components have made this teaching career a reality and I would like to acknowledge all of them. First, I thank the management, members, and all my friends at the tennis clubs I have belonged to or worked at. These include Sunrise, Bissonet-Maned Downs, Driftwood, and Green Acres community clubs in Metairie, Louisiana; the Rivercenter in New Orleans; Tops' l and the Sandestin Resorts in Destin, Florida; and especially the Beach Club in Metairie where I began and Bocage Racquet Club in Baton Rouge where I first taught full-time and am still enjoying a great career.

I also thank the people I have worked with and learned from: Brett, Timmy, Ronnie, Kenny, Tommy, Jerry, Harry, Rick, Jan, Ed, Del, Burgis, Steve and Ann, Rob and Karen, Kathryn, Chad, Kirsty, Jeff, Coach Jerry, Nat, Ashley, Arthur, Melee, Sally, Chris, Richie, Ray, Alfredo, Daddy-Al, Leon, Stephanie, Angel, and especially Jason, my TY, and my partner, Vikki.

More people have helped me through the years I have taught, obviously, too many to name. I give a special thanks to Dr. Bruce and Ona and their family, at whose court I taught my "Wild and Crazy Ladies" in Metairie; Bev, Newt and Ann Reynolds; Miss Carolyn and B.J.; Ben (for going first) and all the great teams and individuals I've coached at Bocage. And of course, I thank Brett Schwartz for making our ideas a reality.

—Chris Dazet

And last together we thank all the staff members at Human Kinetics for their help with this book: Marni, Martin, Cathy, and Boyd (for putting up with us). Our appreciation goes also to the USTA (Dave Schobel and Randy Gregson), LTA (Dianna and Sally), Wilson Sporting Goods (Mike Wallace), and Ms. Jones, and for the photos, Jennifer Abelson, Bocage Racquet Club, and our models, the Gov., Rose, Fanny, Pops, and TY.

Special thanks to Chanda, Mary Joe, and Ken for their generosity and time in providing us with quotes for our book.

Introduction

In the United States, thousands of tennis tournaments are played each week. In each tournament, players with characteristics in common are grouped together: divided by age, team, club affiliation, playing ability, and so on. Of all the aforementioned ways to group players, the fairest is to group them by playing ability. Within this grouping, dozens of classification systems are used to rate the players. The traditional methods of classification involve a letter or a name for each class, such as A, B, C or beginner, advanced beginner, intermediate. These classification systems serve their purpose—grouping like players—but they are broad and subjective. Therefore, the United States Tennis Association (USTA) teamed with the United States Professional Tennis Association (USPTA) and the International Health, Racquet Sportsclub Association (IHRSA) to adopt a new, more objective system called the National Tennis Rating Program (NTRP) which could be used universally to unify the classification of players throughout the United States.

The NTRP classification system is unique in that it defines, in writing, the playing characteristics of each of its levels. Initially, players seeking a general rating in this system have to go to an NTRP Verification Clinic conducted by approved section verifiers who are usually USPTA or United States Professional Tennis Registry (USPTR) certified tennis professionals. Once you've been rated and play in the USTA League, your results are put into a computer program that objectively compares your wins and losses with other players at your level to give you a rating. By defining the playing characteristics and objectively rating the players, the NTRP classification system rates players more accurately, which makes for better, more even competition. As a result, there has been a resurgence in tournament and league competition.

USTA-sanctioned adult tournaments have traditionally been contested by age; however, many players have been reluctant to play these tournaments, fearing they would get clobbered by the best players early on. As a result, more and more tournaments now use the NTRP classification system to determine their various events. For example, before 1990, all the divisions for state-sanctioned adult tournaments in Louisiana were formulated according to age. In 1997, 12 of the 38 state-sanctioned adult tournaments offered NTRP divisions, with more offering NTRP divisions each year. These tournaments give players, who might otherwise have lost in the first round in one of the age divisions, as good a chance as any of the other

participants to experience the tournament. Imagine what it would feel like to be in the semifinals or finals of a tournament! Furthermore, many states offer state NTRP rankings. For example, Colorado gives state rankings to players from the 2.5 to the 5.0 levels in singles, doubles, and mixed doubles. This provides extra incentive and reward for participation. Imagine the satisfaction you would get from being the best 3.0 or 3.5 player in your state! Most of these things are now possible because the new NTRP tournaments give you a chance to compete on an equal playing field.

Created by the USTA in 1981, the USTA League expanded to more than 250,000 participants by 1996. The reasons for the league's explosive growth are as follows:

1. It uses only the NTRP classification system, which ensures equal competition for all participants. Therefore, on any given day, you can beat your opponent.
2. It offers competition from the 2.5 to the 5.0 levels. This gives you incentive to improve your tennis, because you can graduate to a higher level. Imagine the satisfaction you would feel having improved your game enough to be promoted to another level by an objective process!
3. It holds state, regional, and national championships. These championships give you incentive to set competitive goals. Imagine what it would feel like to be an official USTA national champion.
4. It provides a great setting for meeting other players. By joining a team, you may meet a new practice partner or friend. And we all know you can never have enough of either one!

We divide *Competitive Tennis* into chapters that cover each of the levels contested in the USTA League, taking you from the beginning stages of your development, the 2.5 level, to the latter stages, the 5.0 level. Each chapter has four sections: NTRP Guidelines, Objectives, Keys to Success, and Practice Drills. These sections provide you with pertinent information and instruction that relate solely to your situation.

In the NTRP Guidelines section, we (with the help of the USTA) help you identify your playing level and the playing characteristics associated with that level. We give you a fundamental understanding of what you can and can't do, a general awareness of what to expect from your fellow competitors, and a look ahead.

In the Objectives section, we show you the shots and skills you need to develop to improve your game. Some of the objectives apply to the level in which you're reading them, whereas others (which are more difficult to master) apply to the following level but are shots or skills you need to start developing at your level. We explain how and why you need to learn each shot or skill, provide you with building blocks for improving your game, and give you a good preview of what is expected of you at the next level.

In the Keys to Success section, we show you the essential shots and skills and explain the singles and doubles strategies you need to know to be successful at your level. We cover where to hit the ball, where to position yourself, and why you hit the ball and position yourself where you do. By doing this, we create a set of rules that are building blocks to the strategies used at higher levels. At each successive level, we add to the basics you've already learned.

Each chapter ends with two sets of practice drills—one for singles and one for doubles—that help you develop the shots and strategies listed in the Objectives and Keys to Success sections. These drills help you internalize the skills and knowledge you need to be successful, so you're comfortable with them when you play your matches and don't have to figure them out in the heat of battle.

Additionally, each chapter includes a Quick Tips section that lists problems common to your level and their probable solutions. This section provides quick answers to your problems so you can fix them immediately during matches or drill sessions.

When reading *Competitive Tennis*, read the levels immediately preceding and following yours, because they educate you in the natural progressions involved in learning tennis and show you where you've been and where you're going. You know exactly what is expected of you at each level and what to do to improve your game enough to be successful and reach the next level!

Good luck and good tennis!

1

The 2.5 Level

© Claus Anderson

NTRP Guidelines

The verification guidelines for a 2.5-level player, as specified in the NTRP Guidebook, are as follows:

Groundstrokes—Your form on your forehand is developing, and you're prepared for moderately paced shots. Furthermore, because you have grip and preparation problems on your backhand, you often choose to hit your forehand instead.

Serve—You're attempting a full swing on your serve, but your toss is inconsistent. You get the ball into play at a slow pace.

Volley—You're uncomfortable at the net, especially on the backhand side, and frequently use the forehand racquet face on your backhand volley.

Specialty Shots—You lob intentionally but have little control. When receiving the lob, you make contact on the overhead.

Generally, you sustain a rally of slow pace, but you have weak court coverage. This hinders your ability to play consistently, because you don't set up properly for your groundstrokes. In doubles, you usually remain in the initial one-up, one-back formation throughout the point.

OBJECTIVES

Your objectives as a 2.5-level player are basic. To become successful at your level and, consequently, advance to the 3.0 level, you have to conquer five tasks. You must develop consistency and directional intent, learn the defensive lob and how to return high balls, and learn positioning.

Develop Consistency on Your Groundstrokes

Develop consistency on your groundstrokes, because they're the foundation of your game and the building blocks for all the other levels. Consistency is simply your ability to keep the ball in play. However, one fact must be established before we can proceed: Power and consistency are not synonymous for 2.5- to 3.5- and, arguably, 4.0-level players. If players at these levels could hit the ball hard consistently, they would be playing at a higher level. You need only look at the NTRP guidelines for the 4.0- to 4.5-level player to realize that one of the reasons they're able to play at a higher level is that they can maintain rallies at faster paces. Therefore, as a 2.5-level player you first concern yourself with mastering consistency before increasing the speed of the ball. We suggest hitting within a comfortable power range, which means finding a power range within which you can get every ball into play. You'll find very few players at the higher levels who aren't consistent on their groundstrokes, because all points begin from the baseline.

Begin to Learn How to Direct the Ball

Directional intent means that you can hit the ball where you intend. Again, power is not the answer. Your ability to move the ball around the singles court and keep it away from the net player in doubles is more important than trying to overpower your opponent. Although you can win most of your matches at the 2.5 level by being a "human backboard," you must *begin* to learn to control the direction of the ball while you're still at this level. You won't become highly proficient at directing the ball because you can't master directional intent at the 2.5 level. If you could, you wouldn't play 2.5-level tennis. Your ability to direct the ball only slightly gives you an advantage in your matches against other 2.5-level players and puts you well on your way to becoming a 3.0-level player.

Learn to Lob Defensively and to Hit and Return High Balls

Since lobbing and hitting and returning high balls are related, we address both of them in this section.

Defensive Lob

We start with the defensive lob. When hitting the defensive lob, your goal is to land the ball deep in the backcourt. To accomplish this, you must set up with the ball in front of you, so you control the height and the depth of your lob. You control the lob by letting the ball drop below shoulder level, so you stroke through the ball. If you hit the ball above shoulder level, you aren't able to stroke the ball consistently (see figure 1.1, a-b). Note that it isn't always feasible to keep the ball in front of you on a defensive lob, since this shot is often hit while you're running. However, it's a good reference point from which to start learning.

a

Figure 1.1a (a) Player lobbing from below shoulder height (correct form).

b

Figure 1.1b (b) Player lobbing from above shoulder height (incorrect form).

The second phase of the defensive lob involves the coordination of two elements: the effects of the angle of your racquet face and the angle of the upward motion of your stroke on the trajectory of the ball. To become an effective lobber, you must understand how the angle of the racquet face on impact affects the trajectory of the ball. With the angle of your upward swing remaining constant, the more you open your racquet face, the higher and shorter your lobs are (see figure 1.2a). Conversely, the more you close your racquet face, the lower and longer your lobs are (see figure 1.2b). We suggest that you start at a 45-degree angle.

If you keep your racquet face at a 45-degree angle, you can experiment with the angle of the upward swing on the ball, which is the second element of the defensive lob stroke. The angle of the upward swing is similar in effect to the angle of the racquet face. If you swing straight up at the ball, your lobs go higher and land shorter in the court (see figure 1.3a). Conversely, if you swing straight through the ball, your lobs go lower and land deeper in the court (see figure 1.3b). Therefore, to correct short lobs, angle the racquet face at 45 degrees and swing through the ball more. To correct lobs that are

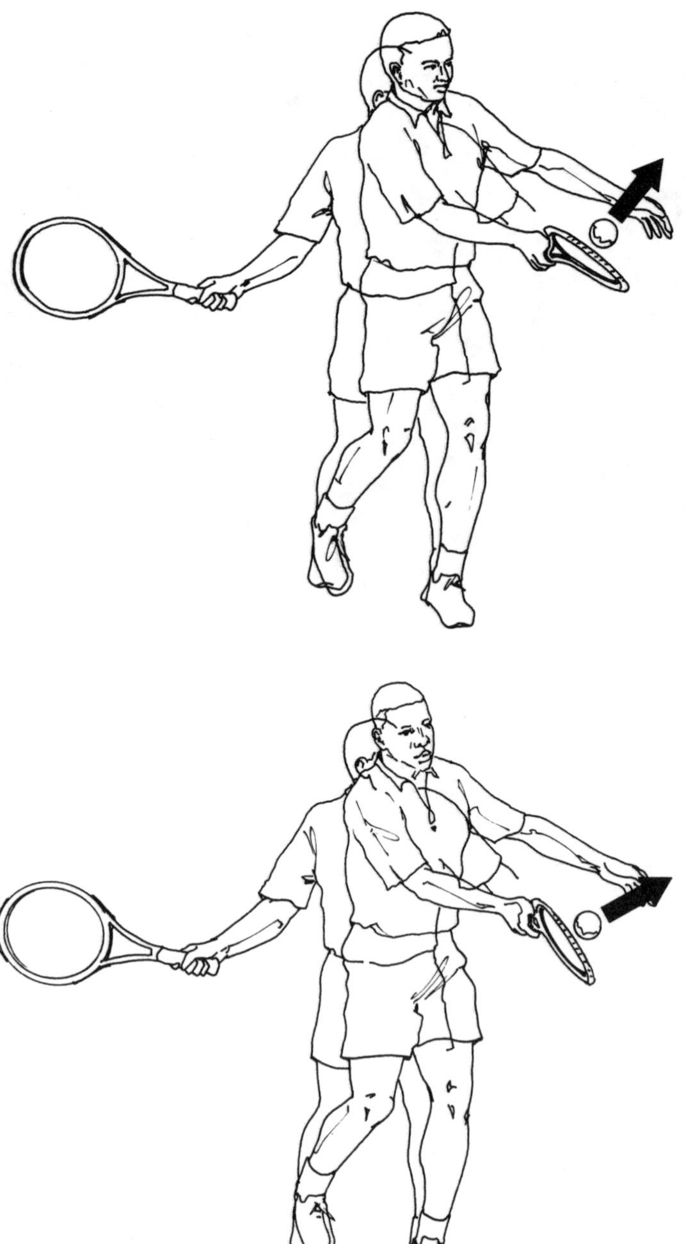

Figure 1.2a-b (a) Player making open-faced contact with lob, sending it upward. (b) Player making less open-faced contact with lob, showing a lower trajectory with the angle of the swing constant.

a

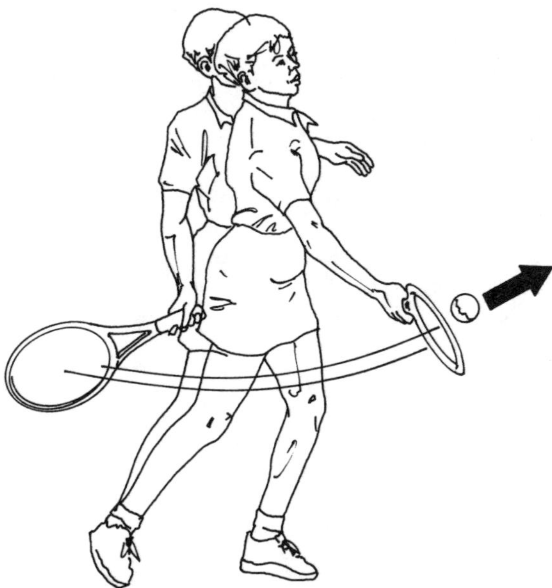

b

Figure 1.3a-b (a) Player hitting straight up for height. (b) Player hitting through the ball for depth with the angle of the racquet face constant at 45°.

going long, start the racquet face at a 45-degree angle and swing up on the ball more. The key is to keep the angle of the racquet face constant so you only have to worry about your upward swing and not both variables: the upward swing and the angle of the racquet face.

The last phase of the defensive lob is the follow-through. Many beginning players are afraid of hitting the ball out, so they stop their follow-through short and don't give the ball a chance to land deep (see figure 1.4, a-c). To give the ball enough speed to land deep in the court, you must make a long follow-through (see figure 1.5, a-c). The key to the follow-through is to keep a steady pace from the beginning to the end of the stroke. This enables you to hit more lobs in play and more easily control their depth and direction. It takes practice to become comfortable with the defensive lob, but if you experiment with its three phases, you'll soon find a range within which you can lob effectively.

a

Figure 1.4a-c Short, choppy follow-through for a defensive lob.

61890

b

c

a

b

Figure 1.5a-c Long, steady follow-through for a defensive lob.

c

Hitting and Returning High Balls

As with lobbing, hitting high balls to your opponent and returning high balls from your opponent requires a lot of footwork. You have to make sure the ball stays in front of you; otherwise you won't give yourself a chance to make the proper swing or control the ball. When returning high balls, back up far enough so you can let the ball drop below shoulder height before you strike it, as you do when you return a lob. If you do this, you'll be able to hit your regular groundstroke, which is a more comfortable and reliable shot. Don't hit the ball from above your shoulders unless you have no other choice, because you lose accuracy and consistency (see figure 1.1b). Also, when hitting a high ball back to your opponent, keep the angle of your racquet face on impact the same as for a groundstroke but swing upward at a sharper angle (see figure 1.6). This arcs the ball higher over the net and deeper into the court, causing it to bounce higher to your opponent. If you can develop this shot, you'll have a weapon that is effective at the 2.5 level.

Figure 1.6 Low-to-high swing for a high ball return with the racquet face square to the net.

Learn the Basic Starting Positions for Singles and Doubles

Positioning is where to stand or move on the court before or during a point to give yourself the maximum chance for success. Although this definition encompasses the starting position and movement during the point, we only address the starting position in this section. (Movement is covered in the Keys to Success section under strategy.) Since every point starts with a serve and a return, we look at these two aspects of positioning first.

Starting Position for Singles

When serving to either the ad or deuce court, stand within 1 yard of the center mark (player A in figure 1.7). This immediately puts you in the middle of the court after you make the serve, which is the proper position for rallying from the baseline. After you serve, don't move into no-man's-land (as the majority of 2.5-level players do), because you won't give yourself enough time to react to your opponent's return and will probably have to hit a difficult shot from your shoelaces (see figure 1.7). Instead, position yourself 1 yard behind the baseline, which gives you enough time to react and improves your chances for an easier shot.

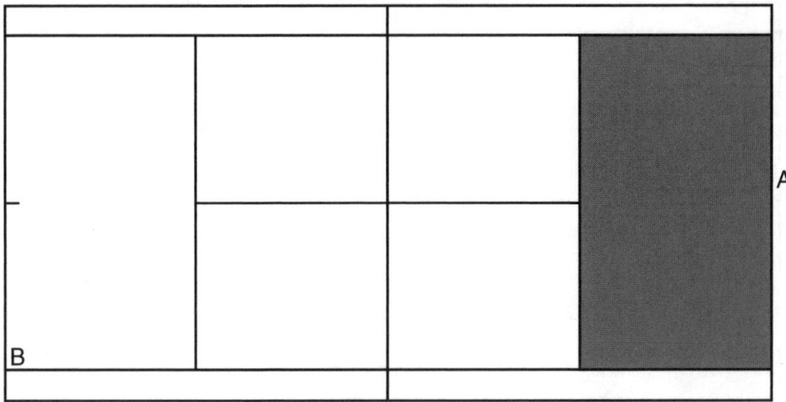

Figure 1.7 Serving position of player A; returning position of player B. The shaded area is no-man's-land.

When returning serve, stand back far enough in the court so you can keep the ball in front of you. A good starting point for the return is to stand closer to the service line against a player who serves short and/or soft and closer to the baseline against a player who serves deep and/or hard. This starting position allows you to control the ball, because you're able to make contact with it in front of your body. Furthermore, it is good practice for future levels, because you'll be able to step into the ball and use your weight to generate more power. Also, set up 1 foot inside the singles line (player B in figure 1.7). This allows you to cover balls hit to your left or right equally well. These singles positions are basic, yet essential, because they are building blocks for climbing the NTRP Ladder.

Starting Position for Doubles

The starting position for serving in doubles is different from singles because you have a different objective. In doubles, you're responsible for the half of the court from which you're serving; therefore, you start halfway between the center mark and the doubles line (player A in figure 1.8). This positions you in the middle of your half of the court after the serve, which maximizes your ability to cover your area of responsibility.

When your partner serves, start 1 yard from the net in the service box on the other half of the court (player B in figure 1.8). This position is closer than we recommend for any other level, because volleying is a weakness at the 2.5 level. Being 1 yard from the net makes

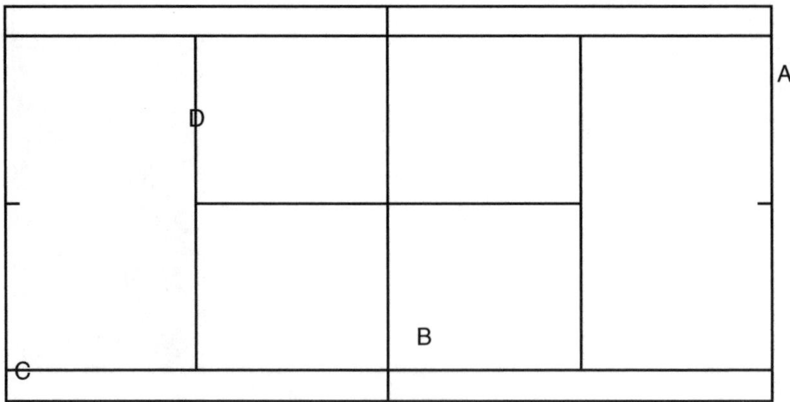

Figure 1.8 Players' positions for doubles.

it easier to volley, because you only need to contact the ball in the strings to keep it in play. Therefore, your net game is more consistent.

When you're returning in doubles, stand back far enough in the court so you can keep the ball in front of you. You do this for the same reasons you do it in singles: to control the ball and to learn the preparation for better power generation. Also, set up with one foot on the singles line (player C in figure 1.8), because it allows you to cover balls hit to your left or right equally well by nullifying the outward movement of the doubles server (player A) as compared to the true singles server (player A in figure 1.7).

If you're the returner's partner, stand in the middle of the service line on your half of the court (player D in figure 1.8). This position helps you accomplish two things. First, if your partner (player C) hits his return to the net person (player B), you cut off player B's angle and give yourself a chance to return his shot (player D in figure 1.9). Second, you can call the serves better. If you follow these basic starting positions, you give yourself a better chance for success.

KEYS TO SUCCESS

The keys to success for the 2.5-level player are threefold. You must develop the proper form on your groundstrokes and service motion, learn to stroke within your power range, and learn basic singles and doubles strategy.

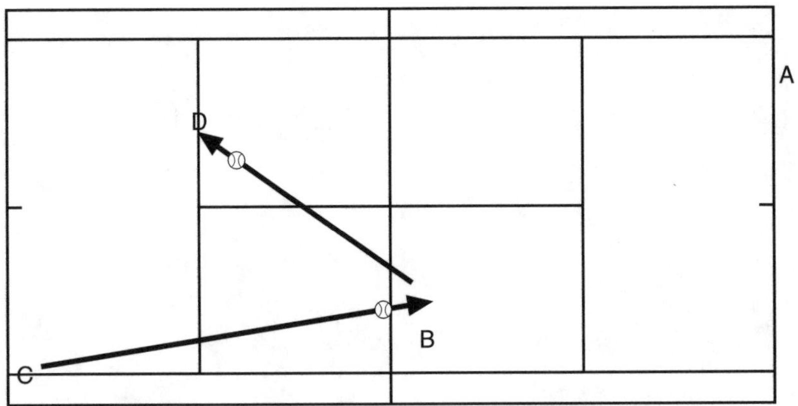

Figure 1.9 Player D cutting off possible angles from player B.

Develop Proper Form on Your Groundstrokes

We attempt to give you food for thought to help expand your knowledge of the proper form and help you correct it by yourself. If you can do this, we believe you'll be a better match player, because you'll be able to self-analyze your errors and, consequently, correct them during your matches.

The first aspect of form that must be addressed is footwork. Footwork is simply setting up the same way for each ball. For example, during a beginner tennis lesson, the professional usually hits the ball perfectly to the student every time, which helps the student enjoy moderate success. However, if the ball is hit away from her, the beginner usually has problems, because she doesn't know how to set up for the ball correctly or where to make contact with it. The proper contact point for hitting groundstrokes is in front of your crossover foot and slightly to the side of your body (to give your arm or arms room to extend), between knee and chest height (see figure 1.10). Therefore, your footwork goal is to move your feet such that every ball is within this hitting area. You can accomplish this by remembering three easy steps:

1. Always bounce on your toes, because it gives you a good start to the ball.
2. Take long steps initially to ensure that you can get to the ball, but take short, choppy steps and bend your knees once you get close. This helps maintain your balance.

Figure 1.10 Player making contact with the ball in the hitting zone.

3. Keep the ball in front of you so you always have a chance to hit the proper stroke. For example, if the ball comes in 10 feet over the net and is going to land on the baseline, it bounces farther behind the baseline than a lower ball of the same speed. Therefore, you have to back up quicker and farther to keep the ball in front of you. This is important because it's easier to hit the ball properly when moving forward than when moving backward, since your weight transfers with your swing when you move forward. Conversely, your weight works against your swing when you move backward because you try to hit the ball in the opposite direction of your body movement (see figure 1.11).

Figure 1.11 Player hitting a groundstroke off her back foot.

If you're successful in accomplishing these three goals, you're able to hit consistently, direct the ball, and generate power on your groundstrokes.

We address the second part of form with a method called quick tips, which players can use to self-analyze their stroking mistakes. We start with groundstroking errors that are common 2.5-level mistakes.

Quick Tips

Identifying Groundstroking Errors

⊖ **Problem**—You're hitting the ball into the net.

⊕ **Solution**—You're probably swinging directly at the ball. To correct this, start your forward swing lower than the ball. You can do this by either lowering your backswing and/or bending your knees more (see figure 1.12). This helps you get under the ball to get it into the air and over the net.

Figure 1.12 Player starting a groundstroke below the ball with her knees bent.

⊖ **Problem**—You're hitting the ball long.

⊕ **Solution 1**—You're probably hitting with the racquet face too open (pointing upward) (see figure 1.13a). In this case, keep your swing the same but slightly close your racquet face (see figure 1.13b). If you've made this change and the ball is still going out, close your racquet face more and try again. This quick tip helps you lower the trajectory of your shot and land the ball in the court more consistently.

⊕ **Solution 2**—If you've closed your racquet face and you're not overswinging, you're probably breaking your wrist at contact, which causes you to hit the ball too hard and lose control. Therefore, firm up your wrist at contact. This takes some variability out of your swing and helps you hit more consistent groundstrokes.

• •

⊖ **Problem**—You're having trouble directing the ball.

⊕ **Solution**—You're probably not aligned with your target. In this case, align your shoulders and hips parallel to the path of your target. For example, if you're a right-hander and want to hit a

a

b

Figure 1.13a-b (a) Player making contact with the ball on a groundstroke with the racquet face open. (b) Player making contact with the ball on a groundstroke with the racquet face less open (more closed).

Figure 1.14 Player aligning his body with a target on a groundstroke.

down-the-line forehand, align your left shoulder and left hip with the target and swing through toward the target (see figure 1.14). This is a good reference point from which to start learning to direct the ball.

Problem—When you attempt to hit the ball down the line, you're hitting it wide.

Solution 1—Check your contact point, because you're probably hitting the ball late. If this is the case, contact the ball earlier in the swing (see figure 1.15). It helps you hit more accurately.

Solution 2—If you're striking the ball early enough, you're probably aiming too close to the line. To correct this, aim 3 feet inside the

Figure 1.15 Player making contact with the ball in front of his right foot on a groundstroke.

line instead of directly at the line. This prevents you from trying to hit too good a shot and helps you keep the ball in play.

Using these quick tips while you're practicing or playing gives you a better understanding of your strokes and helps you out of some tight spots!

Develop Proper Form on Your Service Motion

Developing proper form on your service motion gives you added power and control. We demonstrate the basics of the serve using the following figure sequence.

Figure 1.16 illustrates the proper stance. Your feet are shoulder-width apart for balance, your right foot is directly behind your left (right-handed players), and your left arm is extended and touching the racquet.

Figure 1.17 shows you where to toss the ball. You toss the ball immediately over your right shoulder (1 o'clock), as high as you can reach, and about 3 inches in front of you. Tossing the

Figure 1.16 Service ready position.

Figure 1.17 Where to toss the ball.

ball over your right shoulder is the most natural place from which to hit the ball and allows for maximum power. Contacting the ball as high as you can reach allows for maximum transfer of power from the uncoiling of your body and gives you a better angle down into the service box. Finally, tossing the ball 3 inches into the court forces you to use your body weight on the serve, giving you more power. These three factors combined help you generate more power and give you more control.

Figure 1.18, a-d, shows you the proper toss and service motion. When tossing the ball, hold it with your fingertips for better control, much like a basketball player dribbles a basketball with his fingertips. You start the service motion by simultaneously dropping your hands and the racquet, then start to toss the ball when they separate (figure 1.18a). Once this occurs, your arms progress to a slightly skewed *T* position. When your left arm gets to the *T* position, you toss the ball. At the same time, your right arm starts to bend as if you are throwing a ball (figure 1.18b). Then, with a relaxed wrist, you uncoil upward to the ball and culminate your swing with a wrist snap that is skewed downward at the box (figure 1.18c). Finally, you follow through to the left side of your body (figure 1.18d). These are the basics of the service motion. Remember that the serve is the hardest stroke to learn, and hours of practice are needed to perfect it. We recommend that you hit two baskets of serves before you practice or play a match.

Hit Within Your Power Range

Hitting within your power range means hitting the ball as hard as you can while still keeping it in play on every shot. Once again, consistency takes precedence. Initially, you aren't able to hit the ball very hard and still be consistent. But as you establish a stroke speed you're comfortable with, experiment in practice with increasing the speed of your shots. By trying this in practice, you become more comfortable with increased pace, something you need as you move up the NTRP scale. One thing to remember is that improving shots or pace takes hours of practice and hard work. Also, some people are more athletically inclined than others and improve at a faster rate, but in either case, improvement requires hard work and patience.

a

b

Figure 1.18a-d (a) Hands separating for the toss. (b) Slightly angled *T* position. (c) Racquet snapping over the ball after contact. (d) Follow-through.

c

d

Learn the Basic Strategies for Singles and Doubles

The basic strategies involved in playing 2.5-level singles and doubles are very similar. Both require steady play from the baseline with an eye for changing your strategy when needed. The main difference is the doubles teamwork needed to coordinate the movements between you and your partner with your opponents' shots.

Singles Strategy

At the 2.5 level, take a conservative approach to strategy. You don't want to start the match trying to make things happen. Start by simply keeping the ball in play anywhere in the court. Hit more balls back than your opponent. If your opponent hits five balls back, you hit six balls back. If your opponent hits 10 balls back, you hit 11 balls back. If this strategy doesn't work, it's for one of two reasons. Either you're not executing the strategy properly, which means you're not getting every ball in play, or you're executing the strategy properly but your opponent is better at it than you are, which means you have to modify your game.

You still want to keep every ball in play, but you have to change the height and pace of the ball. First, change the height of the ball, because 2.5-level players have trouble with higher balls. Most of the time, they hit a ball that is shoulder height or higher by swinging overhand instead of hitting their normal stroke. This leads to errors and, ultimately, points for you. Second, move your opponent up and back in the court by varying the pace of the ball, which doesn't mean you hit harder. You hit softer so your opponent has different shots to contend with and has to move forward and backward to hit the ball. This way, you test his footwork ability and sometimes catch him off guard, which translates into easy points for you. If you're really lucky, he'll come to the net, in which case you either hit the ball right at him or lob over his head.

If keeping the ball in play and changing the height and pace of the ball are unsuccessful, your third option is to find a weakness and exploit it. For example, if your opponent has a weak backhand, keep hitting the ball to his backhand. This is the most difficult strategy for you to execute, because you have difficulty directing the ball at the 2.5 level, but try it if none of the other strategies are working. Overall, these are basic strategies, but you don't have to be fancy to win at the 2.5 level.

Doubles Strategy

Since 2.5-level players aren't yet proficient at the net, we suggest a one-up, one-back strategy. Don't go to the net and get into a two-up formation unless you're pulled in by a very short shot (halfway in the service box) and have no other choice (see figure 1.19). Avoid the two-up formation because, at the 2.5 level, you aren't able to volley well enough to win points at the net consistently, and it's extremely difficult for a member of your team to move backward to retrieve any lobs hit by your opponents.

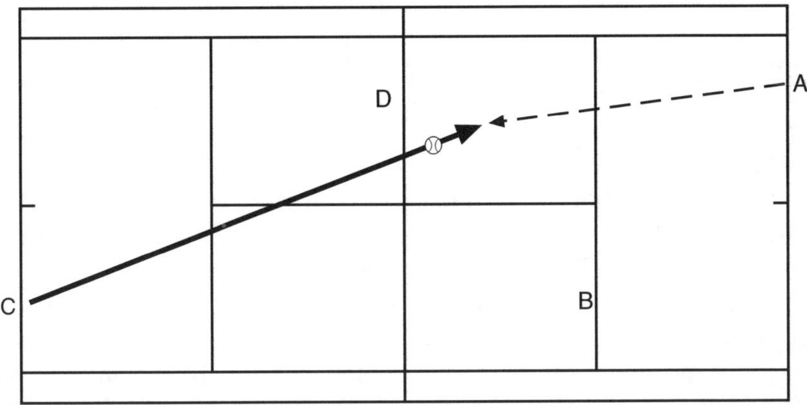

Figure 1.19 Player A being pulled into service box area to return a short ball from player C.

One-Up, One-Back Versus One-Up, One-Back. In this first part of doubles strategy, we show you how to play a one-up, one-back formation against another team playing the same formation. In the one-up, one-back formation, the net player moves forward after her partner's shot passes her opponents' net player and backward after her opponents' return passes her (players B and D in figure 1.20). When you move up and back, you do two things. First, when you move up, you crowd the net (play 1 yard from the net), making it easier to volley. Don't worry about anyone lobbing over your head, because your partner is able to cover it since she's back on the baseline. (If the ball is lobbed over your head, you "switch" by moving diagonally to the service line on the other half of the court to avoid having you and your partner on the same side [player B in figure 1.21]. In this situation, player D makes this same play by advancing to within 1

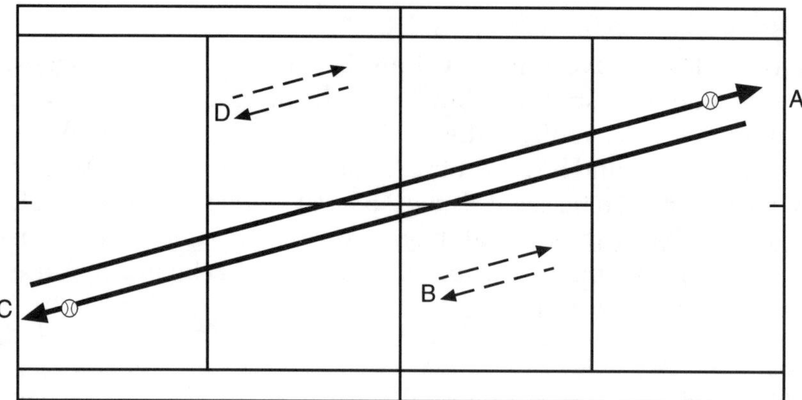

Figure 1.20 Players B and D moving back and forth with the flight of the ball.

yard of the net.) Second, if your opponents hit the ball crosscourt, as the return comes back over the net to your partner, you move to the back third of the service box. You do this because the aim of the 2.5-level player isn't well developed, so you want to give yourself a chance at the ball if your partner hits it to the net person. What governs the net player's lateral movement is her partner's shot. If she hits the ball wide into the alley, you, as the net person, shadow the ball and move forward so you can cover your alley (player D in figure 1.22). If you do this, you're ready for your volleys at the net and can force your opponent to hit to your partner, which leads to your first basic move.

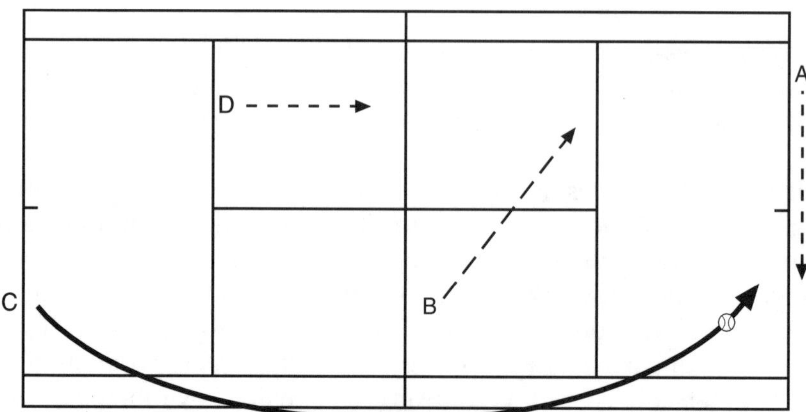

Figure 1.21 Player C hitting over the head of player B. Players A and B switching sides and player D moving closer to the net.

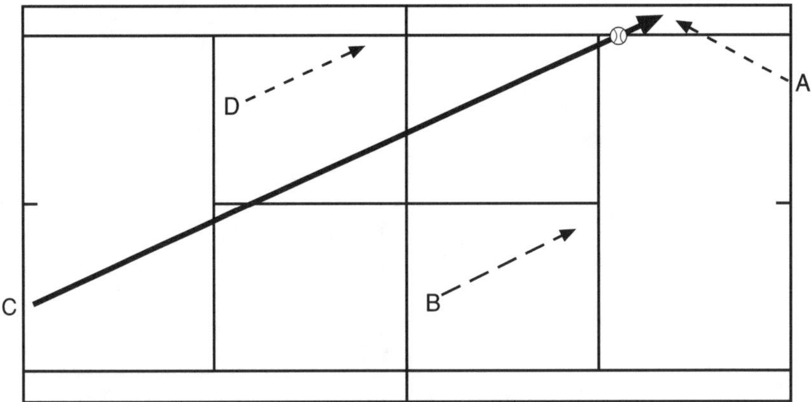

Figure 1.22 Player C hitting a ball wide to player A. Player D moving up and with the direction of the ball to cover her alley (shadowing the ball).

Play the ball back consistently from baseline to baseline. Again, hit more balls back than your opponents. If this strategy isn't working because they're better at it or you're not executing it properly, note where the other team's net player is positioning herself. If she's playing on the service line, which often happens because many 2.5-level players are afraid of getting hit by the ball, hit the ball at the net player, because 2.5-level players don't volley well. If this strategy isn't working, lob over the net player's head. This forces your opponents to hit high balls from the baseline, a liability for 2.5-level players.

One-Up, One-Back Versus Two-Back. Teams at the 2.5 level don't always play a one-up, one-back formation, so note where your opponents are playing. If your opponents are playing a two-back formation (both players on the baseline), stay in the one-up, one-back formation. The net player remains 1 yard from the net for the entire point and doesn't move forward and backward, because he doesn't have to defend against any balls coming from another net player. Rather, he moves laterally with the direction of the ball (player B in figure 1.23). This formation is easier to play against because it takes the pressure off the baseline player, who doesn't have to keep the ball away from a net player. Instead, hecan concentrate on hitting one more ball back than his opponent.

One-Up, One-Back Versus Two-Up. If your opponents are both playing at the net when they get the opportunity, stay in the one-up,

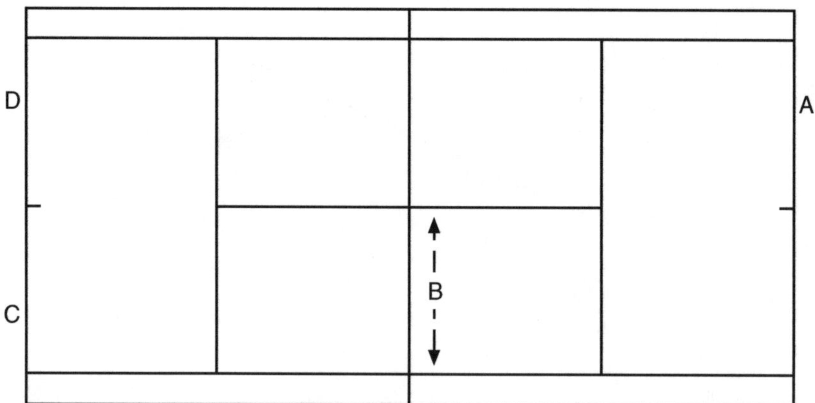

Figure 1.23 Player B moving only laterally with the ball because players C and D are in the two-back formation.

one-back formation and hit at the net players or lob over them. In this situation, your net player plays in the back third of the service box to defend against any balls hit at her by the other team's net people. If you keep the ball in play, this is an easy formation to defeat, because 2.5-level players don't volley or hit overheads consistently and don't hit the ball well while moving.

Two-Back Formation. The last formation is the two-back formation. To be successful at this formation, concentrate on hitting every ball back and not making any mistakes. Let the other team make the errors, which results in them "beating themselves." Try this formation (a) if your baseline player is hitting too many balls to the other team's net player and you're losing games because of it, or (b) if you're making too many mistakes at the net and losing games because of it.

Remember, you want to play a one-up, one-back formation if you can, because it's the easiest formation for you to play and prepares you for the higher NTRP levels by introducing you to the net game. These strategies give you a better chance to succeed, since you'll play the highest percentage tennis possible at the 2.5 level.

PRACTICE DRILLS

The net game isn't a priority at the 2.5 level. It becomes more important at the 3.0 level, thus it's addressed in that chapter. All the drills we suggest are baseline drills, because you have to be a solid baseline player to be successful at the 2.5 and subsequent levels. The best way to practice developing your groundstrokes is with the ball machine, because the ball comes to you the same way every time, and this consistency helps you develop a feel for your strokes. Another way to practice is to drill. Drilling is focusing on one or two aspects of your tennis game through repetition, usually with two or more players; however, drills can be done with the ball machine or against the backboard. If any of the following two-person drills are too difficult, we suggest you do them individually with a ball machine. It helps you develop your stroke and gain confidence in your ability to perform the drill. After you feel more comfortable with your ability, try it again with your partner. *Each drill you do should last about 10 to 15 minutes.*

Singles Drills

The following are baseline drills that reinforce the groundstroking form and basic singles strategy we described in the Objectives and Keys to Success sections.

Rally Drill

This drill is consistent with our first basic singles strategy. You and your drill partner stand on opposite ends of the court at the center mark, 1 yard behind the baseline. One of you starts the ball in play, and your focus for the drill is to keep the ball in play (figure 1.24). Don't try to hit winners, place the ball, or come to the net. Your main concern is to hit the ball back safely into the court. Give yourself some

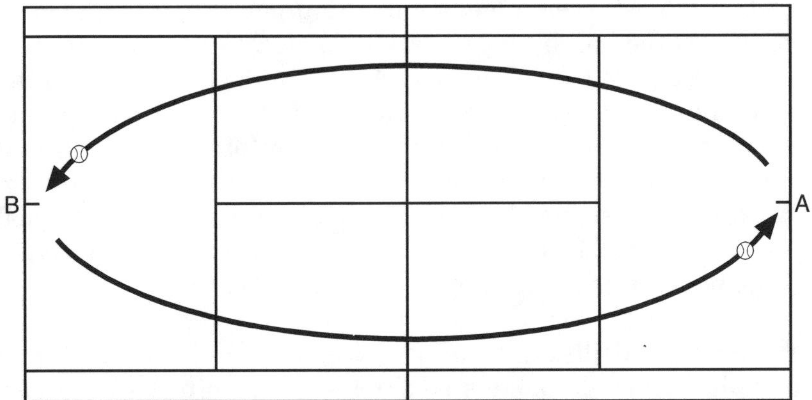

Figure 1.24 Rally Drill in which both players try to keep the ball in play.

goals to attain. For example, each of you tries to hit five balls over the net. As you achieve your goals, increase them, so that you always have something to strive for.

After you become proficient at keeping the ball in play, start trying to change the height and pace of the ball, our second basic strategy. The next two drills help you accomplish this goal.

High Ball Drill

This drill helps you hit high balls to your opponent and return high balls from your opponent. Both players start on opposite ends of the court, 1 yard behind the center mark of the baseline (see figure 1.24). After one player puts the ball in play, sustain a rally by hitting the ball 5 feet or higher over the net. Remember, when hitting a high ball to your drilling partner, swing upward at a sharper angle than normal while keeping the racquet face square to the net. When returning a high ball from your drilling partner, move back far enough to keep the ball in front of you. Then let the ball drop to below shoulder height and take your normal swing. Note that you have to stay on your toes and move your feet quickly to be successful at this drill. This drill is straightforward, but it's extremely helpful for ball control and footwork.

Short Ball Drill

This drill is designed to help you learn to change the pace on the ball. Both players start in the same positions as for the High Ball Drill. Player A feeds a medium paced ball to player B, who returns the ball by hitting a stroke at half- to three-quarters speed. This causes the ball to land shorter in the court (around the service line) (see figure 1.25). Learning this shot is important, because it draws your opponent into an uncomfortable position and can translate into more points for you. Player A practices running forward to hit the short ball. This helps him learn to hit the ball when he's moving forward and running. After player A retrieves the ball, he returns to the baseline for the next shot.

The next two drills are more specific ball control drills that help you exploit your opponent's weaknesses, our third basic singles

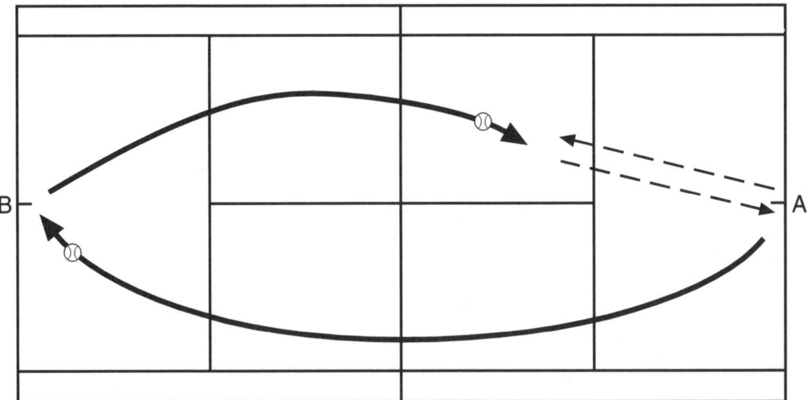

Figure 1.25 Short Ball Drill with player A feeding the ball to player B, who hits a short return to pull player A into the middle of the court. Player A returns to the baseline after he hits.

strategy. These drills are more difficult than the previous three, so you have to be patient while trying to sustain a rhythm. You should have more success at these drills if you're on the upper end of the 2.5 level.

Forehand and Backhand Crosscourt Singles Drills

Start with both players on opposite ends in the deuce court (to the right of the center mark when facing the net), 1 yard to the right of the center mark and 1 yard behind the baseline. In this drill, after one player starts the ball off, you hit the ball crosscourt, forehand to forehand, until one of you misses (see figure 1.26). (This is from a right-hander's perspective and is the reverse for left-handers.) When attempting to hit the ball crosscourt, you must catch the ball earlier and more in front of your crossover foot (left foot for right-handers). To accomplish this, align your left shoulder and left hip with your crosscourt target, which leaves your body slightly open. Then swing through to your desired target.

Next, move to the ad court (to the left of the center mark) and do the same thing with your backhand. When hitting backhands crosscourt, it's easier to start the drill with a forehand stroke. This drill helps familiarize you with some of the basic shots of both the singles and doubles game. Remember, this drill is harder than

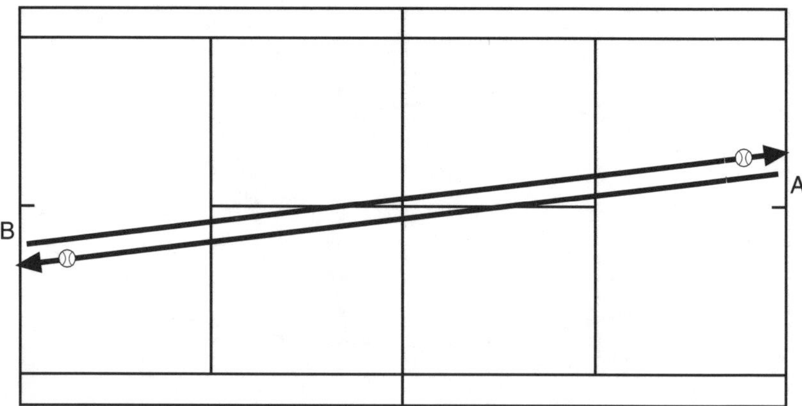

Figure 1.26 Forehand Crosscourt Singles Drill with players A and B rallying crosscourt with their forehands. Reverse for Backhand Crosscourt Singles Drill.

the first three and takes more time to get used to, so stay positive and keep trying.

Down-the-Line Drills

In this drill, both players move 1 yard to the same side of the center mark and start 1 yard behind the baseline. You hit the ball down the line, so one of you hits forehands and the other hits backhands (see figure 1.27). Your goal is consistency in the number of balls you keep in play and the direction of your shots. Remember the quick tips if

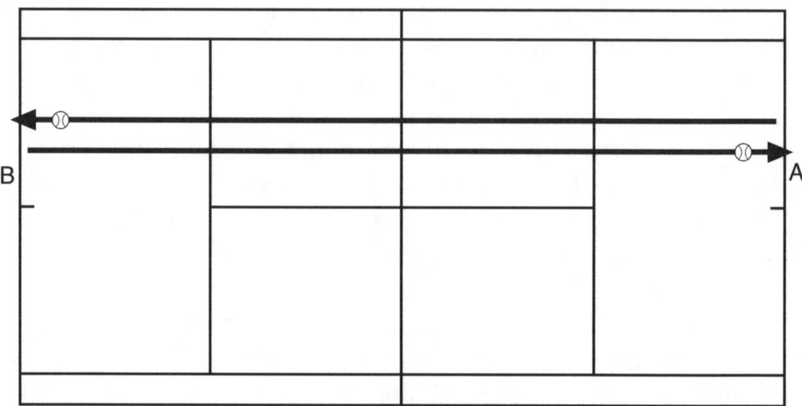

Figure 1.27 Down-the-Line Drill with player A hitting forehands and player B hitting backhands. Reverse for left side of the court.

you're hitting the ball wide. Check your contact point to ensure that you're striking the ball early enough, which helps you avoid the wide error. Also, make sure you're not aiming the ball right at the line. You want the ball to land 1 yard inside the singles line while not swinging too far to that side of the court. After you've practiced one way for 10 to 15 minutes, switch and try it the other way. If you were hitting forehands down the line, hit backhands, and vice versa. These last two drills are practiced by players of all levels and are difficult, but they're necessary for learning to control the ball. If you aren't able to sustain a rally in these drills, use the ball machine to hit your directional shots. For example, to practice the forehand crosscourt, line up the ball machine facing crosscourt (like your opponent would hit the ball in the drill) and hit the balls crosscourt as they come over. Using the ball machine helps you drill more efficiently. After you become fairly proficient at these drills, you are ready to move to the 3.0 level.

Doubles Drills

The following drills are baseline, net, and positioning drills that reinforce the groundstroking form and basic doubles strategy we told you about in the Objectives and Keys to Success sections.

Doubles Crosscourt Drills

This is basically the same as the Forehand and Backhand Crosscourt Singles Drills you did in the singles section. Since we advocate a one-up, one-back formation, it's imperative that you, as the baseline player, consistently hit the ball crosscourt. If you don't, you lose points if you hit to the net player of a good 2.5-level team, and you don't set up your partner at the net for easy put-aways. You can practice this doubles drill with two or four players, but you make more efficient use of your court time with four players. With two players, each of you positions yourself on the singles line to the right of the center mark in the deuce court and rallies the ball crosscourt. By positioning yourself on the singles line, instead of between the center mark and the doubles line, you make it easier to direct the ball crosscourt with your forehand and backhand, because your body is almost always naturally aligned with your target (see figure 1.28).

After you've done this for 10 minutes, switch sides of the court and hit the other way, ad court to ad court. When you become profi-

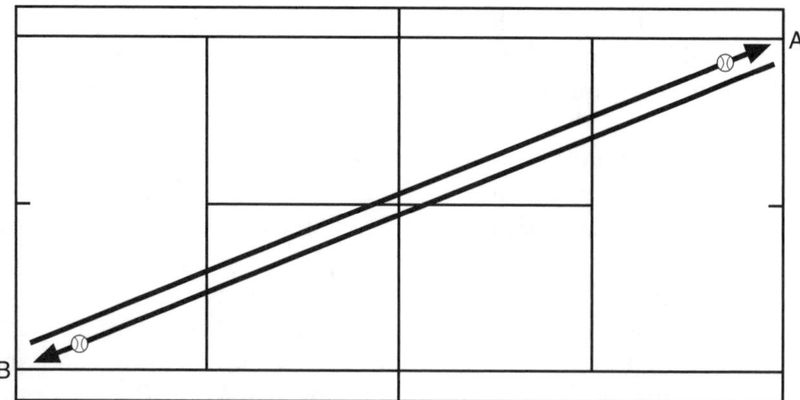

Figure 1.28 Doubles Crosscourt Drill with players A and B rallying forehands and backhands crosscourt.

cient at this technique, you're well on your way to moving up to the 3.0 level.

Serve-Return Drill

This drill involves serving and returning, which is how every point begins. Again, you only need two people for this drill. The server starts halfway between the center mark and the doubles line (the same starting position as in the doubles positioning section). The returner starts back far enough that he can keep the ball in front of him at all times (the same starting point as in the doubles positioning section). The server concentrates on getting the ball into play with the correct form. A good rule of thumb for serving is hands down together and up together, then swing up to the ball, as described in the Keys to Success section on serving. The returner focuses on hitting the ball back crosscourt. If you keep the ball in front of you, you will have no problem reaching this goal. When the returner hits the ball back crosscourt, don't play out the point. Instead, repeat the drill. After one of you serves for 5 minutes, switch positions.

Net Drill

This drill, the only net drill we suggest for 2.5-level players, can be done with two players. Player A stands at the service line and player B stands 1 yard from the net. Player A feeds the ball to player B, who hits the ball crosscourt to where the net player on the other team

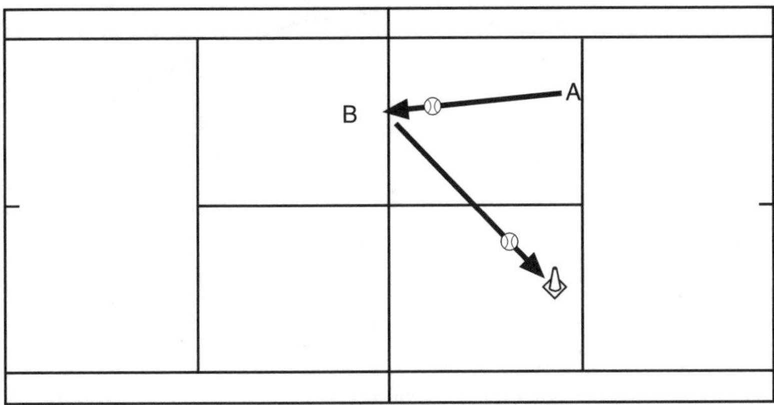

Figure 1.29 Net Drill with player A feeding a ball to player B, who hits a volley to the target on the service line.

would be (see figure 1.29). We suggest putting a target where the net player would be to give you something to aim at. The key is to hit down and through the ball so it goes to the target, or the imaginary net player's feet. This is important, since it's the only way to end the point aggressively at the 2.5 level. After one person has done this for 10 minutes, switch and let the other person try. After you've completed one rotation, try it from the other half of the court. *Note:* This drill is easier if you use a basket of tennis balls.

Lob Drill

This drill teaches you how to lob defensively and can be practiced with two players. Each of you starts on opposite sides of the net, 1 yard behind the baseline. The player who starts the drill drops the ball and hits a lob to the other player, and you continue to lob until someone misses (see figure 1.30). To be successful at this drill, you have to keep the ball in front of you at all times. You have time to accomplish this because all of the balls coming over the net are lobs. When your drilling partner hits the ball, project where it will bounce and adjust accordingly. This is important because, as the baseline player in the one-up, one-back formation, you are responsible for all lobs behind the service line. For example, if you think the ball is going to land away from you and close to the baseline, retreat diagonally to about 5 yards behind the baseline to give yourself enough room to hit the ball. If, after you've moved to 5 yards behind the baseline, the ball actually lands in front of the baseline, move for-

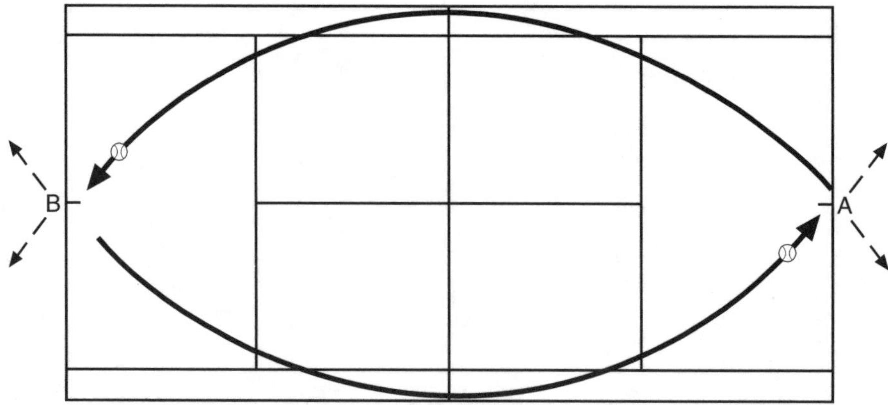

Figure 1.30 Lob Drill with player A feeding a lob to player B, who lobs back to player A. The players' backward movements are diagonal to cover the lob effectively.

ward to hit the ball. The key is to keep the ball in front of you and give yourself a chance to hit the lob properly.

If you're pressed for court time, you can do this drill with four people. Start with two people on each side of the court, positioned halfway between the center mark and the doubles line (see figure 1.31). Do the same drill, keeping the ball on your half of the court,

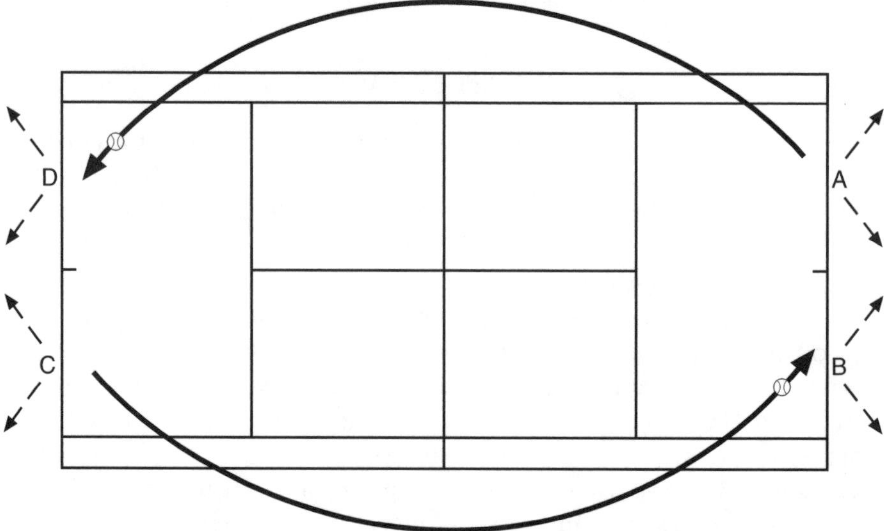

Figure 1.31 Four-person Lob Drill showing backward movements of players to cover the lobs.

between the center mark and the doubles line. It may be difficult at first, but stay with it and you'll get it.

Four Play Drill

The Four Play Drill is done with two doubles teams. The team receiving the feed sets up as if they are serving the ball, one player on the baseline and the other player 1 yard from the net. The team feeding the ball (starting the drill) sets up as if they are returning the serve, one on the baseline and one on the service line. The player on the baseline of the returning team starts the point and lobs the ball over the net player's head or hits the ball deep crosscourt, short crosscourt (inside the service line), or to the net player. Depending on where the baseline player starts the point, the other team reacts and plays out the point. Each person plays her initial position for 5 minutes, then rotates to the next position, giving each player 5 minutes at each position. Let's simulate each situation.

If player A starts the point with a short ball crosscourt, the other baseline player (player C) moves in to the service line and hits the ball back deep crosscourt. Her partner (player D) remains in her original position at the net. You, as player C, don't advance any farther after you return the ball. Instead, you retreat to the baseline, because you and your partner shouldn't both be at the net which leaves no one to cover a lob hit by your opponents. The net player on the other side of the net (player B) remains at the service line, which gives her a chance at the ball if her partner hits a weak reply. The baseline player who originally started the rally (player A) remains on the baseline (see figure 1.32). At this point, everyone is in the position that gives them the best chance to win the point. After player C returns the ball, play out the point with players B and D moving in their respective service boxes (see figure 1.33).

If player A starts the drill with a high ball to the opposing net person (player D), player D hits the volley crosscourt to the net person (player B) (see figure 1.34). This is the only offensive play you make at the 2.5 level. After the initial shot by the net person, play out the point.

If player A starts the rally with a deep shot (past the service line), she stays on the baseline, and her partner (player B) moves forward to within 1 yard of the net. The returner's partner (player D) moves to the back third of the service box to give herself a chance to hit the

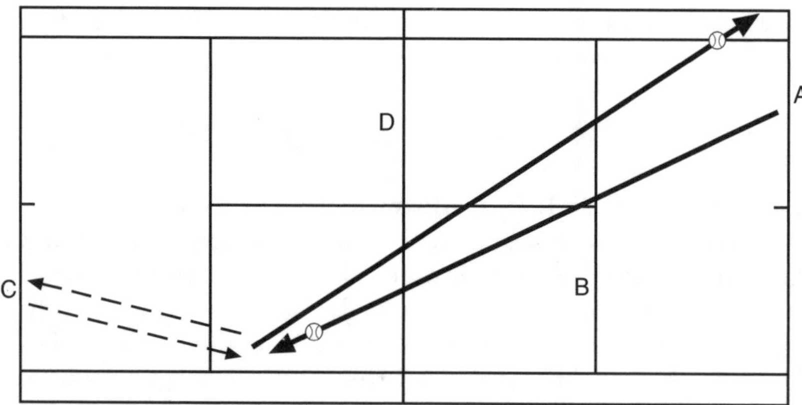

Figure 1.32 Four Play Drill's first play with player A feeding a short ball to player C, who returns crosscourt and retreats to the baseline.

ball if her partner hits a shot to the net player. The player returning the shot (player C) hits the ball crosscourt. As the ball goes back and forth across the net, the net players keep shifting up and back in the direction of the ball until they get a chance for a put-away or one of the baseline players misses (see figure 1.33).

If the baseline player (player A) starts the rally with a lob over the opposing net person's head (player D), the baseline player on the receiving team (player C) immediately runs to the other side of the court (switches) so she can make the return. When she does this, her partner (player D) moves diagonally to the service line on the other

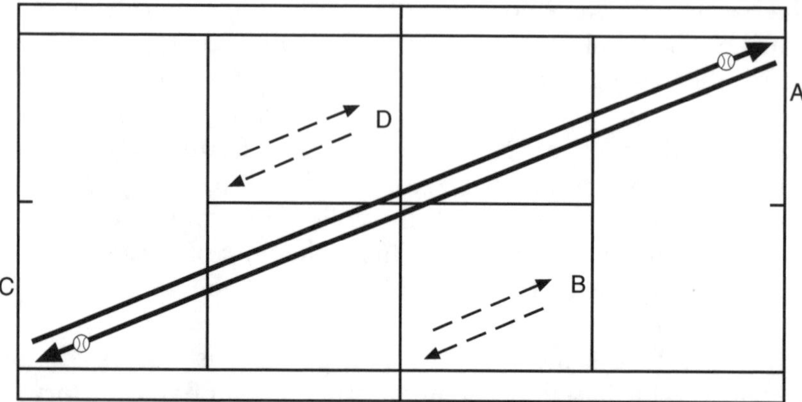

Figure 1.33 Four Play Drill's second play with player A feeding the ball deep crosscourt to player C and players B and D moving back and forth with the ball (shadowing the ball). Player C returns the ball crosscourt to player A.

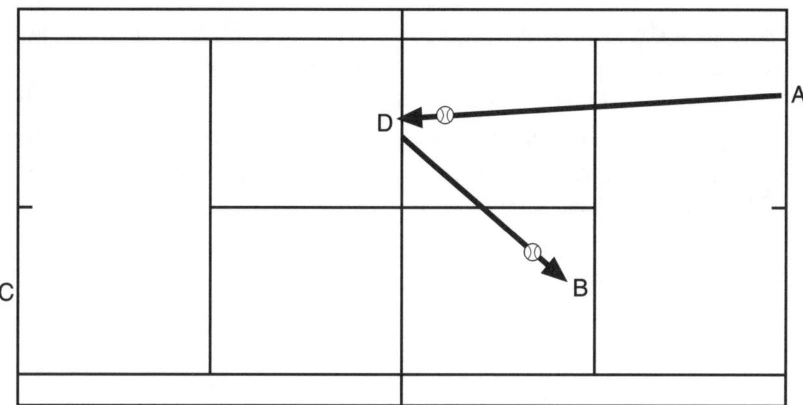

Figure 1.34 Four Play Drill's third play with player A feeding a ball to player D, who volleys to player B.

half of the court. Player A, who started the rally, remains in the back court, and her partner (player B) moves forward to within 1 yard of the net and slightly to the middle to give herself a chance to intercept the return of the other team. She doesn't worry about the other team lobbing over her head, because her partner can cover the lob (see figure 1.35). Once everyone moves to their position after the lob, play out the point, adhering to the basic doubles strategy rules.

These are the drills that help you in your drive to be a better tennis player and advance to the 3.0 level. It's important that you use

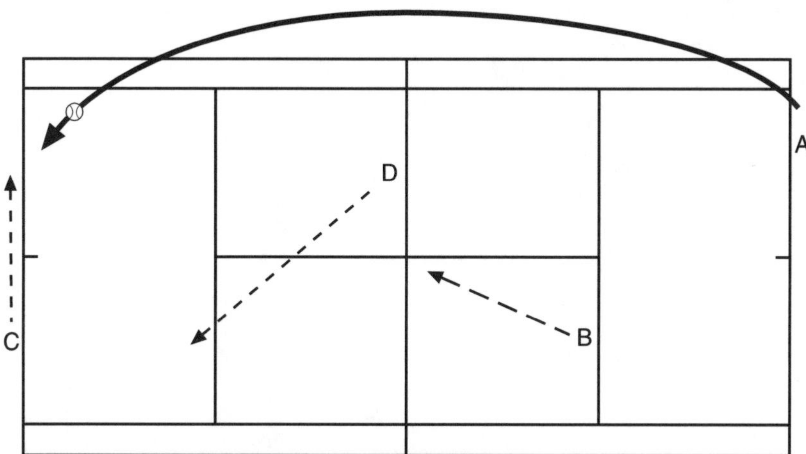

Figure 1.35 Four Play Drill's fourth play with player A feeding a ball over the head of player D, players C and D switching sides, and player B moving closer to the net and the centerline.

our stroking drills at this stage of your development, because good form is the building block of all good tennis players. It's also important that you understand the basics of our situation drills as they apply to your level of tennis, because these are the basics of strategy and positioning, which are modified as you get better. We wish you good tennis and good luck!

2

The 3.0 Level

NTRP Guidelines

The verification guidelines for a 3.0-level player, as specified in the NTRP Guidebook, are as follows:

Groundstrokes—Your forehand is fairly consistent and has some directional intent, but you lack depth and directional control. On your backhand side, you're frequently prepared and are starting to hit with fair consistency on moderately paced shots.

Serve—You're developing rhythm in your service motion but have little consistency when trying for power, and your second serve is often considerably slower than your first.

Volleys—You hit a consistent forehand volley but an inconsistent backhand volley. You have trouble with low and wide shots.

Specialty Shots—You lob consistently on moderately paced shots.

Generally, you're consistent on medium paced shots and developing some directional intent. You approach the net when play dictates, but you're weak at executing net shots. In doubles, your most common formation is still the one-up, one-back formation.

OBJECTIVES

The objectives of the 3.0-level player are naturally a more specific extension of the basics learned at the 2.5 level. At this level, you shore up the basics, begin to learn the all-court game, and become aware of the more complicated strategies involved in playing tennis. It's important to remember that the basics are the foundation that make the all-court game successful.

Consistency

The most important objective, as always, is consistency. You must be able to hit one more ball back than your opponent, and focus on increasing the pace at which you hit the ball. We suggest a slight increase in the speed of your swing, one that doesn't change your basic swing and doesn't make you feel uncomfortable. The reason is that you always want to feel confident about your strokes. You must have confidence in your strokes, or problems will arise in executing your game plan. The way to gain confidence is through repetition in practice.

Placement

Placement is your ability to control the direction and depth of the ball. Directional intent, your ability to hit the ball where you aim, is the first part of this definition and was covered in chapter 1. The second part of the definition of placement is depth. At the 3.0 level, you must begin to learn to hit the ball deep, because depth is the cornerstone of basic match strategy for singles players from the 3.5 level up to the pros and for doubles players from the 3.5 to the 4.0 level.

To simplify the decision process for the 3.0-level player, we define a deep ball as any ball that lands past the service line. In contrast, we define a short ball as any ball that lands in front of the service line. These terms must be understood before we can pursue the strategies of playing tennis, because much of what we say in later chapters will refer to these terms.

You want to hit the ball deep because it limits your opponent's strategic options by pinning him at the baseline, forcing him to play more defensively. For example, if you hit the ball short, your opponent can direct the ball more readily, which forces you to move.

But if you hit the ball deep, your opponent must concern himself more with hitting the ball back than with directing it. Also, if you hit the ball deep consistently, you can force your opponent to hit the ball short, which gives you a chance to direct the ball and run your opponent. In singles and doubles at the 3.0 level, you can still win by hitting the ball short because your opponent isn't likely to put a short ball away or volley well. However, if you hit short balls at the 3.5 level, your opponent will be more aggressive and put pressure on you by hitting drop shots, driving the ball to the corners, or approaching the net. Therefore, depth becomes increasingly important as you climb the USTA Ladder.

Positioning

Positioning is knowing where to stand on the court before the point starts and where to move when the ball is in play. It's important to think of positioning in terms of offense and defense, because during every point you're either on offense or defense. There is no neutral strategy. Therefore, you must learn to move with the ball and your partner during a point.

When you position yourself properly, you accomplish two things. Offensively, you place yourself in a formation that enables you to attack the hitting mistakes or errant strategies of your opponents, which results in put-aways or forces your opponent into a defensive position. Defensively, you align yourself so you cut off your opponents' angles and force them to hit the most difficult shot to put the ball away. Both aspects of positioning maximize your chances for success. However, execution of your shots and strategy ultimately determine the outcome of the match.

The starting positions for the 3.0-level player are as follows.

Starting Position for Singles

The server starts immediately to the side of the center mark, which positions her in the middle of the court after her serve and maximizes her ability to cover the court (player A in figure 2.1).

The returner positions herself as far in or back as necessary to keep the serve in front of her (player B in figure 2.1). This accomplishes two goals: (1) it helps her neutralize the serve and control it better, and (2) it gives the returner a chance to move forward. The forward motion allows her to cut off the serve at an angle and generate power with her weight by stepping into the ball (figure 2.1).

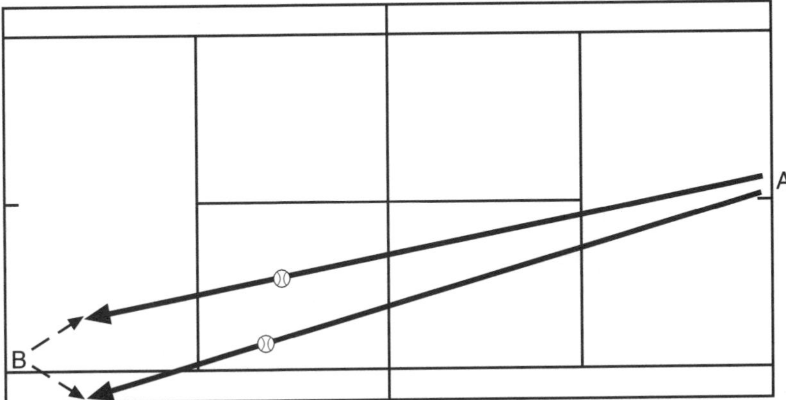

Figure 2.1 Serving and returning positions for singles with player B moving forward to return serve.

The basic premise for this positioning is that it's easier for a player to move forward than backward.

Starting Position for Doubles

When you're learning to play doubles, you must understand that the serving team starts in an offensive position, because the serve is designed to be an offensive shot. Figure 2.2 shows the basic offensive positioning of the serving team (players A and B).

The server (player A) starts halfway between the center mark and the doubles line, which positions him in the middle of his half of the

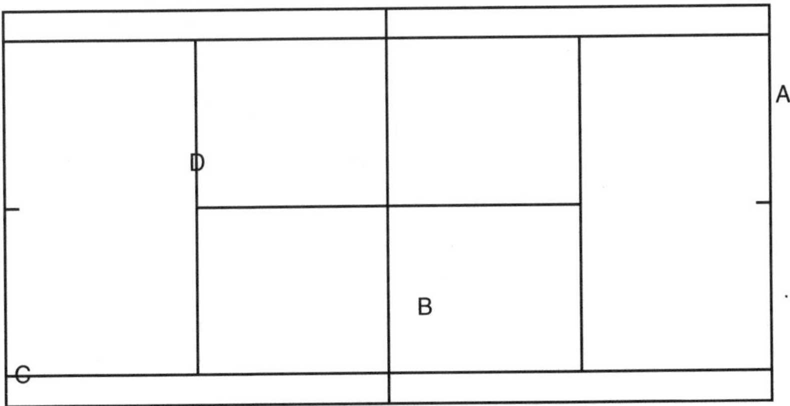

Figure 2.2 Basic offensive and defensive doubles positions for the serving and receiving teams.

court and maximizes his ability to cover that entire area. The server's partner (player B) starts in the middle of the front third of the service box on the other half of the court, putting him in an offensive position where he can put away high volleys or poach (move to the server's side to intercept the ball during the point) on a feeble return.

Conversely, the receiving team starts in a defensive position. Figure 2.2 illustrates the basic defensive positioning of the receiving team. Again, the receiver (player C) starts back far enough so he can keep the serve in front of him, enabling him to control the ball and move forward to cut off the angle of the serve. The returner's positioning in doubles is as important as in singles, if not more so, because the doubles returner has less court in which to return the ball. This means that the nature of the doubles game forces him to be more precise with his returns.

The receiver's partner (player D) stands at the service line on his half of the court, approximately 1 yard from the center service line, where he's able to defend against shots volleyed into the gap by the server's partner and has a better view for calling the serve.

Learn to Attack

Before you can attack effectively, you must know how to attack or approach the net. In its simplest form, the approach shot is a shortened backswing with a lengthy follow-through designed to place the ball deep into the court (see figure 2.3, a-c). You want to place the ball deep into the court to get farther in toward the net and elicit an easy first volley. If your approach shot is hit short, your opponent can keep the ball in front of her and control it, giving her the opportunity to make you hit a difficult first volley.

After you make an approach shot, advance to the net and split-step when your opponent starts his swing (see figure 2.4). The split-step does two things for you. First, it forces you to stop, so you don't run through your first volley. If you run through your first volley, you will hit the ball late. Second, the split-step balances your body so you can move in any direction with ease. By split-stepping correctly, you greatly increase your chances of hitting a good first volley.

Also, you must know when to attack. You must realize that the approach shot isn't designed to win the point. It's designed to set you up for easier volleys and make your transition from the baseline

a

b

(continued)

Figure 2.3a-c (a) Short take-back for the approach shot. (b) Contact point for the approach shot.

c

Figure 2.3 *a-c (continued)* (c) Long follow-through after the approach shot.

Figure 2.4 Player on the left split-stepping and turning to make his first volley.

to the net as smooth as possible. Therefore, be selective in choosing shots on which to approach, because you must make sure you can get far enough into the court to make an effective first volley. The simplest way to view the approach shot is to think of it as responding to being invited in to the net by your opponent. A good reference point for learning when to approach is to attack balls that land short (in front of the service line). Remember that the key for approaching is not the depth of your shot; it's the depth of your opponent's shot. You don't approach the net because you hit a deep shot. Rather, you approach the net because your opponent hit a short shot, and while approaching, you hit a deep ball to force your opponent. This gives you time to get at least to the service line area, because you usually begin your approach inside the baseline, which increases your chances of hitting a successful first volley.

Remember, the key to a good approach shot is knowing not only how to approach, but when to approach.

Develop the Drop Shot and the Overhead

The final objective of the 3.0-level player is to develop two specialty shots: the drop shot and the overhead.

Drop Shot

The drop shot, also loosely referred to as a "dink shot" or "cut shot," is a good singles weapon at the 3.0 level, because a player's inability to move and volley are sometimes the reason he doesn't play at a higher level.

To hit the drop shot, shorten your backswing, relax your hand, and gently bump the ball over the net (see figure 2.5, a-b). To hit an effective drop shot, you have to hit it when your opponent hits a short ball. By hitting the drop shot off a short ball, you don't give your opponent as much time to retrieve the ball and you don't have to hit the ball as far to clear the net, two factors that make the shot easier to execute.

With the drop shot in your arsenal, you can exploit the foot speed of opponents who don't move well by winning free points with shots they can't reach. Furthermore, you can use the drop shot in both singles and doubles to draw your opponents to the net. By doing so, you can exploit two more weaknesses of your 3.0-level opponent: a weak volley and a weak overhead. To exploit a weak volley, drive

a

b

Figure 2.5a-b (a) Player taking a short backswing for the drop shot. (b) Player hitting a soft, short drop shot.

the ball directly at your opponent once they have come to the net. (Make sure they don't get too close to the net, because they'll be in a position to put the ball away.) To exploit a weak overhead, lob over your opponent's head once you've drawn them to the net.

At higher levels, the drop shot is a low-percentage play because the players are faster and hit volleys and overheads better. However, if you learn to hit a drop shot consistently at the 3.0 level, it's an extremely effective weapon.

Overhead

The second specialty shot is the overhead, a constant source of stress for 3.0-level players. The root of your problem, if indeed you have a problem with your overhead, can usually be traced to your preparation or your service motion.

First, if you're not set up properly for the ball, you'll probably miss the overhead, even if you swing correctly. Too often you glide back for an overhead and arrive just in time to hit it. Players at the 4.0 level and higher might be able to get away with this, but you can't. When preparing for an overhead, turn sideways, step backward with your right foot, point your left hand at the ball, and bend your racquet arm to a cocked position behind your ear (see figure 2.6). Now you're ready to move back for the ball. When moving backward, quickly shuffle your feet (move your feet without crossing them) to keep the ball in front of you. This positions you where you can transfer your weight back into the ball, giving you more power and better control.

The second problem is that most 3.0-level players haven't yet developed good service motions, because they let the ball drop too low and push at it (see figure 2.7). Since the overhead is a derivative of the serve, this problem usually carries over. However, the overhead can be easier than the serve, if you let it. An overhead is simply a half serve without the toss. Some professionals teach the half serve as a tool to help beginners learn to serve, because there isn't as much coordination involved in executing it. In hitting a half serve, start with your racquet arm bent and ready to swing while your other arm is in the *T* position, ready to toss the ball (see figure 2.8). With the wrist of your racquet hand relaxed, toss the ball in front of your right shoulder to 1 o'clock and as high as you can reach with your racquet, swing upward toward the sky, and snap your wrist over the ball. The only difference between an overhead and a half serve is that you use your non-racquet arm to

Figure 2.6 Preparation for an overhead.

Figure 2.7 Overhead with a pushing motion off a low ball.

Figure 2.8 Set up for a half serve.

point to the ball for balance and perspective. But you still set up the same as for the half serve, reach as high as you can in front of your right shoulder to make contact, hit the ball at 1 o'clock, snap over the ball, and follow through (see figure 2.9). If you simplify your overhead using these pointers, you'll greatly enhance your chances for success at the 3.0 level and beyond!

KEYS TO SUCCESS

The keys to success at the 3.0 level are learning to hit deep, learning to volley, and learning what strategy to use once the ball is in play.

Figure 2.9 Overhead or half-serve motion with racquet striking the top side of the ball.

Learn to Hit the Ball Deep

Most beginning and beginning-intermediate players aim the ball low over the net because it's a more tangible target and they're afraid to hit the ball out. However, this causes the ball to land short (in front of the service line), since they don't hit hard enough to get the ball to the backcourt. To hit the ball deeper, aim 6 feet over the net, which naturally causes your ball to land deeper in the court. To be successful at this, swing up at a sharper angle while keeping your strings square to the net and making a long, high follow-through (see figure 2.10, a-c). After trying this, you may hit the ball consistently deeper immediately. But chances are, you'll have to experiment with your shots to find the correct feel for your stroke. For example, if you're hitting the ball 6 feet over the net and it's consistently going long, slow your swing by about 20 percent and use the solutions in our Quick Tips section on groundstrokes (chapter 1) to analyze yourself. By experimenting, you'll get a feel for how to stroke the ball deep.

a

b

(continued)

Figure 2.10a-c (a) Player with racquet preparation starting below the ball to hit it higher over the net. (b) Player making contact with the strings square to the net.

c

Figure 2.10a-c *(continued)* (c) Player following through high above the ball to hit it higher over the net.

Learn to Volley

Volleying is hitting the ball in the air before it bounces. Volleying isn't as difficult as groundstroking, but it still requires coordination of footwork and form. Since you hit the ball in the air, you have less time to prepare for volleys than you do for groundstrokes. Therefore, efficiency through quick footwork and proper form is essential for solid volleys.

Develop Proper Footwork on Your Volleys

Footwork on volleys requires two important steps: bouncing on your toes and cross-stepping diagonally.

By bouncing on your toes, you establish a good starting point for making sound volleys, because you can spring to the ball quickly. If you stand flat-footed at the net, you'll have problems with balls that are hit away from you and balls hit right at you.

By cross-stepping diagonally, you put your weight behind the ball (see figure 2.11, a-b). If you step laterally, you'll hit the ball inefficiently because your weight isn't behind the shot. Cross-stepping

Figure 2.11a-b (a) Cross-step on a forehand volley. (b) Cross-step on a backhand volley.

diagonally helps make you a more efficient volleyer because it naturally enhances your control and increases the pace on your volley. Your control and pace improve because you don't have to use as much arm or shoulder. That's how most lower rated players try to generate power on their volleys, usually at the expense of control, so they go hand in hand.

Develop Proper Form on Your Volleys

Form for volleying is straightforward. We always tell our students that "less is more" when they volley, because the more compact you keep it, the more you get out of it. The volley can be broken down into four phases: the grip, the racquet preparation, the take-back, and the "punch."

Grip. For volleys, both forehand and backhand, you use the Continental grip. To locate this grip, hold the throat of the racquet in your left hand (right hand for left-handers), between your thumb and your middle finger, and place the *V* of your right hand on the first bevel of the racquet handle (see figure 2.12). Initially, it feels more comfortable for your backhand volley than it does for your forehand, but if you persevere, it'll feel equally comfortable on both sides.

Racquet Preparation. Using the Continental grip, get into the ready position with your knees bent. Make sure your arms are comfortably at your side and the head of your racquet is at chin height. This improves your form, because you want to keep your racquet head above your wrist as much as possible when you volley (see figure 2.13).

Take-Back. When you take your racquet back, use your shoulders, not your arms. If you start from the ready position with your arms locked and turn your shoulders and hips to the side, you automatically take your racquet back properly because you set it at the right height, a comfortable distance from your body, and as far back as your back foot (see figure 2.14). Also, your racquet face is at the correct angle. Furthermore, turning your hips and shoulders helps your footwork because it forces you to cross-step as your weight shifts to the side of your body from which you hit the ball. Therefore, if you step to the ball, you can't step to it with the wrong foot (look at the player's left foot in figure 2.14).

"Punch." Once you've cross-stepped to the ball, lock your wrist and use your arm to "punch" the volley. We use the term *punch* because you're making a quick motion from a dead stop, not because

Figure 2.12 Continental grip with the *V* of the hand marked.

Figure 2.13 Volley ready position.

Figure 2.14 Player with hips and shoulders turned to the side for a volley.

you're making a punching motion like a boxer. Learning to do this puts you ahead of the majority of 3.0-level players, because most of them swing at their volleys. When you hit the volley, always start the racquet head above your wrist and the ball, because you want to punch down slightly on the volley to impart backspin to the ball. Also, keep your strings square to the target as long as possible on your follow-through (see figure 2.15, a-b). Another way to envision the backspin is to aim at the underside of the ball and make it roll off your strings. This helps you keep your racquet face open on volleys without having to think about too many things. Proper backspin keeps the bounce of the ball low by producing a skidding motion that makes the shot difficult for your opponent to return.

By combining the previous three steps with the punch, you have the tools you need to become a successful volleyer. All you need is practice!

Our quick tips for volleys help you self-check your problems whether you're practicing or playing.

a

b

Figure 2.15a-b (a) Volley take-back starting above the ball with the racquet face open. (b) Volley follow-through with racquet face remaining open and square to the down-the-line target.

Quick Tips

Volleys

⊖ **Problem**—You're volleying the ball into the net.

⊕ **Solution 1**—You're probably swinging down at the ball too much. In this case, slightly open your racquet face and punch through the ball more toward your target (see figures 2.16, a-b, and 2.17, a-b). This helps you volley more consistently because it takes the excess motion out of your stroke.

⊕ **Solution 2**—If you try solution 1 and the ball is still going into the net, your racquet face is probably too closed (see figure 2.18). Keep your same punching motion, but open your racquet face slightly, which forces the ball to come off the racquet higher (see figure 2.17b).

Figure 2.16a-b (a) Flat-racquet-face volley.

Figure 2.16a-b (b) Flat-racquet-face follow-through toward the ground (incorrect form).

(continued)

Figure 2.17a-b (a) Open-racquet-face volley.

b

Figure 2.17a-b *(continued)* (b) Player punching a volley correctly with an open racquet face (correct form).

Figure 2.18 Closed-racquet-face volley (incorrect form).

⊖ **Problem**—You're volleying the ball long.

⊕ **Solution 1**—Your racquet face is probably too open. Keep your same punching motion, but decrease the openness of the racquet face by decreasing its angle. This causes the ball to travel downward at a sharper angle and into the court.

⊕ **Solution 2**—If you try solution 1 and the ball is still going long, check your form. You're probably overhitting (swinging, not punching). In this case, continue to perform solution 1 but shorten your take-back and follow-through (see figure 2.17, a-b). This helps eliminate any excess motion in your stroke.

⊕ **Solution 3**—If solution 2 isn't the answer to your problem, you're probably using your wrist on your volleys (see figure 2.19a). In this case, continue to perform solution 1 but lock your wrist (see figure 2.19b). This helps take the variation out of your swing and keeps the strings square to the ball throughout the shot.

a

(continued)

Figure 2.19a-b (a) Volley with player snapping wrist (incorrect form).

b

Figure 2.19a-b *(continued)* (b) Volley with player maintaining firm wrist (correct form).

⊖ **Problem**—You're having problems directing the ball.

⊕ **Solution**—You probably aren't aligning your body properly. After you've turned your shoulders and hips and set up for the volley, step to your target. This aligns your shoulders and hips with your target and directs the ball accordingly (see figure 2.11a).

• •

⊖ **Problem—**When you try to go down the line, you're volleying the ball wide.

⊕ **Solution 1**—You're probably striking the ball late. In this case, keep your same punching motion but make contact with the ball more in front of you. This causes the ball to travel straighter (see figure 2.20, a-b).

⊕ **Solution 2**—If you try solution 1 and the ball is still going wide, you're probably "overpunching" the ball in the direction of the line. In this case, keep punching the ball the same way but aim more into the court and not at the line. This gives you more margin for error, which translates into a higher percentage of balls hit into the court.

• •

a

b

Figure 2.20a-b (a) Player making late contact on a volley (incorrect form). (b) Player making contact in front of left foot (correct form).

If you find that you're missing your volleys the same way repeatedly, try our quick tips to help you out of any jams you may encounter. We think you'll find them very helpful, especially in match situations!

Learn Strategy

Learning strategy gives you the tactical knowledge necessary to be successful in singles and doubles.

Singles Strategy

At the 3.0 level, take a conservative approach to strategy. You don't want to begin a match by trying to make things happen or by taking unnecessary chances. Leave that to your opponent. Start by hitting every ball back into play. Feel out your opponent to see how consistent he is. If you're hitting every ball back and winning, stick with it.

If you're hitting every ball back and losing, change your strategy. By losing, we don't mean trailing by a close margin. For example, if you're down 3-2 in the first set, you're playing a tight match and may just have lost some close points. However, if you're down 4-0 in the first set, your opponent's strategy is obviously giving you problems and you need to change yours.

First, check your opponent's mobility. He may be slow afoot, which is highly likely because court coverage is one of the limiting factors for 3.0-level players, but you don't know for sure unless you move him around the court. If you hit the ball away from him and he hits weak replies or doesn't reach the ball at all, it's a good indicator of poor mobility.

To hit the ball away from your opponent, picture his side of the court with a triangle in the middle of it (see figure 2.21). Hit the ball on the outside of the triangle, which forces him to move. As you move him around the court, hit the ball into the part of the court that you've opened up. If your opponent happens to come to the net on any balls, hit the ball right at him or lob over his head. In either case, you force him to hit shots that 3.0-level players aren't comfortable with. You'll be able to score easy points or control the points, because your opponent is more concerned with getting the ball into play than with moving you around or hitting to your weakness. Remember, you still have to keep the ball in play to be successful at

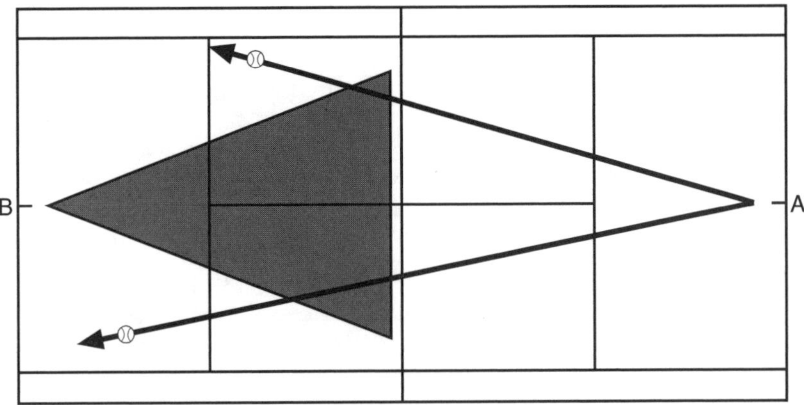

Figure 2.21 Player A hitting on either side of the triangle on player B's side of the court.

this strategy. If this strategy is working, stay with it until your opponent learns how to defend it.

If you've executed this strategy properly and given it enough time to work (four or five games) but it's unsuccessful, then your opponent moves well and / or hits the ball well on the run, and you have to modify your approach again. Your next alternative is to locate your opponent's groundstroking weaknesses. For example, if you see that your opponent doesn't hit a backhand very well, play the ball to his backhand for most of the point, since he won't be able to do much with the ball other than hit it back defensively. In this case, he doesn't put much pressure on you to hit shots you're uncomfortable with. After a while he may overcompensate for his backhand by recovering to the backhand side of the center mark, which opens up the court for you to change the direction of the ball by hitting it to his forehand side.

Each of these three strategies—hitting every ball back, moving your opponent around, and playing to his groundstroking weaknesses—is successful against certain types of players. However, you may have to use a combination of two or three of them against others. Be persistent in figuring out which strategies are successful during a match; as you get better, you'll find that figuring out how to win is as much fun as winning.

Doubles Strategy

Doubles strategy becomes more involved at the 3.0 level because you begin to see different formations. Therefore, we cover how to play the one-up, one-back formation, our formation of choice for 3.0-level players, against the one-up, one-back; the two-back; and the two-up formations. Also, we introduce you to how and when to play the two-up formation.

One-Up, One-Back Versus One-Up, One-Back. As at the 2.5 level, we suggest a one-up, one-back formation because the volleying proficiency needed to play a two-up formation effectively is still deficient at the 3.0 level. Here, we show you how to play successfully against another team that employs a one-up, one-back formation. The two keys to this formation are the steadiness of the baseline player and the "headiness" of the net player.

To start the match, you, as the baseline player, hit every ball back deep to the other team's baseline player. By accomplishing this goal, you protect your partner and team by keeping the ball away from your opponents' net player and denying her any advantage, because she's essentially taken out of the point. Also, if you hit the ball deep, you create opportunities for your net player, because it forces your opponents' baseline player to hit shots that are difficult to control. If the opposing baseline player has trouble controlling the ball, he will inevitably hit easy balls to your net player that are put away. So the steadiness of the baseline player actually controls and sets up the point.

On the other hand, as the net player, you don't control and set up the point; you react to the ball and try to end the point. You react to the ball because your position relative to the net changes as the ball travels back and forth across the net. Let's look at how to change your position properly from both the offensive and defensive perspectives.

Defensively, we know from our positioning section that you start on the service line (in a defensive position) when your partner is returning because you want to close the gap and cut off the angle of the net player. However, once your partner returns the ball, you move forward to the front third of the service box (about 2 yards from the net) (player D in figure 2.22). Before moving forward, you must wait until you know that the ball is past the other net player, because if you leave too soon, you won't accomplish your original objective—to cover the gap and cut off the angles. As the rally continues, move with the ball between the back third and front third of the service box (player D in figure 2.22). Also, follow the flight of the ball (shadow the ball). If the ball is hit into the alley (line 1), move for-

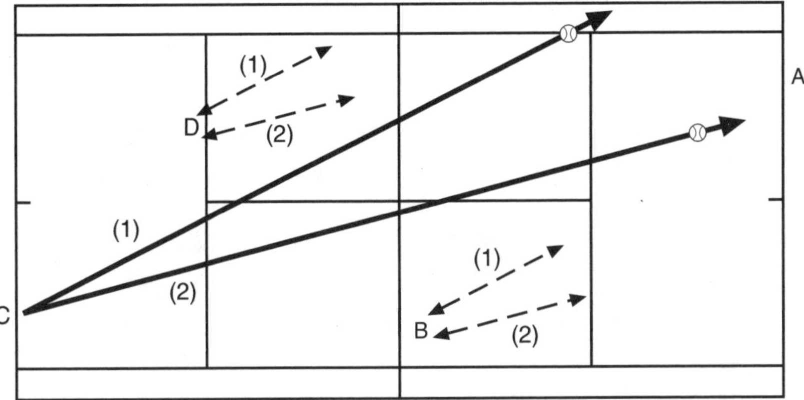

Figure 2.22 Player C hitting a wide crosscourt groundstroke and player D moving toward the net and the doubles alley (1). Player C hitting a crosscourt groundstroke to the middle of the court and player D moving toward the net and closer to the middle of the service box (shadowing the ball) (2).

ward toward the alley (player D in figure 2.22). If the ball is hit toward the middle (line 2), move forward toward the middle (player D in figure 2.22). By following the ball, you cut off your opponents' angles and give yourself the maximum chance for success.

Offensively, when your partner is serving, you start in the front third of the service box (in the offensive position) (player B in figure 2.22). You move back and forth with the ball from the front third of the service box to the back third, the same as when you start at the service line. When you're in the offensive net position, your goal is to intercept the ball when you can get your racquet on it. Don't be afraid that you're "hogging" the court; however, use discretion on the balls that you do poach (intercept). In other words, take the balls that you think you can volley effectively. For example, if you're on the forehand side and your opponents are hitting the ball low to your backhand, you'll have a hard volley and would be wise to let the ball go to your partner at the baseline. In general, you want to take what you can get.

When the ball does come to you, you have two options at the net, depending on the height of the ball. First, if the ball comes to you at a height where you can volley the ball offensively (a good reference point is chest height or higher, although it can be as low as the top of the net if you have good form), hit the ball through the net person (he's usually on the opposite half of the court) (see figure 2.23). This

Figure 2.23 Net player volleying a high ball through the opposing net player.

affords you the chance to end the point immediately, because you hit the ball a short distance and with authority at the feet of the net player, who may have the reflexes to get the ball back but probably lacks the stroke discipline to actually pull it off.

Second, if the ball comes to you at a height where you can't hit the ball offensively (usually chest height or below), volley the ball back to the baseline player, which keeps the point alive and helps you avoid having to try a shot that you aren't ready to execute (see figure 2.24). If you try a crosscourt volley on a ball that is below your chest, more often than not one of two things happens: (1) you hit the ball into the net because you try to hit too good a shot; (2) you pop the ball up in the direction of the net person, which puts you at a disadvantage, because the net person hits the ball back at you from an offensive position. So play defensive tennis on balls hit below your chest.

If you stick to these simple rules, you'll find that you'll win more points at the net—a building block to greater doubles success!

We've covered what to do from the baseline and the net in all situations except when your opponents lob. This situation involves

Figure 2.24 Net player volleying a low ball back to the baseline player.

"switching," which is what you, as the one-up, one-back team, do when the ball is hit over your net player's head. In this situation, you do exactly the same thing we showed you earlier in figure 1.21 (chapter 1).

One-Up, One-Back Versus Two-Back. Now let's look at how to play a one-up, one-back formation against a two-back formation. Basically, your task is simple. The net player on your team plays in the front third of the service box at all times and poaches on anything he can get. As the net person, you don't need to move forward and backward with the ball, as you do when you're playing against a one-up, one-back formation, because you don't have to cover the gap or worry about the net player. You simply stay in an offensive position. The goal of the baseline player is still the same: to hit every ball back deep. However, she can now concentrate on hitting the ball to the weaker baseline player on the opposing team because she doesn't have to keep the ball away from the net player. "Switching" is also important when playing against this formation because your opponents are more than likely lobbing often, so be ready for it. In this situation, you switch a little differently than you did against the one-up, one-back formation. For example, if you're player D and the ball goes over your head where you can't reach it, you move laterally to the other side of the court, remaining in the front third of the service box (see figure 2.25). This is different from moving diagonally back to the service line, which is what you do against the one-up, one-back formation. You stay close to the net because the two-back team can't immediately hurt you on your partner's return. Therefore, you take minimal risk by staying close to the net.

If you're unsuccessful with this strategy, bring one of your opponents to the net by hitting drop shots. You want to bring them to the net because they're probably poor volleyers if they stay back all the time. If you're successful at bringing your opponents to the net, hit the ball to them; it helps you score some cheap points.

If neither of these strategies works, you can play the two-back formation. You only do this as a last resort, though, because your opponents are probably better at it than you are since it's their initial choice of formation. If you choose to go to a two-back formation, bring a lot of water and a lunch, because you'll be on the court for a while. A word to the wise: In the long run, you're better off playing the net than playing two at the baseline, because you only hinder your development at the net by playing the two-back formation.

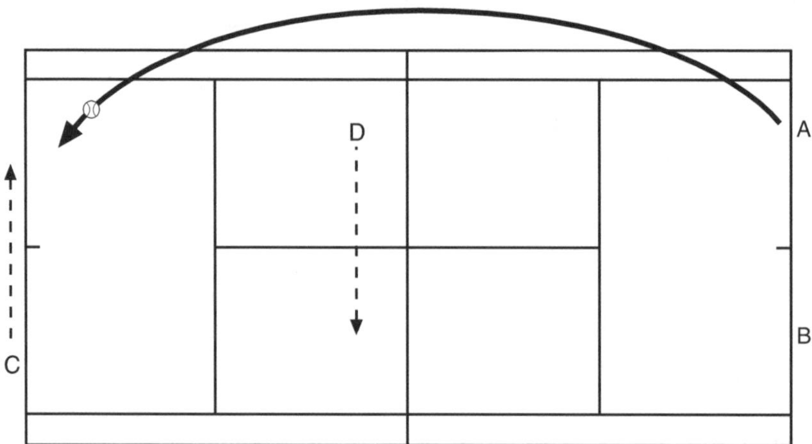

Figure 2.25 Player A lobbing over player D. Players C and D switching sides, with player D remaining in the front third of the service box.

One-Up, One-Back Versus Two-Up. The last formation an opponent can use against you is the two-up formation. At the 3.0 level, this formation isn't hard to defeat, because 3.0-level players don't play the net well enough to execute it and don't retreat well enough to retrieve balls hit over their heads effectively. Therefore, when your opponents get into a two-up formation, your net person backs up to the service line into a defensive position and your baseline player either drives the ball straight at them or lobs over their heads. Caution: If you're the net person, be ready for the ball to come at you if your partner hits a weak shot. If you're losing points because the other team is hitting the ball through your net person, either your baseline player isn't hitting the ball well enough or the other team is very good at the net (in the latter case, they shouldn't be playing 3.0-level tennis). In this situation, play a two-back formation and mix up your shots between lobs and low drives. Both are shots that your opponents aren't confident in returning, which forces them to hit weak replies you can attack. For example, if you drive the ball low at your opponents' feet and they pop the volley into the air short and to your forehand, move in and hit an offensive shot from high to low to put more pressure on them at the net. If you execute properly, you win the point outright or at least receive another weak reply.

If you lob to your opponents, the same course of action applies to weak or short replies off their overheads. If they're not hitting any weak replies, keep the ball in play and try to outlast them.

The Two-Up Formation. The only formation we haven't covered from your perspective is the two-up formation. You only use this formation in two instances. First, if you're drawn up to the net by a drop shot or short shot and have no other choice but to come to the net (player A in figure 2.26), hit your approach shot deep to player C and move into the back third of the service box. At this point, make your split-step and get ready to volley. When the ball comes back, remember the rules we've laid down concerning the height of the ball. High balls go through the net person (player D), and low balls go to the baseline player (player C). If your opponents are playing a two-back formation, hit to their weaknesses or hit short balls to make them hit the ball on the move and pull them in to the net. To guard against the lob, both net players (A and B) stay in the back third of the service box (see figure 2.26). If your opponents lob over your heads, you need to communicate verbally with each other. The

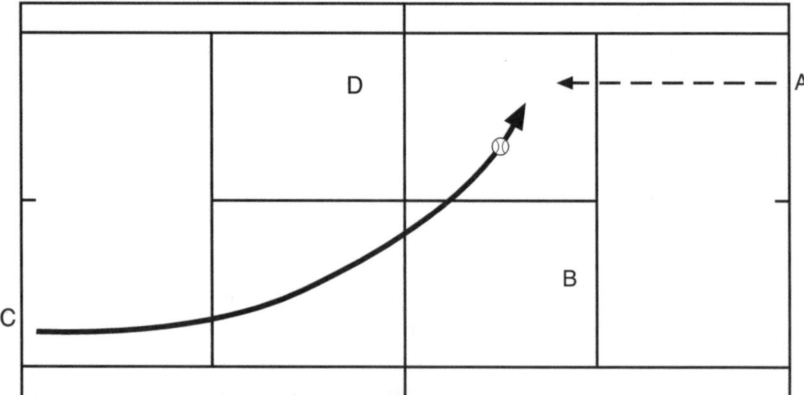

Figure 2.26 Player C hitting a short ball to player A, who comes up to the back third of the service box to join player B.

general rule is that you're responsible for your own lobs. This means that when the ball is lobbed over your head, you have to go get it. The person making the call takes most of the lobs. When one of you successfully retrieves a lobbed ball, continue moving to the baseline so you can return to the one-up, one-back formation.

The other instance in which you play a two-up formation is as a last resort. If you've tried everything else and nothing works, you have nothing to lose. Play the formation the same as if you're drawn in to the net: with both players in the back third of the service box, communicating on the lobs.

Generally, for both singles and doubles, you initially take a conservative strategic approach to your match. Don't try to create points or make things happen; rather, get a feel for the match and for how your opponent(s) play. Based on how you're performing and what your opponent(s) are doing to combat your strategy, adjust accordingly as the match progresses.

PRACTICE DRILLS

At the 3.0 level, groundstrokes are the most important aspect of a successful game. Therefore, most of the drills we suggest in this section are solely baseline drills or involve all aspects of the game of tennis with an emphasis on groundstrokes. However, we also feel it's important to the development of your game that you begin to learn how to approach the net and how to volley. A few drills focusing on these aspects of your game are also covered in this section. As was the case in the Practice Drills section of chapter 1, if any one of the two-person drills is too difficult, we suggest you try it individually on a ball machine to help you develop your strokes and gain confidence in your ability to perform the drill. Each drill lasts 10 to 15 minutes.

Singles Drills

The following singles drills are mainly baseline drills with a focus on directional control and movement.

High Ball Drill

The High Ball Drill is exactly the same as the High Ball Drill in chapter 1, but you'll do it better at the 3.0 level because your skill level is better. This drill helps you keep the ball in play, which is consistent with our first basic singles strategy. It also helps you work on getting depth on your groundstrokes. By hitting the ball 5 feet over the net, you accomplish two goals. First, you hit more balls into play because you hit fewer balls into the net. Second, you hit the ball deeper more frequently, which causes your opponent problems. If you're hitting the ball 5 feet over the net but it's consistently going out during the drill, refer to our Quick Tips section on groundstrokes in chapter 1. It will steer you in the right direction. Remember, to be successful at this drill, you have to move your feet and keep the ball in front of you, which helps you land the ball deeper in the court. Begin the drill by setting accomplishable goals, such as hitting five balls each safely into the court. As you reach these goals, raise them so that you're constantly striving to improve.

Once you feel comfortable with this drill, try a variation of it that adds competition. From the same starting positions, put the ball in play and rally. You score a point if your drilling partner hits a ball that lands in front of the service line or outside the singles court. Play to 11 points. The game forces you to hit the ball past the service line, which is how we define a deep ball at the 3.0 level. You'll be surprised at how well you do after you play it a few times!

Triangle Drill

This drill focuses on directing the ball, which is our second basic singles strategy. Again, you and your drilling partner start at opposite ends of the court, 1 yard behind the baseline. Both of you pretend there's a triangle in the middle of the other side of the court and avoid hitting the ball into it (see figure 2.27). This forces you to direct the ball away from the middle of the court and, consequently, away from your opponent. It also gives you and your drilling partner practice hitting balls while you're on the run.

In this drill, you have the freedom to direct the ball anywhere you want, as long as it is outside the triangle. It is an excellent drill for learning how to move the ball around the court and helps you capitalize on an opponent whose weakness is speed. However, you need more specific drills to capitalize on your opponent's groundstroking weaknesses.

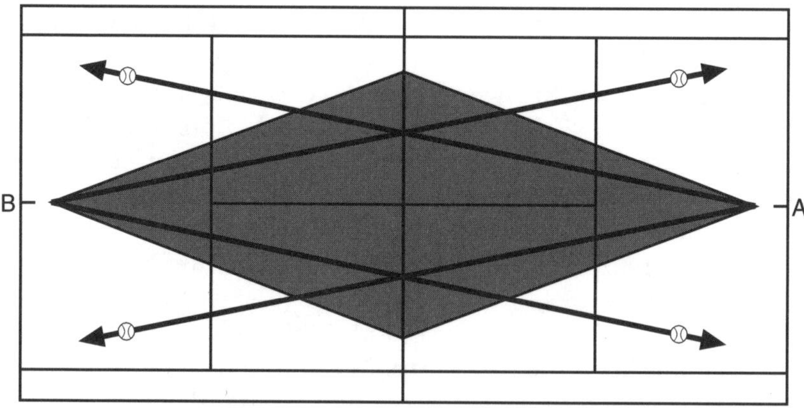

Figure 2.27 Triangle Drill with players A and B keeping balls outside their opponent's triangle.

Recovery Drills

The next two drills, the Recovery Drills, give you practice in directing the ball to specific spots and recovering to the middle afterward. They're essentially the same as the Forehand and Backhand Crosscourt Singles Drills and the Down-the-Line Drills introduced for 2.5-level players in chapter 1. These drills, however, are only recommended for players at the upper end of that level. At the 3.0 level, you'll have greater success with these drills because your execution is better, one factor that separates you from the 2.5-level player, and will continue to improve as you perform these drills. Another factor that separates you from the 2.5-level player is that you can anticipate the ball better and therefore judge the bounce and move to the ball better. Thus, you can modify the drills so that you practice judging and moving to the ball while you drill. To do this, start in the middle of the court for each drill and pretend you don't know where your drilling partner is going to hit the ball. Then, after you move out and hit the ball, recover back to the middle and get ready for the next shot, just as you do in a match (see figure 2.28). For instance, let's say you're doing the Forehand Crosscourt Drill. You both stand 1 yard behind the baseline in the middle of the court. You start by hitting the ball crosscourt to your drilling partner's forehand. Your partner then moves from the middle of the court to the ball. After hitting the ball, she returns to the center. When she returns the ball, you do the same. This is excellent practice, because the only way to continue improving your judgment and movement to the ball is by seeing and running to more balls in a match-type situation. (By the way, these two drills are performed from the 2.5 level all the way to the professionals, so get used to them.)

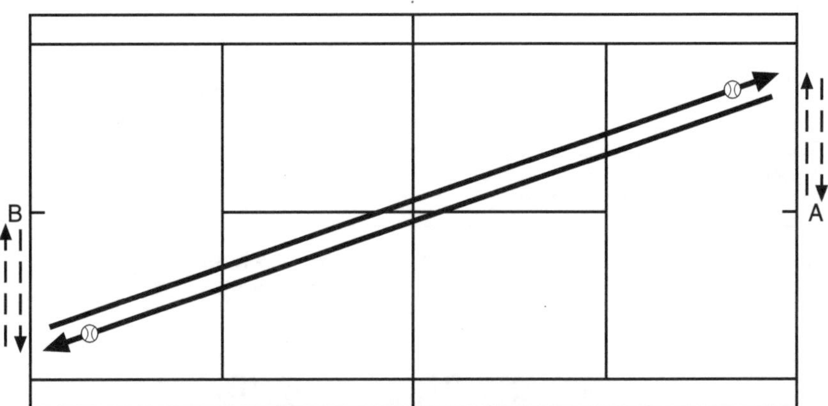

Figure 2.28 Recovery Drills with players hitting their groundstrokes and returning to their original positions after each shot.

Directional Movement Drill

Another, harder variation of the Recovery Drills, which should only be tried by players at the upper end of the 3.0 level, is the Directional Movement Drill. In this drill, both players start in the middle of the court at opposite ends, 1 yard behind the baseline. The player who starts the drill (player A in figure 2.29) puts the ball in play crosscourt. The other player (player B in figure 2.29) moves to his right and hits the ball down the line. Each player hits the ball in the same direction throughout the drill (figure 2.29). For example, the player who starts the drill with a crosscourt shot always hits the ball crosscourt, and the player who receives the ball and hits it down the line always hits the ball down the line. The main key to success in this drill is recovering to the middle after you hit the ball, because if you don't, you aren't able to hit the next shot and the rally ends. This drill gives you practice hitting the ball on the run, recovering after your shot, and changing the direction of the ball, all of which are important to climbing the NTRP Ladder. This is not an easy drill, so keep your head up and keep trying.

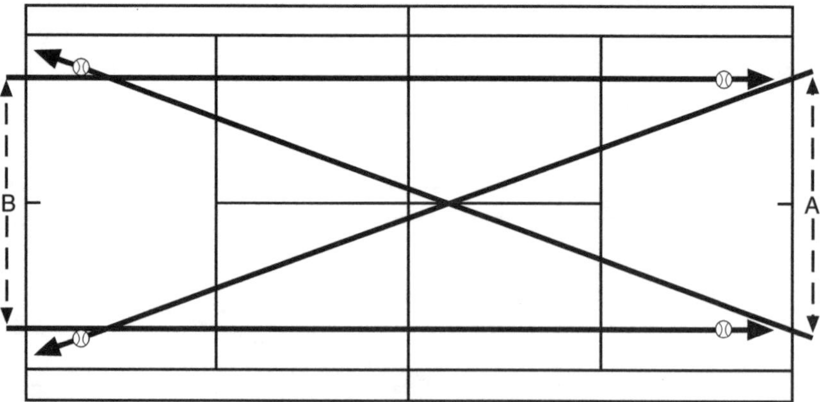

Figure 2.29 Directional Movement Drill with player A hitting all groundstrokes crosscourt and player B hitting all groundstrokes down the line.

Approach Shot Drill

This drill is designed to help you work on keeping the ball deep and approaching the net. In singles and doubles at the 3.0 level, you only come in to the net if you're drawn in by a short ball; otherwise, you stay back. However, at the 3.5 level, you'll look to come in to the net more often, especially in doubles. Therefore, you need to begin developing your skills in approaching the net.

In this drill, both players start in the middle of the court at opposite ends, 1 yard behind the baseline. One player starts the drill by hitting a groundstroke into play. The object is to rally the ball deep (behind the service line). As long as you rally the ball deep, your drilling partner must stay on the baseline. If you hit the ball short (on the service line or in front of it), she must hit an approach shot and come to the net. Once one of you is pulled in to the net, play out the point. As the person approaching the net (player A in figure 2.30), your focus is to hit the ball deep up the line and shade toward the side of the court where you approached. By doing this, you give yourself the best chance to cover the court (see figure 2.30). For example, if you approach crosscourt, you leave yourself vulnerable to a higher percentage down-the-line passing shot because you'll have a difficult time covering the side of the court where you approached. On the other hand, if you hit the short ball and are being attacked (player B in figure 2.30), your goal is to drive the ball back low to the attacker's feet. (A good guideline for driving the ball low is to keep in mind that if you miss the shot, you want to miss it into the net.) By driving the ball low, you force the attacker to hit a difficult volley, to which she probably hits a

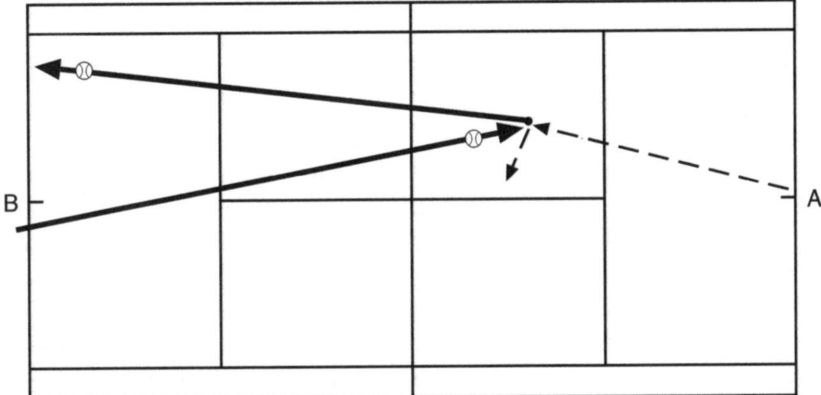

Figure 2.30 Approach Shot Drill with player B hitting a short ball after a rally and player A moving up, hitting an approach shot down the line, and shading to the middle, after which the point is played out.

weak reply. In this case, you have an easier next shot with which to force your opponent. This drill is basically a starter kit for learning to approach the net. After you've become proficient at this drill, make a game of it by playing the first person to 11 points wins!

Other Drills That Still Apply

Chapter 1: Rally Drill, Short Ball Drill

Doubles Drills

The following doubles drills cover the basic aspects of every facet of the game.

Recovery Drills

This is a modified version of the Doubles Crosscourt Drills for the forehand and backhand covered in chapter 1. The focus is different in that you want to practice your judgment of and movement to the ball. It can be done with two or four players on the court at the same time. If you do it with four players, you make more efficient use of your court time. You start the drill with all four players 2 yards to the right or left of the center mark (depending on whether you're in the deuce or ad court) and 1 yard behind the baseline. Two players hit forehands crosscourt and two hit backhands crosscourt. The drill is performed simultaneously, which means that two balls are in play at the same time. This drill differs from the 2.5-level drill in that you move back to your original starting position after hitting the ball (see figure 2.31). After you've done 10 minutes or so on one side, switch and do the drill from the other side. Remember the quick tips on your groundstrokes. To hit the ball crosscourt, align your hips and shoulders with your target and make contact with the ball early. The key is to judge where the ball will bounce and get there before it does, so that you have plenty of time to prepare. Also, hit the ball 5 feet over the net, which helps you land the ball deep in the court. These are important drills because the whole one-up, one-back formation is based on them!

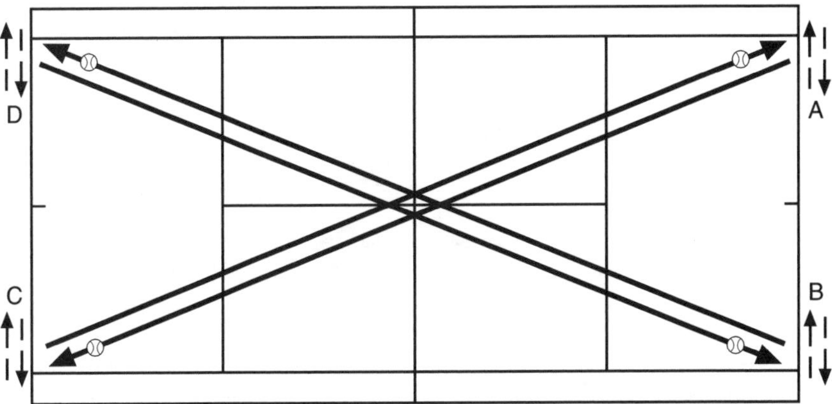

Figure 2.31 Recovery Drill with all four players hitting crosscourt groundstrokes and then moving back to their original positions.

Volley Rally Drill

The volley becomes increasingly important as you climb the USTA Ladder. The 3.0 level is an excellent point to start working hard on your volley, because it isn't that important to your success at this level. That way, you have time to become comfortable with it before you move to the higher levels. This drill can be done with two or four players on the court, but again, you make more efficient use of your court time with four people. With four participants, everyone starts 1 yard inside the service line of a different service box. Your goal is to volley the ball crosscourt to your partner (see figure 2.32). You're not playing to win the point! You simply want to keep the rally going and work on your form. This means that even though you know which side the ball will probably come to, you still need to return to the ready position after you make your volley, which forces you to hit from a game-type situation. After drilling to one side for 10 minutes, switch and drill the other way. Remember, it's easier to start the drill on the backhand side with a forehand. Don't underestimate the effectiveness of this drill. It helps you work on your form and on your crosscourt volley, which is a necessity at higher levels.

A variation of this drill is to volley straight ahead. With all four players starting 1 yard inside the service line of a different service box, one player puts the ball in play and you volley straight ahead. Once again, the focus is on keeping the ball in play with the proper

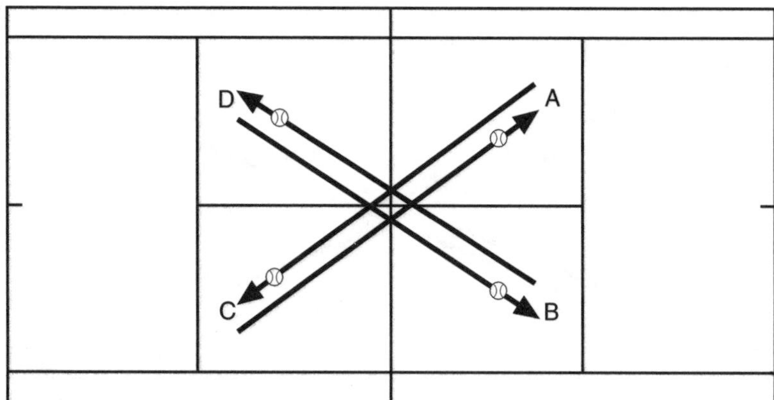

Figure 2.32 Volley Rally Drill with players A and C volleying back and forth crosscourt at the same time as players B and D.

form and on returning to the ready position after each shot. By doing this drill straight ahead, you give yourself needed practice on your form and directional skills.

Doubles Approach Shot Drill

Although this drill is listed as a singles drill, you need to work on teamwork also. The following drill helps you in this regard. Start with all four players 1 yard behind the baseline in a standard two-back formation. One team puts the ball in play, with the goal being to hit the ball deep. Remember to aim 5 feet over the net. When one team hits the ball short, the other team makes the approach shot and both players come to the net. You play out the point from there (see figure 2.33). The team approaching focuses on hitting their approach shots deep (to force a weak reply) and split-stepping when the other team goes to hit the ball (to prepare yourselves for the first volley). Also, if you don't get to the back third of the service box on the approach shot, move there as a team after your first volley. The team being attacked focuses on driving the ball low at the other team's feet (to force a weak reply). We know it's easier to hit a lob in this situation, but you need practice in developing the low drive. So grit your teeth, and give it a try. After you get the hang of the drill, play the first team to 11 points wins.

A scoring game that you can play with this drill is the 3-2-1 game. You play it exactly the same as above, except you score multiple

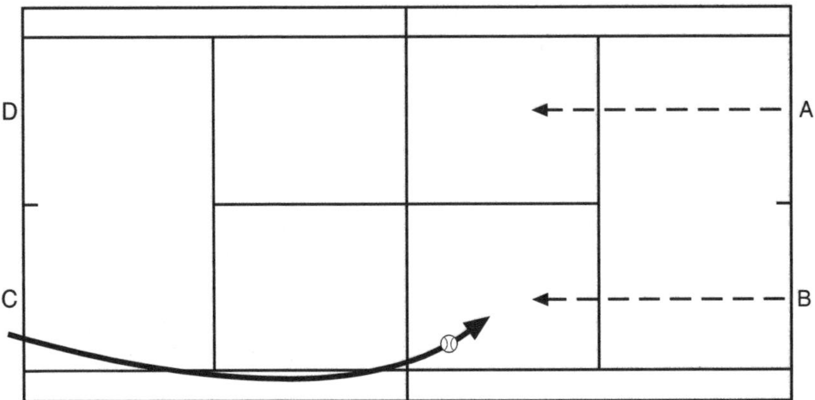

Figure 2.33 Doubles Approach Shot Drill with player C hitting a short ball and players B and A approaching the net together. In this diagram, player B is hitting the approach shot.

points if you win the point while you're at the net. The incentive in this game is to hit the ball deep so the other team doesn't have a chance to come to the net and score multiple points. Scoring is as follows: one point if you win the point from the baseline, two points if you win the point at the net but don't hit a winning volley, three points if you come to the net and win the point with a volley. The last shot hit determines the point value. For example, if both teams are rallying from the baseline and one team hits the ball into the net or out of bounds, you get one point. If your team gets pulled in to the net and the other team hits the ball into the net, you get two points. If your team gets pulled in to the net and you hit a winning (nonreturnable) volley, you get three points. All the games are fun and make your drill session more interesting.

Standard Doubles Drill

Another drill that uses the 3-2-1 scoring system is the Standard Doubles Drill. It starts with a one-up, one-back versus a one-up, one-back formation, the standard doubles formation at the 3.0 level. To start, one of the baseline players puts the ball into play crosscourt, and you play out the point. The scoring for this drill is as follows: If you're a baseline player and you win the point, you score one point. If you're an original net player and you win the point at the net, you score two points. If you're the baseline player, get drawn into the net by a short ball, and win the point with a volley, you score three points. The last shot hit determines the point value.

The strategy in this drill is twofold. First, keep the ball deep so the baseline player doesn't have the opportunity to come to the net and score three points. Second, keep the ball away from the net person so he doesn't get the opportunity to hit a winning volley and score two points. Using the scoring system, keep track of the score and play the first team to 11 points wins. When someone makes a multiple-point shot, analyze what you did to give them the opportunity to score big. It'll give you some insight into your mistakes and help you become a more aware player!

Return Drill

The Return Drill focuses mainly on what to do with your return off a weak first or second serve (most 3.0-level players have a weak second serve). In this drill, the serving team starts in the offensive doubles position and the returning team starts in the defensive doubles position. Player A, the server, serves the ball, and player C, the returner, has one of three options (see figure 2.34).

First, she can hit the ball short and wide (into the alley) (line 1 in figure 2.34). This is the strategic play if: (a) the server is a weak net player, (b) the server is slow in her forward movement, (c) the other

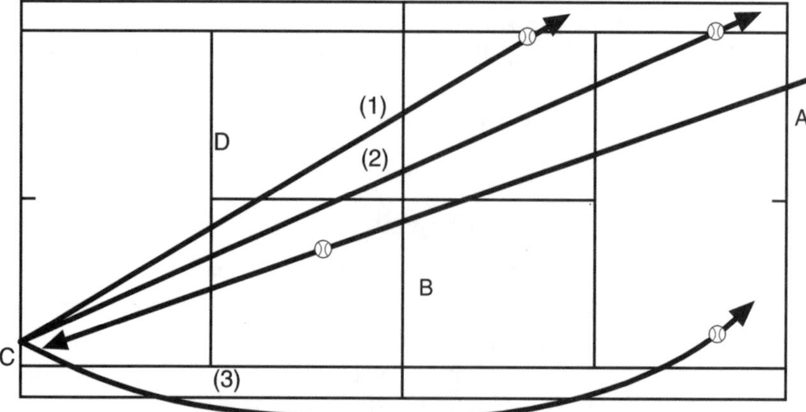

Figure 2.34 Return Drill with player A serving to player C, who hits one of three options: a short, wide return (1), a deep crosscourt return (2), or a lob over the net person (player B) (3).

team is weak in the two-up formation, or (d) the other team starts in a two-back formation and you want to draw them out of it. These are all good options if used in the proper situation.

Second, she can drive the ball deep back to the baseline player (line 2 in figure 2.34). This is a good strategic play if: (a) the server is a good net player and you don't want to draw her in, (b) the net person volleys fairly well and you want to keep the ball away from her, or (c) you want to set up your net person for an easy volley.

The last option is to lob over the net player's head and is only used against a one-up, one-back formation (line 3 in figure 2.34). This is a good strategic play if the server (a) moves slowly or (b) doesn't hit high balls well on the run.

It's important to develop these shots because the more diversity you have in your game, the more weapons you have in your arsenal to win a match. After choosing one of these three options and making your return, play out the point with all players reacting to the choice. After 5 minutes in one position, rotate clockwise one position and continue to do so every 5 minutes until everyone has played each position. This gives each player practice at serving and returning. After you've completed the rotation, switch and do the same drill to the backhand side. Once you get the hang of the specific shots, you'll be surprised at how well you actually execute these strategies!

The final 3.0-level doubles drill is essentially the same as the Four Play Drill covered in chapter 1, except it is easier for you to execute. Refer back to this drill in chapter 1 and pay close attention to the movements that you're expected to make in each situation, because they're your guide to high-percentage winning doubles at the 3.0 level!

Other Drills That Still Apply

Chapter 1: Lob Drill

These are all the basic singles and doubles drills you need to know to improve your game at the 3.0 level. It's important that you realize the context of these drills and why we recommend you do them. Your understanding of these drills and their situational applications helps you become not only a better tennis player, but a smarter tennis player. So get to work now, and good luck!

3

The 3.5 Level

NTRP Guidelines

The verification guidelines for a 3.5-level player, as specified in the NTRP Guidebook, are as follows:

Groundstrokes—You have good consistency and variety on your forehand on moderately paced shots. Also, you have good directional intent. On the backhand side, you have directional intent on moderately paced shots, but you have problems with high or hard shots and return difficult shots defensively.

Serve—You're starting to serve with control and some power.

Volleys—You're playing more aggressively at the net but have difficulty putting away volleys. You use the proper footwork and show some ability to cover wide shots. On forehand volleys, you direct the ball. On backhand volleys, you control the ball but have little offense.

Specialty Shots—You're developing approach shots, drop shots, and half volleys. You place the return of most second serves and are consistent on overhead shots that are within reach.

Generally, you're consistent on moderately paced shots and can direct the ball. You have improved court coverage and are starting to look for the opportunity to go to the net. In doubles, you're developing your attacking skills and teamwork.

OBJECTIVES

Now that you've clawed your way from the 2.5 to the 3.0 to the 3.5 level, you have a fairly sound understanding of the fundamentals of stroking and strategy. However, your objectives as a 3.5-level player change now because your competition becomes multidimensional. For example, in doubles you now play against a few teams that play two-back, but you mainly play against teams that play the one-up, one-back and two-up formations. The catch is that they play these formations better, quicker, and smarter than at the 3.0 level. You can bet that at the 3.5 level, a successful two-back team, a rarity that becomes rarer as you climb the NTRP Ladder, hits every ball back, moves fairly well, and lobs exceptionally well. You can also bet that a successful team that plays predominantly the two-up formation moves forward and backward quickly, approaches well, and volleys consistently and with authority when needed. This is something you haven't seen before but will see more of as you climb the NTRP Ladder. The way to combat the diversity of these specialists at this and subsequent levels is to diversify yourself. To be successful, you have to add more specialized shots and strategies to your knowledge of the fundamentals of stroking and strategy. The good news is that we've already gone over some of the tools you need to be successful at the 3.5 level in the 3.0-level chapter, which makes it easier for you to assimilate into the 3.5 level!

Consistency

The most important objective, once again, is consistency. In the preceding chapters, we referred to consistency purely from a groundstroking perspective, because consistency from the baseline is what you need to win. We're now going to broaden our view of consistency to include all aspects of the game. The new additions are serves, volleys, approach shots, and overheads. Consistency on all these shots plus groundstrokes is what you need to be successful and move to the 4.0 level. Developing consistency on these shots takes practice, but think of it as the means to the end—the end being your ability to win matches by varying your shots or changing your strategy to outsmart your opponent!

Ball Control

Ball control is the ability to hit with directional intent and depth but also to adjust the height of the ball. Notice that directional intent and depth were the 2.5- and 3.0-level objectives, respectively, on which you now have a good handle for moderately paced shots. Now you only need to learn to adjust the height of the ball to have total ball control. At the 3.5 level, controlling the height of the ball becomes more important because net play becomes more important. For example, when your opponent plays the baseline, you hit the ball 5 feet over the net because you want to keep the ball deep. On the other hand, when your opponent rushes the net, you want to hit the ball 1 foot over the net to attack his advance. Obviously, this is more important for doubles than for singles, because most of your doubles at this level are played at the net. Controlling the height of the ball becomes increasingly important as you climb the USTA Ladder, because the game becomes faster and more precise.

Change the Way You View a Match

The third objective is to change the way you view a match. In the preceding chapters, we described in great detail where to stand and move before and during the point, but not how to think. We still want you to abide by those rules, but we also want you to think about each point in terms of offense and defense. To help you do this, we provide you with some general working knowledge that will govern what to do in each situation. For example, in the preceding chapter, we told you to hit high volleys at the net player's feet (offensive shots) and low volleys back to the baseline player (defensive shots), but we didn't explain them in great depth. We just told you that they work. And they do. But at this new level, you need to know that an offensive shot is used to win the point or force your opponent to hit a weak reply, and a defensive shot is used to help you play the percentages and to recover when you're out of position. For example, you can no longer lob just because someone comes to the net. You have to assess your position, your opponents' position, and your opponents' shot to determine whether to hit an offensive or defensive shot. You have plenty of options now, and you must exercise those options accordingly. We show you how to do that in this chapter.

Learn How to Hit Backspin From the Baseline

Learning to hit backspin helps diversify your offensive and defensive games. Offensively, you use backspin on your approach shots to give yourself more time to get to the net (because the ball travels slower when hit with backspin) and to make the ball stay lower to the ground, which makes your opponent's passing shots (attempts to hit the ball past you at the net) more difficult. Also, you use it from the baseline to change the pace and bounce of the ball, which upsets the rhythm, timing, and ultimately the confidence of your opponent. Defensively, you use it to buy time to recover when you're pulled off the court.

Hitting backspin is easy. Hitting good backspin isn't. To make it easier to envision, think of the backspin shot from the baseline as an elongated volley where you're turning your shoulders more and following through longer. Let's go over it step by step. First, turn your shoulders and start with your racquet 6 inches higher than the ball. The racquet is higher than the ball because your downward swing is what puts the backspin on the ball. Second, open the face of the racquet so the ball goes over the net when you swing downward (see figure 3.1a). We equate this principle to golf. In golf, you swing down on the ball, but the loft of the club determines how high it goes. The more loft it has, the higher and less far the ball goes. The less loft it has, the lower and farther the ball goes (see figure 3.2). For backspin drives of waist height or higher, use less loft to hit the ball down into the court. For backspin drives of waist height or lower, use more loft (open the racquet face more) and swing downward more to put some air under the ball and get it over the net. Third, cross-step to the ball to position yourself and use your weight efficiently (see figure 3.1b). Finally, with a firm wrist, swing slightly downward through the ball, as if it is rolling off your strings, using only your arm (see figure 3.1c). If you use your body too much, you upset the timing of your shot. If you think about using just your arm, your body naturally comes through the shot the way it's supposed to.

At the 3.5 level, the backspin drive is sporadic. Some players can do it, some can't. However, very few players do it well. If you learn to do it well at this level, you give yourself a decided advantage. Nonetheless, it's a shot that you must definitely begin to learn at this level, because it adds variety to your game and your shot selection.

a

b

Figure 3.1a-c (a) Player turning his shoulders and opening his racquet face to hit backspin with the racquet face starting higher than the ball. (b) Player cross-stepping to hit backspin shot with an open racquet face at contact.

c

Figure 3.1a-c (c) Downward follow-through after the backspin shot.

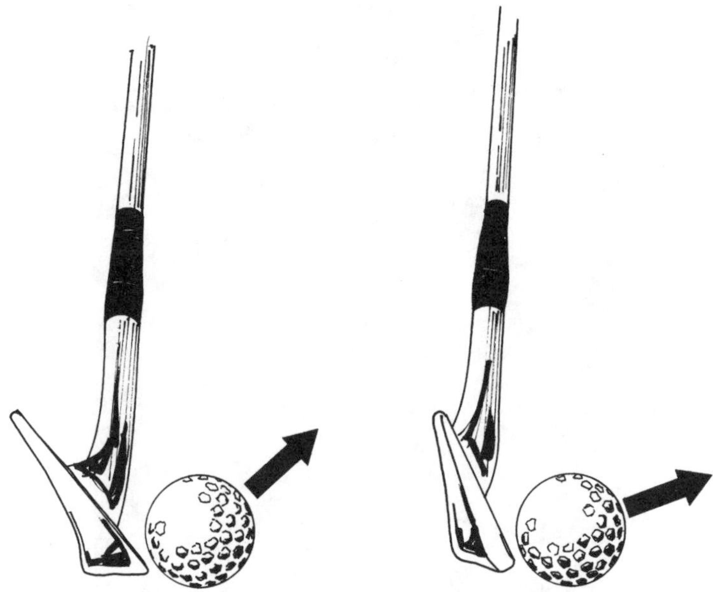

Figure 3.2 Lofts (open face = higher trajectory, closed face = lower trajectory).

Learn How to Serve With Spin

A prerequisite for learning to serve with spin is to make sure you're using the proper grip. If you're not using the correct grip, learning to serve with spin is extremely difficult. The correct service grip is the Continental grip, in which the *V* of your hand is placed on the first bevel (see figure 2.12). You can achieve this grip by pretending to shake hands with the racquet.

The service motion involves the turning of your wrist and arm through the ball (called pronation). By varying the degree to which you pronate your arm, you change the spin on the ball. In figure 3.3, the server turns her arm fully through the ball and hits a flat serve. In figure 3.4, she turns her arm slightly less through the ball, causing the racquet to contact the ball at a slight angle and impart a slice (sidespin). This causes the ball to curve to the left when it hits the service box. The spin is useful in creating an immediate

Figure 3.3 Player hitting a flat serve.

Figure 3.4 Player hitting a slice serve.

offensive advantage for yourself. For example, if you're a right-handed player serving into the deuce court, you can pull your opponent off the court wide and open up the court (see figure 3.5), or you can serve down the middle and jam your opponent (spin the ball into her body), which forces a weak reply (see figure 3.6). If you're successful at executing one of these options, you immediately put yourself in an offensive posture and take control of the point. Professionals are adept at putting spin on their serves, which is one of the reasons breaking service is so difficult at their level.

If your grip is incorrect, it negatively affects the pronation of your arm when you serve, limiting your ability to impart spin to the ball. For example, if you use a semi-Western grip (a frying pan grip) to serve, the racquet face already faces the target and you have to turn

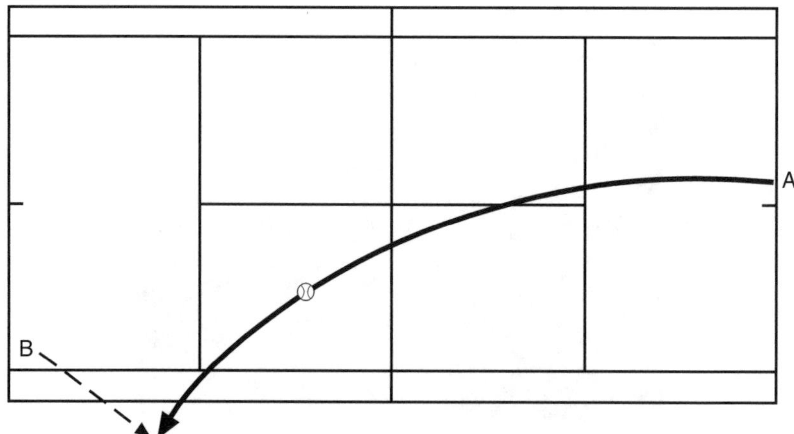

Figure 3.5 Player A slicing a serve to player B, pulling her off the court.

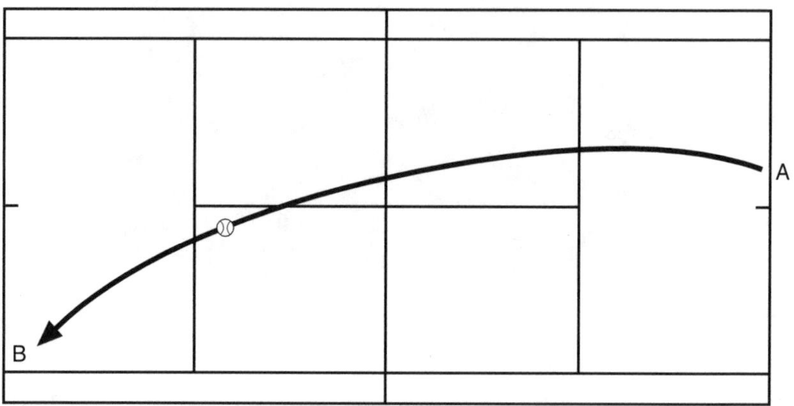

Figure 3.6 Player A slicing a serve into player B's body.

the racquet the wrong way to pronate your arm or else you can hardly turn your wrist at all (see figure 3.7). As a result, your serve is less consistent and less powerful, because you don't give your wrist a chance to follow through properly.

We don't recommend that you try to serve with spin in your matches until you're consistent at it. Instead, practice the proper serve by hitting baskets of balls until you're comfortable with it. Then hit it in practice and practice matches to gain confidence in it. When you feel confident that you can do it consistently in a match, you're ready to use it and improve your serving potential.

Figure 3.7 Incorrect pronation of the wrist during a serve due to an incorrect grip.

Learn How to Hit Low and Wide Volleys

Low and wide volleys are shots that you definitely want to learn at the 3.5 level because they are a must for success at the 4.0 and higher levels, especially in doubles. The reason these shots become more critical is that you approach the net more as you move higher up the NTRP Ladder. You attack weak serves and serve and volley, which means that you're in transition. When you're in transition, you have to go through the midcourt to get to the net. The midcourt is the area from 2 yards behind the service line to 2 yards in front of the service line. If you can't hit low and wide volleys, you can't make it through the midcourt, and your success is limited by your opponent's ability to take advantage of this weakness. We explore the midcourt game more later in this chapter.

Learn the Offensive Lob

The offensive lob, a specialty shot, is merely a combination of lobbing defensively and hitting the ball 5 feet over the net. It's used when your opponents are at the net and are: (a) slow and/or short and can't jump very high, or (b) playing on top of the net.

There are two kinds of offensive lobs. One is the topspin lob, which we don't recommend at this level because it's too involved for your skill level. The other kind of offensive lob is one with no spin. One way to hit this shot is simply to put less arc on the ball than you would on a defensive lob. To do this, start with the 45-degree angle we suggested for the defensive lob in chapter 1, but close your racquet face more than you do for the defensive lob. Another way to hit this shot is to put more arc on your groundstroke. To do this, use the same swing as you did to hit the ball 5 feet over the net in chapter 2, but open the racquet face more and don't swing as hard. Either way helps you accomplish your goal of getting the ball over your opponents' heads by using a low trajectory (see figure 3.8). If you're successful at getting the ball over your opponents' heads, you'll more than likely win the point, because the ball bounces away from them instead of straight up in the air, as it does on a defensive lob, making

Figure 3.8 Offensive lob with less loft on the racquet face, causing the ball to go lower over the opponent's head.

it more difficult for them to retrieve. If your opponents are smart, they'll back up to cover this play; however, this puts them on the defensive at the net, in which case you either drive the ball low at their feet or hit defensive lobs.

The above scenario is a good example of how thinking offensively and defensively can benefit your game. It's also a good illustration of how outsmarting your opponent makes the game more fun than just trying to hit every ball back!

KEYS TO SUCCESS

At the 3.5 level, the keys to success still involve the fundamentals, but they now include more of the technical and mental aspects of tennis. You still need the fundamentals, but you have to have more. You have to think offensively and defensively. You have to know when to attack, when to change your game plan, and when to retreat. In short, you can't be a one-dimensional player at this level and expect to be successful and move up to the next level.

Learn to Hit All Your Shots Consistently Deep

At the 3.5 level, you need to have depth on all your shots: groundstrokes, serves, volleys, approach shots, and overheads. This doesn't mean depth is appropriate on every shot, because there are times when angle shots and drop shots come into play. But you must be able to hit the ball deep when necessary. We've already discussed at length why you should hit your groundstrokes and approach shots deep, so let's focus on serves, volleys, and overheads.

Serves

We define serving deep as landing the ball in the back quarter of the service box. This becomes increasingly critical as you climb the ladder because your opponents become more versatile. They have different ways to attack weak serves that land short in the service box. For example, a good singles baseliner returns a weak serve into one of the corners, to your groundstroking weakness, or approaches the net, immediately putting you on the defensive. Your opponent dictates the point, and you're a pawn. A doubles example is a good net team that approaches off a short second serve, forcing your team into a defensive formation after the first shot. This is one of the most common reasons for 3.5-level players losing their serve. The only way to learn to serve the ball deep is to correct any fundamental problems you have and experiment with your serve by hitting baskets of balls.

Volleys

Short volleys (volleys that land in front of the service line) back to your opponent also put you at a disadvantage, because you allow your opponent to control the ball. If you hit a short volley, the ball stays in front of your opponent and doesn't force him to move, giving him a choice of two offensive shots: a low passing shot or an offensive lob. On the other hand, a deep volley pushes your opponent back and forces him to hit one of two shots: a low ball at your feet, which is a difficult shot when moving backward, or a defensive lob. It also gives you control of the point. You have a much better chance at success if your opponent is forced to hit low balls and defensive lobs than if he has the choice of hitting low-ball passing shots and offensive lobs. If you're having problems hitting deep volleys, reread the section on volleying in chapter 2, fix any fundamental problems you find, and practice volleying at targets placed deep in the court. This will increase your proficiency at volleying deep!

Overheads

Short overheads can also get you into trouble, but not as easily as short serves and volleys. Because the overhead is the most offensive shot you can hit, you can misfire and still not be in immediate trouble. However, your opponent can easily nullify the effect of a short overhead, because it gives him a chance to drive the ball at your feet or hit a more effective lob. This puts you on equal footing because you've lost your advantage. Your best chance for success on your overhead is to hit it away from your opponent, but this isn't always possible. If you have to hit the ball to your opponent, force a weak reply by hitting the ball deep.

Learn to Hit Low Balls to Your Opponents When They Are at the Net or Approaching

The low ball is used by players at the 4.0 level and above to neutralize or defend against an opponent who attacks the net. However, at the 3.5 level it's used to neutralize or attack an opponent who attacks the net, because 3.5-level players have trouble volleying low balls. For example, in doubles, if your opponents are at the net, what are your options? You can hit the ball either at your opponents or over them, because if they position themselves correctly, it's difficult to hit the ball past them. So if you choose to hit the ball at them, you want to make them play the most difficult shot you can. Is that a high ball or a low ball? Naturally, it's a low ball, because it forces your opponents to volley the ball defensively from below the level of the net. A high ball gives them a chance to put the ball away. So if you can't hit the ball over or past your opponents, you have to hit the ball at them and still make them play a difficult shot, which is the low ball. Thus, because players come to the net more in doubles, playing the ball low is a more important shot for doubles than for singles. However, don't discount its usefulness in singles.

To hit the ball low, you only need to adjust your swing a small amount. Take the low-to-high swing you normally use to hit a deep groundstroke and flatten it out some. In other words, don't swing from low to high at as sharp an angle. If you try this and find that you're hitting too many balls into the net, slightly increase the angle on your low-to-high swing. Another way to look at it is that you want to hit the top of the ball to make it go low over the net and you want to hit the bottom of the ball to make it go deep into the court. Hitting the ball in this manner automatically causes you to make the necessary adjustments in your swing. Whichever method you try, the low ball is a shot you need to experiment with to learn how to hit it efficiently. So if you can't get it right away, don't give up on it, because it's a shot that wins a lot of points at the 3.5 level and one that is a must at higher levels.

Develop Low and Wide Volleys

These shots are important because you spend a lot of time in the midcourt or transition area at this level. In the midcourt area, you aren't close to the net, which leaves more space for your opponents to hit the ball low and/or wide. Furthermore, your opponents at this level are more capable of hitting the ball at your feet when you approach the net. Therefore, you need to gain proficiency at the low and wide volleys to enable you to play through the midcourt to position yourself at the net.

Low Volleys

First, let's look at the low volley. There are three keys to hitting the low volley.

First, you must have balance. The correct form is to bend your knees as you go down for a low volley (see figure 3.9a). The common error is to bend at the waist (see figure 3.9b). By bending your knees, you keep your upper body above your lower body, which maintains your balance.

Maintaining balance is important for enabling you to keep your racquet head up on your volley, the second key to hitting the low volley. The lower the ball, the more you need to bend your knees to keep the racquet head up. The more upright you stand, the more you have to drop the racquet head to make a low volley. Keeping the racquet head up is important because the more you drop the racquet head, the greater the tendency to pop the ball up. Remember from the section on volleying in chapter 2 that ideally you want the ball to stay

a

Figure 3.9a-b (a) Player bending at the knees with the racquet head up (correct form).

b

Figure 3.9a-b (b) Player bending at the waist with the racquet head down (incorrect form).

low when it bounces, so you can force your opponents to hit the ball up, giving you an easy high volley. If you pop the ball up, it's a "sitter," or an easy shot for the other team to take advantage of, and more than likely won't result in an easy volley for you. Therefore, you want to avoid hitting pop-ups on your low volleys.

The third key to hitting the low volley is to open the racquet face slightly and keep it moving parallel to the ground (see figure 3.10). This causes the ball to travel upward off your racquet and is necessary for your volley to clear the net. If you're performing all the other parts of the low volley properly and the ball is still going into the net, you need to open your racquet face more to give it more trajectory to clear the net. On the other hand, if your racquet face is too open and you're popping the ball up, close your racquet face a little more to make the ball move through the court.

These three steps help you accomplish the goal of hitting your volleys back deep and low and turn your low volley into a strength rather than a weakness!

Wide Volleys

Next, let's look at the wide volley. The two keys to the wide volley are the split-step and the shoulder turn. As well as being the basic

Figure 3.10 Player hitting a low volley with an open racquet face and the racquet moving parallel to the ground.

fundamentals of approaching the net, they are the two most important parts of hitting the wide volley.

First, split-step to provide balance from which you can spring to the wide volley. If you're still moving when approaching the net or aren't in the ready position to hit a volley, you can't move to the side quickly enough to allow for good form on a wide volley. Therefore, you're already at a disadvantage before you start.

Second, turn your shoulders to position your body correctly. If you turn your shoulders for a wide volley, your momentum causes you to cross-step in the direction of the ball, enabling you to make the shot (see figure 3.11). We often see players neglect the cross-step in favor of stepping with their outside foot. You want to avoid this error because it shortens your reach. Compared to stepping with your outside foot, a diagonal cross-step gives you an extra shoulder's width of reach, because your outside foot is on the same side as the ball (see figure 3.12, a-b). Therefore, take advantage of the natural reach that good form provides by making your cross-step. After

Figure 3.11 Shoulder turn for a volley.

taking care not to make these two common preparatory errors on the wide volley, hit your volley as you normally do.

Learn to Put Away Short Lobs

A short lob is one that lands inside the service line. It's important to learn to put away these balls because they give you a high-percentage chance to end a point, and you have to capitalize on such opportunities. There are two keys to putting away short lobs with your overhead.

The first key is having enough confidence in your overhead to hit it with pace (which comes through repetition) and to place the ball where you want it to go (which also comes through repetition). When you want to hit the ball to the baseline (singles or doubles) or through the net player (doubles), hit the overhead with pace. Since you have more space in which to land the ball in these situations, you need pace to force a weak response or hit a winner. When you hit an angle overhead (singles or doubles), take pace off the ball because you have less space in which to hit and you don't need to hit the ball hard to force a weak response or hit a winner. In either case, becoming proficient at putting away short lobs requires a lot of practice.

a

b

Figure 3.12a-b (a) Cross-step. (b) Incorrect step to a volley. Note the amount of reach lost compared to the cross-step.

The second key is knowing where to hit your overheads to put them away. At times, there's a definite place to hit your overhead based on your opponents' position. In singles, there's always an open space in which you can put away your overhead. You just have to choose the side to which you want to angle the ball (see figure 3.13). In doubles, if you see a hole in your opponents' position, hit your overhead into the open court. If you don't put the ball away, you at least force your opponents out of position and open another hole in which to hit the ball. If they're in proper position in relation to the ball, you always have three options on your overhead. If the ball is lobbed short and in the middle of the court, your opponents will align themselves equidistant from the center mark to give themselves the best chance to cover the court. When they align themselves in this manner, hit the overhead down the middle or angle it into either alley (see figure 3.14). If you don't put the ball away on your first overhead, you open up the court for a better chance to put the next ball away.

If the ball is lobbed short and to your right, your opponents will align themselves more to cover the angle overhead in the left alley. Your three options are to hit the angle overhead crosscourt, hit the overhead on an angle down the middle, or hit the overhead on a slight angle into the right alley (see figure 3.15). These are the "soft spots" in their coverage.

If the ball is lobbed short and to the left, your opponents will align themselves more to cover the overhead in the right alley. Your three

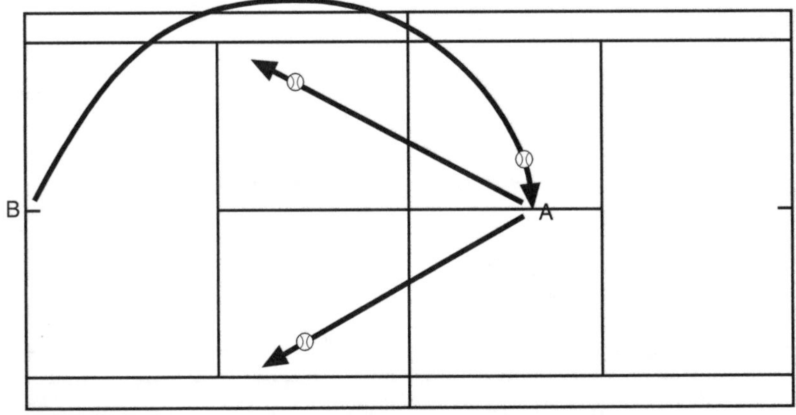

Figure 3.13 Player B hitting a lob to player A, with player A angling off the overhead to the open court.

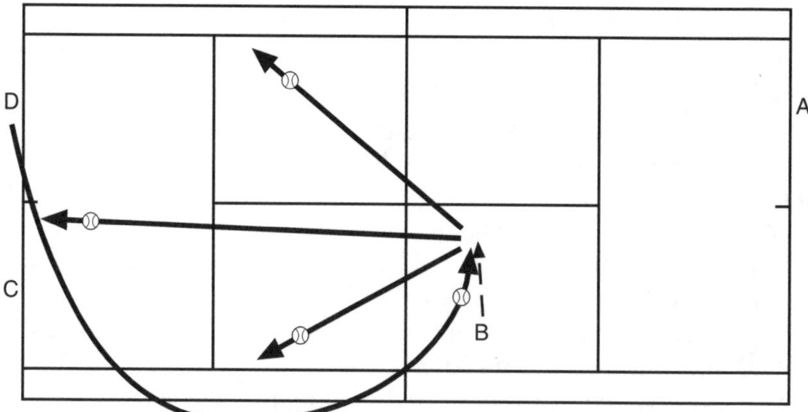

Figure 3.14 Player B returning a lob from player C or D by hitting an overhead from the center to one of the three soft spots in the coverage (the two angles or the middle).

options are to hit the angle overhead crosscourt, hit the overhead on an angle down the middle, or hit the overhead on a slight angle into the left alley (see figure 3.16). By hitting into the soft spots in your opponents' coverage, you give yourself the best chance to put away their short lobs. *Note:* In this explanation, we cover the proper defensive positions to play against lobs hit to the middle or to either

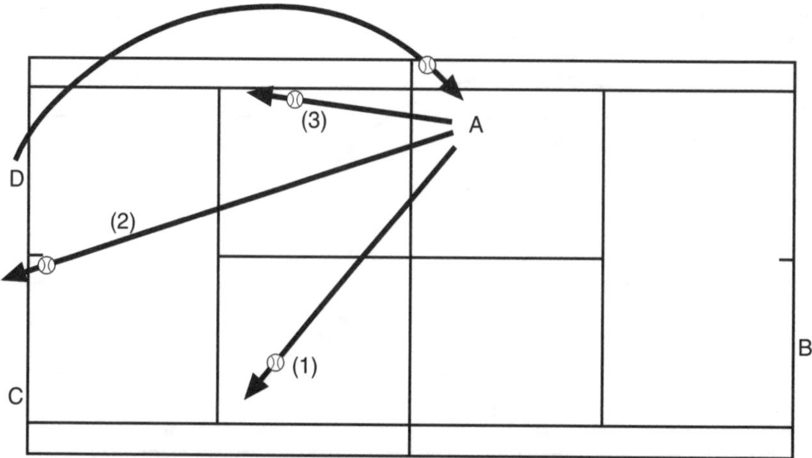

Figure 3.15 Player A in the deuce court returning a lob from player C or D by hitting an overhead with a sharp angle to the left alley (1), down the middle (2), or with a slight angle to the right alley (3).

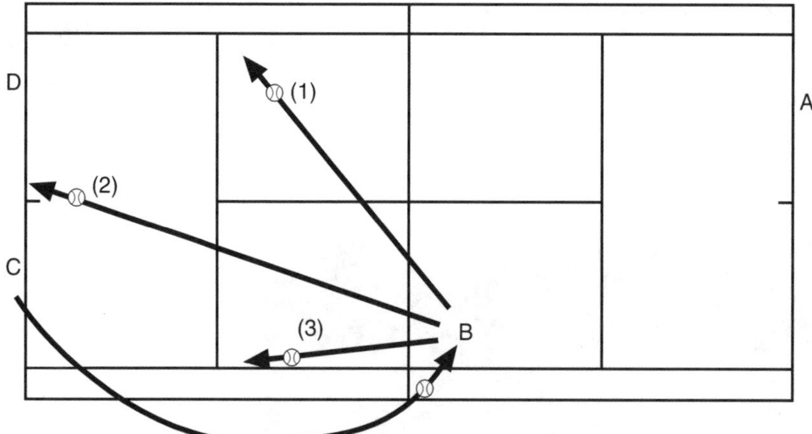

Figure 3.16 Player B in the ad court returning a lob from player C or D by hitting an overhead with a sharp angle to the right alley (1), down the middle (2), or with a slight angle to the left alley (3).

side of the court. The general rule for lob coverage is the closer to the doubles line the ball lands, the more toward the opposite doubles line you have to cover.

Our Quick Tips section on overheads helps you put away short lobs in practice and in matches.

Quick Tips

Overheads

⊖ **Problem**—You're hitting your overheads into the net.

⊕ **Solution 1**—You're making contact with the ball too far in front of you, which causes your racquet face to point at the ground on contact (see figure 3.17). In this case, set up with the ball 3 inches in front of your hitting shoulder and as high as you can reach (right shoulder if you're right-handed) (see figure 3.18). This helps you to contact the ball in the correct hitting zone.

⊕ **Solution 2**—If solution 1 doesn't work, you're probably contacting the ball too low, which causes your racquet face to point at the ground on contact (see figure 3.19). In this case, contact the ball as

Figure 3.17 Player hitting an overhead too far in front of her with the racquet face pointing at the ground on contact.

Figure 3.18 Player hitting an overhead in the correct hitting zone.

Figure 3.19 Player letting an overhead drop too low, with the racquet face pointing at the ground on contact.

high as you can reach. This forces you to swing up to the ball and follow through toward your target (see figure 3.18).

Solution 3—If solution 2 isn't the answer, you're probably pulling your head and shoulders down before you contact the ball, which causes your racquet face to point at the ground on contact (see figure 3.20). In this case, keep your left arm pointed at the ball until the point of contact. This automatically forces you to keep your head and shoulders up.

Problem—Your overheads are going long.

Solution 1—You're overhitting the ball. In this case, don't swing as hard at the ball. This brings the pace of your swing in line with your stroke.

Solution 2—If solution 1 isn't working, you're probably hitting the ball behind your head (see figure 3.21). In this case, set up with the ball about 3 inches in front of your hitting shoulder. This helps

Figure 3.20 Player hitting an overhead, pulling his head and shoulders down, with the racquet face pointing at the ground on contact.

Figure 3.21 Player hitting an overhead with the ball behind his head.

you contact the ball with your racquet facing your target (see figure 3.18).

Figure 3.22 Player hitting an overhead with an open racquet face (incorrect form).

⊕ **Solution 3**—If you have no luck with solution 2, your racquet face is probably facing the sky at contact (as opposed to facing your target) (see figure 3.22). In this case, cover the ball with your wrist at contact. This causes you to hit the ball down into the court (see figure 3.18).

• • • • • • • • • • • • • • • •

⊖ **Problem**—You're hitting your overheads wide.

⊕ **Solution 1**—You're probably hitting with your shoulders square to the net (see figure 3.23a). In this case, turn your left shoulder (for a right-hander) to the net while the ball is in the air (see figure 3.23b). This helps you hit the ball straight, because the ball goes in the direction your shoulders are pointing.

⊕ **Solution 2**—If solution 1 isn't successful, you're probably hitting the right side of the ball (for a right-hander) (see figure 3.24). In this case, focus on hitting the back of the ball on contact. This makes the ball go straight rather than to the side (see figure 3.18).

⊕ **Solution 3**—If solution 2 isn't working, you're probably dipping and turning your head and shoulders (see figure 3.25). In this case, point your left arm at the ball until the point of contact. This keeps your head and shoulders from dropping and turning and helps you hit the ball straight (see figure 3.18).

If you find that you're missing the overhead the same way repeatedly, use our quick tips to help you work through your problem.

Figure 3.23a-b (a) Player setting up for an overhead with shoulders square to the net (incorrect form). (b) Player turned sideways for an overhead (correct form).

Figure 3.24 Player hitting the right side of the ball on an overhead, causing a wide error.

Figure 3.25 Player hitting an overhead, dropping his shoulder and turning his head, causing a wide error.

These tips are most helpful in match-type situations, because they are easy solutions that can get you out of some tight spots.

Learn Strategy

The fifth key to success is learning strategies that help you to be successful in both singles and doubles.

Singles Strategy

Once again, the ability to hit every ball back into play is a must. However, this alone will not win you as many matches as it did at the 3.0 level, because most of the more advanced players at the 3.5 level can hit every ball back plus do more. Therefore, to be the one to hit the last ball back into play, you have to think offensively and defensively. You have to play the game as it presents itself. This means that when you have a chance to play offensively, you take advantage of it and force your opponent's hand. And when your opponent hits an offensive shot, you play a smart defensive shot and recover to the middle, rather than trying to create an offensive shot that isn't there. In this section on singles strategy, we show you what kind of offensive and defensive shots to hit in specific situations. We also talk about how you approach a match.

Offensive Shots. When playing 3.5-level singles, the three basic singles strategies outlined in chapter 2 (consistency, moving your opponent, and playing to your opponent's weaknesses) are good building blocks from which to start; however, they won't bring you the measure of success you're looking for by themselves. In general, players at the 3.5 level are more consistent, move better, and have fewer weaknesses. That's why they're rated a level higher! You still want to play consistently, move your opponent, and play to their weaknesses. That works against a low-level 3.5 player. However, for a mid- to upper-level 3.5 player, that's all just part of the game; it's not a single strategy you can depend on. *Therefore, for simplification, we assume that your opponent is consistent and moves fairly well but has some weaknesses that can be exploited.*

The primary determining factor between offensive and defensive tennis is your ability to hit the ball deep into the court. (At the 3.5 level, we redefine deep as any ball that lands between 1 yard behind the service line and the baseline.) If you hit the ball deep every time, your opponent has little chance to play offensive tennis. There are several reasons for this. First, it's too difficult for a 3.5-level player to hit the ball *consistently hard* from the baseline. If she could, she wouldn't be a 3.5-level player. Therefore, she commits too many errors if she employs an offensive strategy from too far back in the court. Second, by hitting the ball deep, you often force your opponent to hit the ball off her back foot, and this forces her to hit the ball defensively. Obviously, when she hits defensive shots, she can't hit offensive shots. Third, if you hit the ball deep and move your opponent, you again force her to hit the ball defensively. And we already know that you can't hit offensive shots when you're forced to hit defensive shots. On the other hand, if you hit the ball short, your opponent has a variety of offensive shots from which to choose, because she's in prime position to force your hand. These are the reasons why hitting the ball deep is your primary goal on every point.

Now that we've covered the need for depth on your groundstrokes, let's put it into the context of our offensive and defensive theme by showing you how points are played in certain situations.

Assuming that both you and your opponent are at the baseline, you want to hit the ball deep at a moderate pace to force a return you can take advantage of. This is the same as jockeying for position. Once your opponent hits the ball short, you think offensively. We defined a short ball for the 3.0-level player as any ball that lands in front of the service line. However, since 3.5-level players are generally quicker and judge the bounce of the ball better, we define a short ball at this level as any ball that you can get both feet inside the baseline to hit. This gives you more discretion and more opportunities to approach the net.

Once you've forced the short ball, you have three offensive options: drive the ball into one of the corners, hit an approach shot and go to the net, or hit a drop or "dink" shot.

The first option, driving the ball into one of the corners, is the most common option for the 3.5-level singles player. It allows you to play aggressively without putting the entire point on the line by approaching the net. Most 3.5-level singles players choose this option because they're not comfortable covering the whole net by themselves—a direct result of lack of confidence in their volleying skills. This option allows you to win the point outright or take control of the point by moving your opponent from the center of the court. Once you move your opponent from the center, you hit the ball into the open court on your next shot. When you're dictating the points in this manner, you're playing aggressively and employing more than just the three basic strategies we spoke of in chapter 2. You're effectively taking advantage of your opponent's weak shots, which are created by the depth of your groundstrokes.

The second option is to hit an approach shot and go to the net. As stated earlier, most 3.5-level singles players don't feel comfortable approaching the net because they lack confidence in their volleying skills. For those in this category, the only way to gain confidence in your singles approach is to practice the approach and to use it in match play. However, many players at this level enjoy playing the net. For those players who expose themselves to a little more risk, the rewards can be greater, because approaching the net and successfully executing your volleys translates into easier put-aways.

For example, if you approach down the line off a weak second serve and move your opponent from the center, more often than not you force your opponent to hit a defensive shot. With this defensive shot, your opponent is trying to neutralize your attack. In this situation, he's forced to be precise. For example, let's say your opponent lobs defensively (which often happens because he's not in a position to lob offensively). If the lob goes over your head, it'll be high and you'll have plenty of time to retrieve it. On the other hand, if the lob is short, you'll have a high-percentage chance of putting your overhead away because the ball is close to the net and your opponent is out of position.

Another example is your opponent hitting the ball at your feet. If you hit a good approach shot, this is a hard shot for him to execute because he's on the run. In this situation, he's playing the ball at your feet to make you hit the most difficult volley possible. If he succeeds, he has a chance to recover and win the point. However, if he fails and hits the ball high, you hit the ball into the open court and win the point. The most important factor here is choosing the right shot on which to approach, so you can force your opponent into making a defensive shot. When you do this, your opponent won't have a chance to win the point on the next shot (unless you miss), but you will. (For example, besides approaching on a short ball, you can hit a deep, high ball that your opponent has to play defensively and gives you ample time to get to the net. This usually results in a successful approach shot, which we define as any approach shot that gets a defensive reply.)

Approaching the net sounds too good to be true, doesn't it? Sometimes it is. The big risk for a good 3.5-level player in approaching the net is hitting a poor approach shot, because you put yourself at the mercy of your opponent. He can hit a passing shot, a low ball, or an offensive lob, any of which can end the point without giving you much chance to make a play. Thus, you lose a point before it even begins. Without a good approach shot, you have a low-percentage chance of winning the point from the net.

The final option is to hit a drop or "dink" shot. This option is usually set up by the other two options. Typically, if you've been driving the ball into the corners or approaching the net with regularity on your opponent's short shots, he starts to anticipate what you're going to do. You use the drop shot to win points by keeping your opponent honest (if you see that he is overanticipating your shots), surprising him, or running him (if he's slow). However, this shot comes with a warning. It's one of the lowest percentage shots you can hit and should be used sparingly. Also, don't try to hit this shot from deep in the court, because it gives your opponent too much time to retrieve the ball. If your opponent gets to the ball with any time to spare, it usually spells trouble for you!

Those are your three offensive options when someone hits the ball short. The other three offensive shots you can choose from—the low ball, the passing shot, and the offensive lob—are for use against someone who attacks the net. Your shot selection depends on your situation. The only time these options present themselves is when your opponent hits a poor approach shot or volley and you have a chance to set up in a position to execute them.

The first option when your opponent hits a poor approach shot or volley is to hit a passing shot. Your main goal here is to hit the ball away from him so he can't make a play on it. Your two choices are to hit the ball down the line or crosscourt. When hitting the passing shot, don't hit the ball deep. Just get the ball past your opponent, and if it goes deep, so much the better. Also, you want to hit the ball low when attempting a passing shot. You do this as insurance, because if your opponent does get to the ball, he still has to make a difficult volley from below the level of the net, which keeps you in the point. Again, don't try this shot if your feet and body aren't properly set. You only hit the passing shot when you're in a position to control your shot.

The second option is to hit a low ball at your opponent's feet. This play isn't as aggressive as the passing shot, but it also isn't as risky. As long as you keep the ball low, your chances of winning the point are excellent. Hitting the low ball is a conservative play in that you're merely controlling the height of the ball while forcing your opponent to hit a shot that is very difficult for 3.5-level players. Thus, we think the low ball is the most effective shot you can hit for the amount of risk you take. Also, you can use it to set up easy passing shots or offensive lobs. For example, when your opponent is at the net, you can drive the ball at his feet to force him to hit a weak volley (one that bounces high with no pace). After he hits the weak volley, you have an easier time hitting the more aggressive passing shot or offensive lob.

It's always a good play to use the low-ball shot against your opponent when she's at the net. However, it's easier to hit this shot in certain situations. For example, if your opponent is standing at the service line, it's easier to hit the ball at her feet than if she's standing right on top of the net, because you have more room in which to land the ball and don't have to hit it as precisely. Therefore, the best time to hit the ball low is when your opponent is approaching the net, because she usually won't advance past the service line to make her first volley. Beyond that, you have to look at the tendencies of your opponent. Check where she plays when she's at the net. If your opponent never advances past the service line, you can give her fits all day long by hitting the ball at her feet. If she advances all the way to the net, it might be too difficult to hit the ball at her feet because she's so close to the net. It might be easier to lob the ball over her head. In any case, the low-ball shot is a good play if executed properly.

The third option off a poor approach shot or volley by your opponent is the offensive lob. Your main goal here is to hit the ball over your opponent's head so she either can't retrieve the ball or retrieves the ball and leaves you with another offensive shot. For the offensive lob to be successful, you have to hit the ball low or just over your opponent's head. The risk with this shot is that if you don't get the ball over her head, she'll have an easy put-away. Also, although it can be successful in some circumstances, we don't recommend hitting this shot off an approach shot by your opponent. We recommend waiting to hit the offensive lob until your opponent has closed to the net after a volley, because there is more room behind her in which to land the ball. The offensive lob is a lower percentage shot than the other offensive shots (except the drop shot), but it's a great shot to have if you can execute it consistently.

The forehand drive, approach shot, drop shot, passing shot, low ball, and offensive lob are the six offensive shots that you should be aware of at the 3.5 level. You already hit five of these shots with some proficiency because we've demonstrated them in this and earlier chapters. The lone exception is the passing shot, which is new, but you are somewhat familiar with it because it's an extension of shots we've already covered.

Defensive Shots. Defensive shots are equally as important as offensive shots in match-type situations. Defensive shots are shots you hit when you're out of position and trying to stay in a point. There aren't many of them because there aren't many ways that you can get out of position. Remember, if you hit your groundstrokes deep on every shot, you'll seldom have to play defensive tennis. But if you hit the ball short often, you'll have to play more defensive tennis than you want.

Let's start with the baseline. When you're rallying from the baseline and your opponent forces you away from the center of the court where you don't have sufficient time to recover, you have two defensive options.

The first option is to lob the ball deep. When you're pulled off the court, your main goal on your next shot is not to hit a winner, but to provide yourself enough time to recover back to the center. By lobbing defensively, you give yourself time to recover while the ball is in the air (see figure 3.26). This works against forehand and backhand drives and approach shots.

The second option is to hit a groundstroke high over the net into the middle of the court or crosscourt (see figure 3.27). The height of the ball gives you time to recover to the middle. Directing the ball to the middle or crosscourt cuts off any angles your opponent might have created with her offensive shot. For example, if you hit a low groundstroke down the line (line 2) instead of a high ball crosscourt or down the middle, your opponent can easily force you out of the middle of the court by hitting her next shot crosscourt into the open court (line 3) (see figure 3.28). Once your opponent gets you running, you're at her mercy unless you hit some excellent defensive shots. *Note:* Although this is a good defensive play against a forehand or backhand drive where your opponent stays on the baseline, it is not a good defensive play against an approach shot because you leave your opponent with an easy high volley.

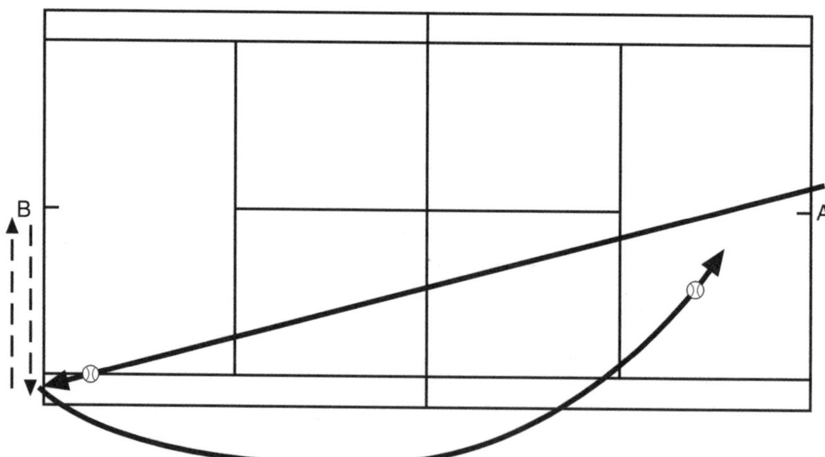

Figure 3.26 Player B hitting a defensive lob when pulled off the court by player A's offensive shot, with the dotted line showing player B's movement back to the center after the lob.

Although these two options sound simple, you need only look at what they do to your opponent to measure their effectiveness. After your opponent has worked to set up a shot she can hit offensively, you effectively neutralize her aggression with a good defensive shot. She now has to work to get into a situation where she can play of-

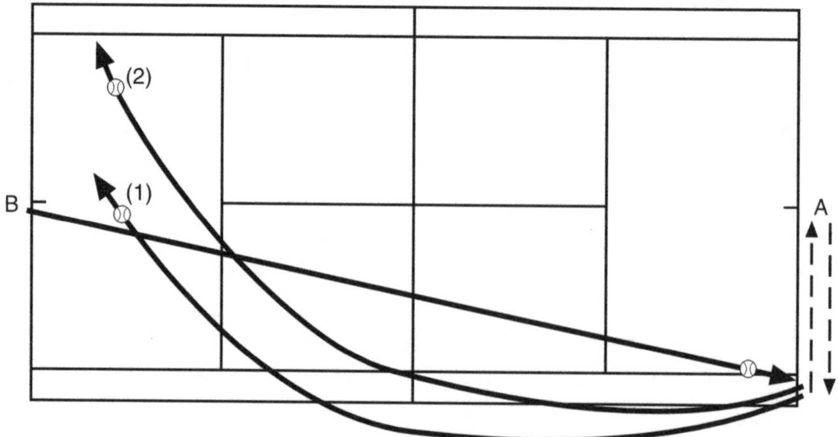

Figure 3.27 Player A hitting a high groundstroke down the center of the court (1) or crosscourt (2), with the dotted line showing player A's movement back to the center to recover after the shot.

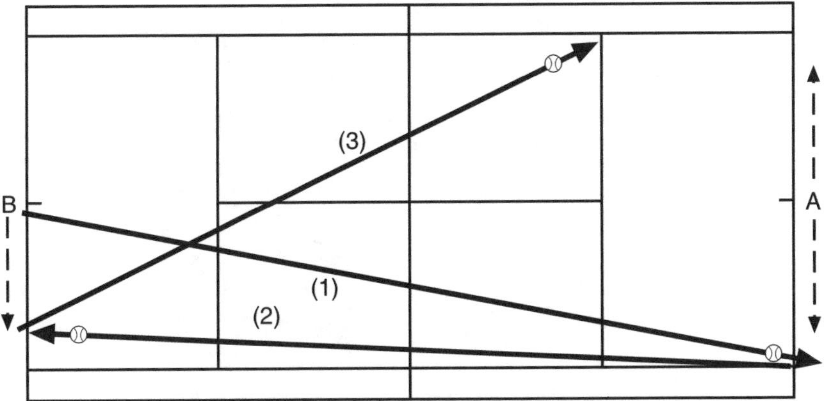

Figure 3.28 Player B hitting an offensive shot to player A's backhand corner (1). Player A hitting a groundstroke down the left line (2). Player B hitting crosscourt into the open court (3).

fensively again. Over the course of a match, this is very disheartening and can sap your opponent's confidence, which could prove to be the deciding factor in the match.

Another defensive shot you can hit is the defensive overhead. You hit this shot when you're at the net and the ball goes over your head, but you're still able to catch up with it and hit an overhead. Your main goal on the defensive overhead is to play the ball deep into the court so you can return to the net or retreat to the baseline. Most of the time, the ball is behind you when you hit this shot, but that makes the shot easier to execute, because your preparation is a little different for a defensive overhead than for a regular overhead. On the defensive overhead you only take the racquet back half as far as you do for a regular overhead because you want to hit up on the ball to give it some trajectory so it will land deep into the court (see figures 3.29 and 3.30).

After hitting the defensive overhead, you must determine whether you return to the net or retreat. You return to the net if you've returned the ball deep and haven't been pushed too far into the backcourt. You return to the baseline if you've hit the ball short and/or your momentum carries you too far into the backcourt. Either way, by hitting the overhead defensively, you keep yourself in the point with a high-percentage shot.

The shots described are the three most important defensive shots for you to know at this level. Once again, these shots are just varia-

Figure 3.29 Abbreviated preparation for the defensive overhead.

Figure 3.30 Defensive overhead after contact with the ball going high over the net and deep into the court.

tions of shots you already know. To gain confidence in them, you have to put them in context and practice them in game situations.

Approaching the Match. Now that we've covered your offensive and defensive options and the situations in which you use them, we need to address your approach to the match. As stated earlier, you need to do more than just hit the ball back every time, but your strategy is to take no more risks than are necessary to win the match. When you start the match, you have to feel out your opponent, assessing his consistency, mobility, and strengths and weaknesses. If you play someone at the lower end of the 3.5 scale, you may not have to do much more than you did at the 3.0 level to win the match. However, chances are you're going to have to use some or all of the offensive and defensive options we've just discussed. If this is the case, start the match by hitting the ball deep and giving yourself time to identify your opponent's weaknesses.

For simplicity, let's group weaknesses into two categories: groundstroking weaknesses and net game weaknesses. If your opponent has groundstroking weaknesses, you can easily exploit them by hitting the ball deep to whichever side is weakest. If that doesn't work, you have to move the ball around to better expose his weakness. If it's truly a weakness, it will manifest itself. For example, if you've detected that your opponent has a stroking deficiency on the forehand side, hit to that side to force him to miss or to hit a short ball. If he hits a short ball, choose the offensive option you're most comfortable with. For instance, if you like to play the net, you hit an approach shot off the short ball and go to the net. By playing this way, you're playing to the strongest part of your game. The most common option at the 3.5 level is to drive the short ball into one of the corners so you can control the point. This is playing to your strength if you like to play the baseline. However, we caution you not to play too one-dimensionally. Once you get on the offensive, you use a mix of the three offensive options for short balls to keep your opponent off guard. You want to play mainly to your strengths, but you also need to keep your opponent off balance.

You'll find that you win easy points when you surprise your opponents with different shots. Also, you soften them up, because they aren't as quick to anticipate your next move.

If your opponent has net game weaknesses, chances are he avoids playing the net, so to exploit those weaknesses, you have to bring him to the net. The way to force him to the net is to hit drop shots or balls that he isn't able to play offensively and isn't able to retreat to the baseline after hitting. After you bring him to the net, hit the ball low at his feet, because it's the shot that gives him the most trouble and is the least risky for you to hit (especially if your opponent doesn't play the net well). A player with limited ability at the net is likely to miss many of these shots, and if he doesn't miss, he'll probably hit a ball that you can play more offensively. If you feel confident, you can try some of the other offensive options or continue to hit the ball low at his feet. Either way, you'll probably be successful.

By identifying the groundstroking or net weaknesses of your opponent, you can use the offensive strategies we've just described; however, you aren't always in position to play offensively, which is why we've shown you the defensive options and the situations in which you employ them. You want to play defense more as a situational response than to use it as a strategy. The problem with using a defensive strategy is that you have to be extremely good at it to be successful. Essentially, you're saying to your opponent, "You can run me around the court and consistently put me in situations where I have to hit very precise shots to win or stay in the point." We're not saying that you can't do this successfully, because you can. But the more offensive weapons your opponent has, the more trouble you'll have executing your strategy. For example, if your opponent likes to come to the net and hits deep approach shots, you have to lob the ball over his head most of the time when he approaches. If the ball doesn't go over his head, he has an easy overhead with which to end the point or force you into hitting another lob. This strategy is only successful if you can hit so many good lobs that he stops coming to the net, because you have taken away the strength of his game. If your opponent doesn't have many offensive skills, you might be successful; but you'd better pack a lunch, because you're going to be on the court for a long time.

In general, we believe you learn to play both offensively and defensively as the situations arise. Knowing when to go for or lay off of a shot increases the percentage of good plays that you make, which increases the quality of your tennis. It also forces you to play multidimensionally, which gives you more ways to win a match.

Doubles Strategy

At this point, we strongly suggest that you reread the doubles keys to success in chapter 2, because they're the fundamentals of strategy and positioning for all one-up, one-back tennis and are still applicable to 3.5-level doubles. The difference at the 3.5 level is that players execute the strategy and position themselves better than 3.0-level players because they have more experience and confidence in the one-up, one-back formation. Therefore, we don't cover the basics of that formation again, but we point out the slight differences in what it takes to be successful in that formation at the 3.5 level. Instead, we focus more on the offensive transition from the one-up, one-back formation to the two-up formation and on how to defend against this transition, because it becomes a key element of the doubles game at the 3.5 level. We also show you how to play the two-up formation.

One-Up, One-Back Versus One-Up, One-Back. In this section, we cover the key points of the one-up, one-back formation versus the one-up, one-back formation and the strategic adjustments you need to make at the 3.5 level.

In the one-up, one-back formation, the points are set up by the baseline player. At the 3.0 level, you wanted the baseline player to play the ball crosscourt consistently on each shot without regard for the depth. If she hit the ball deep, so much the better; but her main focus was to keep the ball away from the net player and to keep her team in the point. This changes at the 3.5 level. You can no longer play the ball crosscourt without regard for the depth because your opponents have more skills and move better. Therefore, as the baseline player in this formation, you not only have to hit the ball crosscourt consistently, but you also have to hit it deep consistently. Otherwise your opponents approach the net on short balls and play the two-up formation, putting you at a disadvantage. On the other hand, if you hit the ball consistently deep every time, you're going to set up your partner for easy put-aways at the net and you're going to get short balls. So the key change at the 3.5 level is to add depth to your crosscourt consistency.

The second adjustment you have to make at the 3.5 level is that the net person must play more offensively at the net. Since 3.5-level players are better volleyers than 3.0-level players, they play more aggressively. At the 3.0 level, we said that the net person takes the ball if it comes to her or if she gets to the ball and hits an effective volley. At the 3.5 level, you do exactly the same thing, except you move more at the net. Make sure that the opposing baseline player knows you're there. Make her think about you and not the shot she needs to hit. You do this by poaching and faking.

When you poach, you cross to the middle of the court to intercept your opponents' shot (see figure 3.31). Poaching enables you to catch your opponents off guard and out of position for an easy put-away. Also, it forces your opponents to think about what you're going to do on each shot and not about what shot they have to hit. This causes your opponents to make unforced errors.

You can poach in two ways: You can tell your partner that you're going to poach or you can use your discretion as the point is being played. Usually when you tell your partner that you're going to poach, you poach on your opponents' return of serve. You do this because it's a premeditated play, and you have to give your partner a definite time when you're going to go. Otherwise, your partner is left guessing when you're going to poach. Also, if you poach and your momentum carries you to your partner's half of the court, she has to be ready to switch sides. By telling your partner when you're going to poach, you're ensuring against a communication breakdown. The other option, poaching without telling your partner, is an instinctive move. When you use this option, the key is to put the

Figure 3.31 Player poaching in doubles to cut off a groundstroke.

ball away or force your opponent into a defensive shot, because if you don't, your team will be out of position with two people on the same half of the court. To help you move more efficiently in this situation, follow this rule: If the net person who's poaching doesn't cross over to the baseline player's half of the court, she remains on her half; if the net person does cross over to her partner's half of the court, she continues to that half of the court and the baseline player switches to the opposite half of the court. By following this rule, you won't get caught with both of you on the same side of the court.

The other way to attract your opponents' attention is to fake like you're going to poach. When you fake to the middle, you do it long before your opponents are going to hit the ball, because you want them to see you before the ball gets to them. You want them to think you're poaching so they worry about you before they actually hit the ball. This affects your opponents in a couple of ways. First, it makes them nervous, because they constantly have to worry about whether or not you're going to poach. This forces your opponents to make errors, because it takes their attention away from hitting the ball. Second, you can use your opponents' nervousness to your advantage by faking toward the middle and forcing them to hit the ball right to you. This results in easy put-aways because you're waiting for the ball.

Overall, poaching and faking help break down your opponents' confidence. When they start to make errors, they become tentative. The more tentative they get, the less confidence they have, which results in more errors. It becomes a vicious cycle that works to your advantage, so take the time to learn how to fake and poach effectively.

Hitting the ball deep from the baseline and playing more aggressively at the net are the two main differences between the 3.0 and 3.5 levels for the one-up, one-back versus the one-up, one-back formation. You may not have noticed that we didn't talk much about offensive and defensive tennis in the one-up, one-back section. The reason is that there's not much offensive and defensive tennis to talk about in this formation. The only two offensive moves are when the net person poaches or fakes to force the other team's hand and the baseline player of the team being poached against hits a passing shot down the alley. And the only defensive moves are the opposing team's reaction to the poaching or faking, which is a defensive lob or a high crosscourt return when the baseline player gets pulled out of position. Other than that, there are no offensive or defensive moves that weren't covered in the doubles section of chapter 2. The offensive and defensive moves come into play when one of the teams advances to the net in a two-up formation. That's when the fun starts!

Transition From One-Up, One-Back to Two-Up. As you play doubles at higher levels, it becomes increasingly important to learn to play more offensively. To play doubles more offensively at the 3.5 level, you have to learn to do two things: (1) to make the transition from the one-up, one-back formation to the two-up formation, and (2) to play the two-up formation.

First, we focus on the transition from the one-up, one-back to the two-up formation. At the 3.5 level, there are three ways to accomplish this offensive goal. You can approach the net on a short shot from your opponents, on a weak serve by your opponents, or on a lob hit over the opposing net player's head. Let's look at the first option.

Since both teams usually start every point from the one-up, one-back formation, the principles stated earlier in this section still apply. As the baseline player, you set up your partner for an easy volley by consistently rallying the ball crosscourt and deep, and at the same time, you set yourself up with short balls on which you can approach the net. Remember that at the 3.0 level, you didn't want to approach the net off a short ball unless you had to, because you didn't want to play the two-up formation. However, at the 3.5 level, you look for short balls on which you can approach the net because you want to play the more offensive two-up formation.

Once your opponent hits the ball short, you, as player A, make your approach shot deep crosscourt and head toward the net. When your opponent (player C) goes to hit the ball, split-step so that you're ready to volley (movement 1 in figure 3.32). The thing to remember here is that you have to cover the lob if it is hit over your partner's (player B's) head (movement 2 in figure 3.32). This is the only time you're responsible for a lob that is hit over your partner's head, because you're in a better position to retrieve the ball. The reason is that while you're advancing, you're not as far into the court as your partner, who is already at the net. Since you're responsible for the lob on the first shot, you don't want to advance to where your partner is standing at the net. You want to stop a few steps behind him, then, if your opponents don't lob, you can volley, move forward, and follow the direction of the ball to find your correct position (movement 3 in figure 3.32). (Following the direction of the ball and team movements are covered in depth in our explanation of the

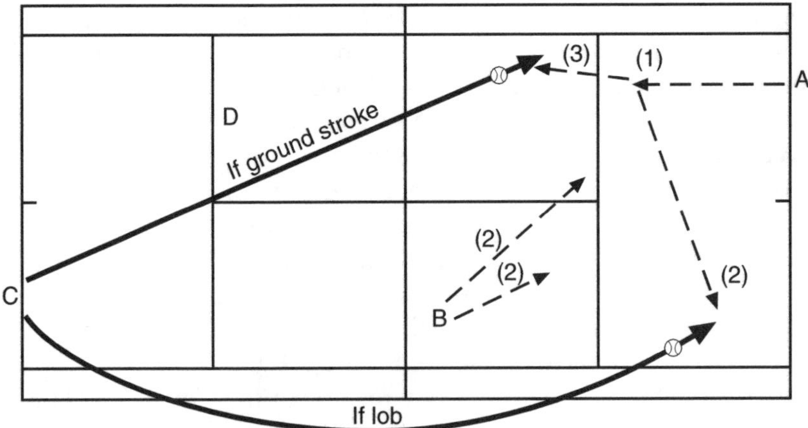

Figure 3.32 Player A approaching the net and split-stepping a few steps behind player B (1). If the return shot from player C is a lob over player B, player A moves behind player B to cover and player B switches (2). If player A sees the return is a groundstroke, he volleys and moves up to join player B, who moves back a step, because he now has to cover his own lobs (3).

two-up formation.) After you've done this, you've successfully made the transition from the one-up, one-back to the two-up formation.

The second way to go from the one-up, one-back to the two-up formation is to approach off a weak second serve by your opponent. This is essentially the same play as approaching off a short ball by your opponent because, fundamentally, you do the same thing we showed you in the preceding explanation. The difference is that you immediately put pressure on your opponents' serve—the first ball put into play—giving them no chance to get into a rhythm or get comfortable on their serve. This translates into unforced errors by your opponents and free points for you, because the immediate pressure plays on their minds and forces them to panic and rush their shots. Just think how much you dislike it when someone does this to you. This, more than any other reason, is why players lose their serve at the 3.5 level.

The third way to go from the one-up, one-back to the two-up formation is to lob over the net player's head. This can be done during a rally or off your opponents' first or second serve, but you have to be careful. First, as the baseline player, you have to make sure the ball goes over the net player's head. To do this, watch how he reacts to your lob. If he doesn't move and sets up to hit an overhead, you stay on the baseline. If he turns his back to you or switches to the opposite half of the court, you advance to the two-up formation. Once both you and your partner are at the net, play at the service line, because your opponents' next shot is probably a lob (especially if the person covering it is hitting a backhand). By positioning yourselves in the back third of the service box, you give yourselves the maximum chance to succeed, because you make it easier to hit overheads or retrieve lobs hit over your heads.

Approaching off a short shot, a weak second serve by your opponents, or off a good lob are your three offensive options in the transition from the one-up, one-back to the two-up formation. If you don't take advantage of these shots, you let your opponents off the hook instead of making them pay for one of their mistakes. For example, if you and your opponents are both in a one-up, one-back formation and your opponents hit a short ball, you can either approach the net and get into the two-up formation, which puts pressure on your opponents and forces them to play defense, or you can hit the ball back to them and return to the baseline, which lets them off the hook and puts no pressure on them. Teams that advance and put pressure on their opponents are usually the teams that win, provided they can volley well enough to play the two-up formation.

Two-Up Formation. The two-up formation is the last standard doubles formation you need to learn. After you make a successful transition from the one-up, one-back to the two-up formation, your goal is to stay in this formation until the other team makes an error or until you put the ball away. You accomplish this goal by maintaining control of the net until one of these two things occurs. The way to control the net is to play high-percentage tennis by positioning yourself correctly and knowing where to hit the ball.

The correct positioning for the two-up formation depends on where the ball is on the court, because you, as a team, have to follow the direction of the ball. We've already touched on how to follow the ball in chapter 2, but now we need to be more specific, because you need to move to certain positions according to where the ball goes on the court. For simplicity, we divide the court into thirds (see figure 3.33). The first position we cover is when the ball is hit into the middle of the court (area 2). When the ball is in the middle of the court, you, as players A and B, stand the same distance from the net and "pinch" the middle, which gives you equal coverage of the court (see figure 3.34). This positioning leaves no holes into which the other team can hit and essentially forces them to play

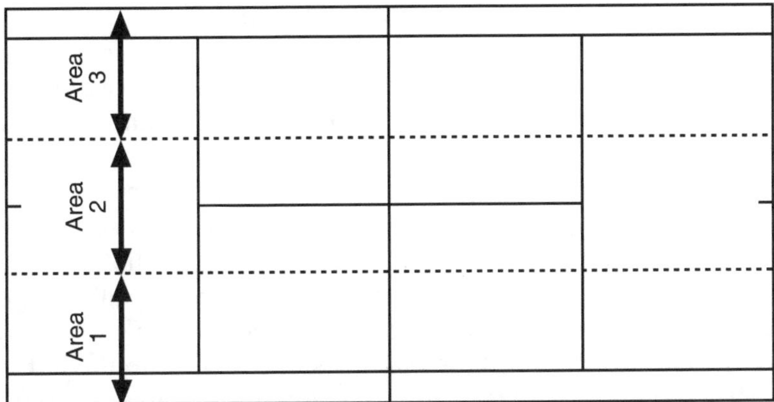

Figure 3.33 The three areas of the court into which the ball can be hit.

the ball to the middle. The key here is to communicate on the balls hit down the middle. If you can do that, you hold the net and force your opponents into trying some things that they don't want to try. When the ball goes to the deuce court alley (area 1), the net person on the left side of the court (player B) moves forward a step and toward the alley to the same degree as the angle of the ball. The other net player (player A) moves toward the middle (see figure 3.35). This is where the infamous imaginary rope theory comes into play. According to this theory, you pretend there's an imaginary rope tied between you and your partner that keeps

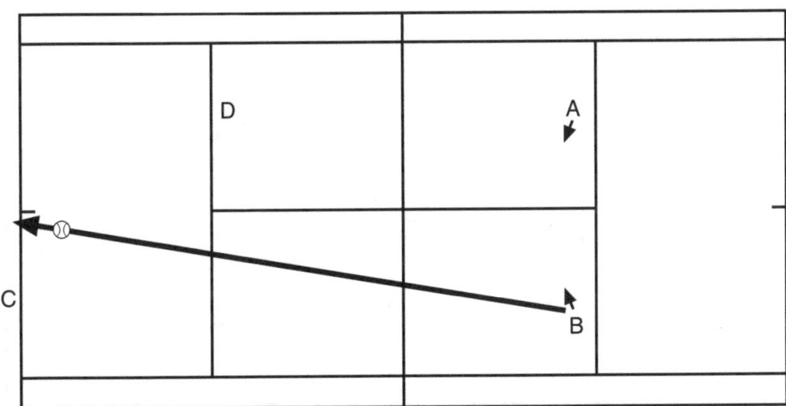

Figure 3.34 Players A and B pinching the middle when either of them hits the ball up the middle to player C.

you the same distance apart at all times. If your partner moves two steps toward the alley, you have to move two steps toward the alley. By doing this, you move in sync with each other and don't leave any holes in your positioning for your opponents to exploit.

There are several reasons why you, as player B, move toward the alley at the angle of the ball. First, the alley is your responsibility. You don't want to give your opponents a free shot down the alley, because there's no one behind you to get the ball if it goes past you. The best way to do this is to follow the angle of the ball. The further into the alley the ball goes, the further to the left you go. Second, you want to take away the down-the-line shot and force your opponents to hit the ball crosscourt, where you have the help of your partner. By doing this, you take away the other team's chances of hitting a winner and force them to hit the ball back to your team, so you can control the net. Third, by moving up a little, you put yourself in a position to play an offensive shot if a high ball comes to you. When moving forward, be aware that once you've made the transition to the two-up formation, you're responsible for covering your own lobs. So if the ball is lobbed over your head, you have to be ready to retreat.

On the other half of the court, you, as player A, move toward the middle. This is important because, if you don't move toward the middle, there will be an opening in the middle of your team's positioning left by player B's movement toward the alley. We all

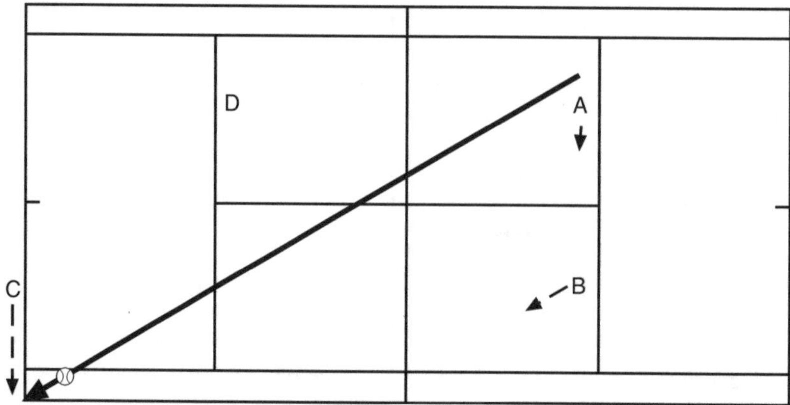

Figure 3.35 Player A hitting a wide ball to player C, with player B moving to the left alley and player A moving to the middle of the court.

know how many times you've heard or read that you should hit the ball down the middle against a team playing the two-up formation. So you have to cover that middle! By moving toward the middle, you do leave a small opening for the other team to hit the ball crosscourt, but if you move your opponents on your approach shot, they're forced to try a difficult, low-percentage shot. So what you're essentially doing is covering the areas that are the easiest to hit to and forcing your opponents to hit to the more difficult areas or to be more precise with their shots into the easier areas. That's how you play smart doubles!

We've just covered how to move with the ball when it's hit into the left alley, so we won't cover how to move with the ball when it's hit into the right alley, because you simply make the same movements from the other side. If you follow these simple team movements for the two-up formation, you'll improve your doubles game, because you'll play smarter tennis and make it harder for your opponents to beat you.

Now that you know how to make the transition from the one-up, one-back to the two-up formation and how to play the two-up formation, we need to look at the two-up versus the one-up, one-back and the two-up versus the two-back formations.

Two-Up Versus One-Up, One-Back. We cover the two-up versus the one-up, one-back formation first because it's the formation you'll most likely play against when you're in the two-up formation. When you make the transition to two-up against a team that plays the one-up, one-back formation, hit your approach shot crosscourt to the baseline player on the other team, which calls for your team to shift to the side of the court at the angle of the ball. The strategy is very simple from here on. Volley the low balls (those below your waist) defensively to your opponents' baseline player, and volley the high balls (waist-high and above) offensively through the net player by hitting to her feet or into any gaps in your opponents' alignment. When you get a high volley at the 3.5 level, it's imperative that you hit 85 percent of the balls into these areas, because it's an offensive opportunity to end the point; otherwise, you have to wait for your opponents to miss or to hit another high ball to have a chance to win the point. And the good teams don't miss that often!

The other play that your opponents can use is the lob. If they lob and the ball lands short, hit your overhead with pace through the net player (she's more than likely retreating to the baseline) or angle it off into the open court. If she returns the ball and retreats to the baseline, employ the strategies described in the following section for use against a two-back team. If the lob is hit over your head but you're able to hit it in the air, play a defensive overhead deep to your opponents' baseline player and return to the net. By doing this, you maintain control of the net. If the lob is over your head and you can't hit it in the air, play a defensive lob deep to your opponents' baseline player and use the one-up, one-back versus one-up, one-back strategies we've already covered.

The other side of the coin is to play from the one-up, one-back formation against a team that plays the two-up formation. To do this successfully, you have several options, the most important of which is on your opponents' approach shot when they are in transition from the one-up, one-back to the two-up formation.

When your opponents approach crosscourt, your most prudent shot is to hit the ball low and crosscourt at the feet of the player approaching the net and have your net player move from the front third (offensive position) to the back third (defensive position) of the service box. This is the most prudent shot for three reasons. First, it's an offensive shot at the 3.5 level because players at this level have trouble with low volleys. This translates into outright misses and/or weak volleys that you can hit with offensive groundstrokes. Second, you have plenty of room in which to land the ball, because the approaching opposition player ends up somewhere around the service line for her first volley. Thus you have more margin for error because you don't have to hit the shot as precisely. Third, if the approaching opposition player makes the first volley successfully, she moves farther into the court, making it easier for you to lob over her head on the second ball. These are the three reasons why hitting low and crosscourt is the most prudent shot you can hit against a team that is in transition.

Your other option off your opponents' approach shot is to lob deep over the head of the player who starts at the net, because you have more room in which to land the ball. If you get the ball over the opposing net player's head, it causes your opponents to end up in a one-up, one-back formation and takes away their immediate offensive threat. It also gives you a chance to play offensively.

To play offensively in this situation, you have to know when to attack off the lob. *(The following applies to all lobs hit against the one-up, one-back and two-up formations.)* When you hit a lob from the one-up, one-back formation, you have to look at the net player whose head the ball is going over. It's most important for your net player to do this, because it tells her what to do. If your opponent stays in place with her racquet above her head, she's probably going to hit an offensive overhead. As the net person, you immediately retreat on your half of the court until your opponent starts her motion, at which point you stop and split-step wherever you are on the court and read your opponent's shot. This gives you a chance to return the ball. If she hits a short overhead that is weak, you return the ball low and move back in to the net. If she hits an overhead that is deep, you lob the ball defensively and continue to move to the baseline. The key is to make one shot in your transition area (which is probably in no-man's-land) and then move forward or backward, depending on the overhead your opponent hits.

If your opponent moves back slowly, as though she can get the ball, hold your ground to see what kind of shot she hits, because she'll probably hit a defensive overhead from this position. This shot doesn't threaten you and allows you to hold your position at the net.

If your opponent turns and runs with her back to the net to retrieve the lob, your net player holds her ground and your baseline player advances to the net into the two-up formation. This allows you the luxury of taking the offensive from a defensive situation. When you get into the two-up formation, you play at the service line, because the next shot is likely to be a lob, and you want to be ready for it.

Hitting the ball low to an opponent who is approaching the net and lobbing over an opponent who is already at the net are the two highest percentage plays you can make when your opponents come to the net.

Once your opponents have made the transition to the two-up formation, you have the same two options as when they were in transition, except you have to hit the low ball more precisely and the lob less precisely because your opponents are closer to the net. If you choose the low-ball option, hit the ball down the middle or crosscourt to the player who makes the approach shot, because she's probably farther from the net than her partner. If you choose to lob the ball, you still lob over the player who was originally at the net, because she's probably a step closer to the net. Once you've done this, all the movements described in the preceding section apply.

Two-Up Versus Two-Back. The last scenario is the two-up versus the two-back formation. When your opponents drive the ball to you in this scenario, the best play is to volley the ball to the middle of the court. There are three reasons for playing the ball to the middle when you're the two-up team. First, because it's the largest part of the court, you don't have to go for too much when hitting this shot. Second, you cause confusion between your opponents as to who takes the ball, which translates into some free points and some weak returns. Third, you open the outside of the court on the side from which the opposing player moves to hit the ball. This is the most important reason for hitting to the middle, because you displace your opponents and create an opening in the alley into which you can hit an offensive shot, providing your only real chance to play offensively off the volley. Otherwise, you continue to hit the ball down the middle, and it's just a matter of which team misses first.

When your opponents lob against you, you have three options. First, play the short lobs offensively by hitting the ball with pace through the baseline players or by taking the pace off the ball and angling it into the alley to open up the middle of the court. You have to experiment with each option to see which one works best against your opponents. Second, if the lob isn't too far back in the court, play a defensive lob and move back in to the net, because you don't want to give up the net if your opponents are giving it to you. Third, if the ball goes deep into the court, play a defensive lob and continue the point in the one-up, one-back formation, looking to come to the net on a short ball.

When playing from a two-back formation against a two-up formation, your best strategy is to attack the middle. You do this for four reasons. First, you hit to the largest part of the court compared to hitting into the alleys, which gives you a bigger target. Second, you hit to the lowest part of the net, which is 3 feet high in the middle compared to 3 feet 6 inches in the alleys; therefore, you make fewer mistakes when you hit the ball low over the net. Third, you cause confusion between your opponents as to who takes the ball, leading to free points and weak replies on balls that do come back. Fourth, you make it harder for your opponents to hit angle shots, because they're harder to hit from the middle of the court than from the outside (the alleys). Thus, attacking the middle when your opponents are in two-up and you're in two-back is your best option, but it isn't the only option you have against a two-up team. You can also hit the ball low over the net, which is an offensive shot at the 3.5 level. Although this shot is used in conjunction with attacking the middle, it is also used successfully to hit to the outside of the court, provided you hit the ball low consistently, because it forces your opponents to miss or hit weak replies. On the other hand, if you hit the ball high when you play to the outside, you give your opponents plenty of offensive options to hurt you with.

Your other options are to lob either offensively or defensively, depending on your situation. You obviously want to hit a defensive lob when you're pushed back in the court or when you're not balanced enough to drive the ball. This gives you a chance to recover to where you have the option of driving the ball low or lobbing offensively. If the other team plays right on top of the net or hits a weak shot that you have time to set up for, hit the offensive lob. For both the offensive and defensive lobs, if you successfully lob the ball over your opponents' heads and force them to turn and run for the ball, go to the net as a team (the two-up formation). Those are your options in the two-back formation. The key to playing this formation against any other formation is that you have to return every ball back into play. If you don't play consistently and move well on the baseline, this strategy is difficult to execute successfully.

Approaching the Match. The last area we cover is your strategic approach to a doubles match. The most important thing to do when formulating your strategy is to assess your strengths and weaknesses. This dictates your approach to the match.

If both you and your partner play the net and move fairly well, you probably want to get to the two-up formation as often as possible, because you'll play to your strength and be in an excellent position to dictate the match. With this strategy, you hit the ball deep when you're on the baseline and look to approach on a short ball. You also attack weak second serves and go to the net. Once you get to the two-up formation, play percentage tennis the way we showed you in the two-up versus one-up, one-back and two-back sections. If you're achieving your goal of getting into the two-up formation and you're losing badly, change your strategy to the one-up, one-back formation, where at least one of the players on your team is at the net. Remember what we said in earlier chapters: You don't change your strategy if you're down 4-1 and every game goes to deuce, because you're playing competitively. You're just losing the big points! However, if you're lucky to have the one game that you've won, you obviously need to change your strategy.

If both you and your partner play the net reasonably well but are more confident from the baseline, play the one-up, one-back formation. This formation still gives you the chance to play offensively from the net, as well as making you more confident about your game, which helps you on the big points. Again, if you're playing the one-up, one-back formation and losing badly, change your formation to whatever feels more comfortable for you, which is probably the two-back formation. However, look at what the other team is doing successfully against you, because that might alter your formation choice. For example, if the other team is rushing the net and playing the two-up formation, you might consider changing to the two-up formation. The rationale is simple. Provided that you feel moderately comfortable at the net, you take away the strength of your opponents and force them to play a formation that isn't as comfortable for them. In this situation, you force them to play the baseline in either the one-up, one-back or the two-back formation. So think about why you're losing before you choose a new formation. Once you change your formation, play it the way we showed you in earlier sections of this chapter.

If neither of you is comfortable at the net and you both like to play the baseline, you still start in the one-up, one-back formation, because you have a chance to play more offensively with one player at the net. Then, if you're losing badly, change to the two-back formation. This puts you in a more comfortable situation, but you concede the net to the other team and essentially give up all your offensive options except the low ball and the offensive lob. Executing this strategy properly requires a great deal of precision and patience, and the teams that are the best at it usually only play from this formation. Your only other option is to play from the two-up formation, but since you're not comfortable at the net, this should be your last resort.

The formations described above are the optimal approaches you should use based on your strengths and weaknesses. However, each team is different, so use this section as a guideline in experimenting to find what works for you as a team. We think you'll find that these formation guidelines apply most of the time.

PRACTICE DRILLS

At the 3.5 level, groundstrokes are still the most important aspect of the game, but you must do more with them than you did at the 3.0 level. You have to know how and when to hit them offensively and defensively. You also have to play a more diverse game by knowing how and when to play offensively and defensively in the other aspects of the game, such as approaching the net, volleying, and hitting overheads. We've put together a set of situation drills so you can practice these shots as you'll have to hit them in matches.

Singles Drills

The following singles drills cover all areas of the game with emphasis on how and when to use each shot offensively and defensively.

Approach Shot Combination Drill

In this drill, you and your drilling partner start at opposite ends of the court, 1 yard behind the baseline. One of you starts the rally with a forehand crosscourt (right-hander), and you continue the rally crosscourt until one of you hits the ball short. When the ball lands short on your side of the court, make an approach shot down the line and shade to the same side of the net (player A in figure 3.36). The person being attacked (player B) hustles to the other side of the court and sets up to play an offensive shot. If he doesn't have time to set his feet, he plays a defensive shot. When player B starts to swing at the ball, split-step and get ready for the volley. Then play the point to its completion.

This drill has four main focuses. First, you practice hitting the ball deep to keep your opponent from approaching the net. You do this by hitting the ball 5 feet over the net (as you practiced in the High Ball Drill in chapter 2). Second, when the ball lands short on your side of the court, you practice your approach shot down the line and split-step, which is one of the offensive plays we discussed for 3.5-level singles. Third, you practice shot combinations in which you pull your opponent to one side of the court and attack into the open court. And finally, you practice moving to the ball and deciding what shots to hit and what shots work best against a player who

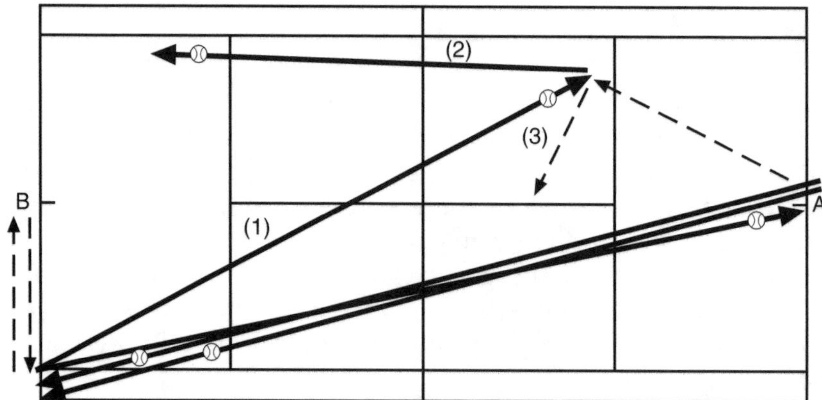

Figure 3.36 Approach Shot Combination Drill with players A and B rallying crosscourt until one of them hits a short ball. In this case, player B hits a short ball (1) and player A moves up and approaches down the line (2), then moves up to the net by shading toward the same side of the court as the approach (3).

is approaching the net. After doing that for about 10 minutes, switch and do the same drill with backhand crosscourts.

Attack the Second Serve Drill

In this drill, you start with one player serving from the center mark and one player returning. The server hits a second serve, and you, as the returner, have to choose from one of the three offensive options covered earlier in this chapter. Option 1 is to drive the ball into one of the corners to force your partner away from the middle. When you choose this option, recover to the middle after you hit the ball and hit the next shot into the opening you create. Your drilling partner defends against this shot with a high groundstroke return or a lob to give herself time to recover. Option 2 is to hit a deep approach shot down the line and go to the net. This is essentially the same play as in the last drill, except your drilling partner isn't pulled off the court when you attack. Therefore, she has a little more time to get to the ball, and you should expect a few more offensive shots than in the last drill. At the net, hit your first volley into the opening you create. Option 3 is to hit a drop shot. When you choose this option, recover to the middle of the court and hit an offensive shot off your drilling partner's next shot. The low ball is always a good offensive shot, but on a drop shot, the offensive lob also works extremely well because your drilling partner's momentum carries her close to the net. If you're the person retrieving the drop shot, shorten your backswing and play an approach shot up the line. In all these options, you play out the point. This drill covers the three offensive options to use off a weak second serve. As you're drilling, vary the options to keep the server off guard and help you get the most out of the drill. After you've drilled for 9 minutes at one position, switch and play the other position.

Defensive Baseline Drill

In this drill, one player starts on the junction of the baseline and the ad court singles line (the singles line to your left on your side of the court if you're facing the net). The other player starts 1 yard behind the baseline in the center of the court. Player A starts the drill with a feed to the deuce court (opposite side of the court from where player B is standing). You, as player B, retrieve the ball from the opposite side of the court and hit one of the two defensive options you have from that position. Option 1 is to return the ball with a high, deep groundstroke to the middle of the court, which gives you time to recover back to the middle. If you succeed, you essentially take the advantage away from player A. If you fail, player A has the advantage and hits an offensive shot into the open court. Option 2 is to return a defensive lob deep to the middle of the court, which also gives you time to recover back to the middle (see figure 3.37). If you succeed, you again take the advantage away from player A. If you fail and hit the lob short, player A practices angling his overhead away from you. After the initial return of the feed, play the point out and score it with the 2-1 scoring system. In this system, player B, who has to play defensively on his first shot, scores two points every time he wins a point because he starts at a disadvantage. Player A, who feeds the ball, scores one point every time he wins a point because he starts with an advantage. Play the first one to score 11 points wins, then switch positions and play to 11 points again. After playing two games from the ad court singles line, start the drill on the deuce court singles line and play two more games.

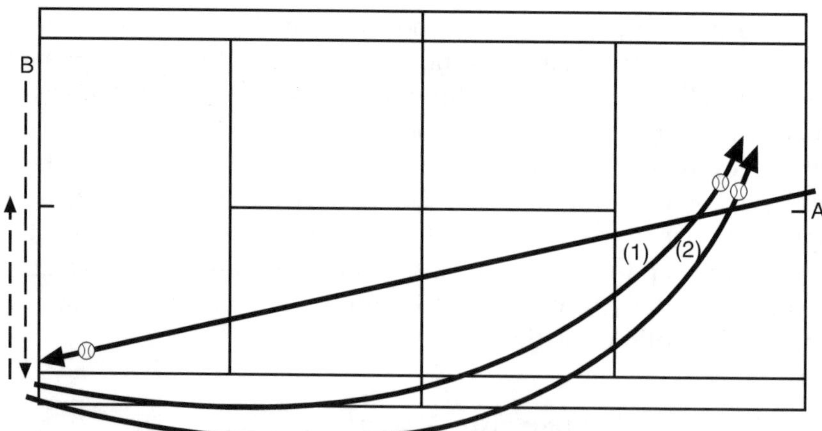

Figure 3.37 Defensive Baseline Drill with player A feeding a deep ball to the opposite corner of player B's court and player B hitting a high groundstroke (1) or a defensive lob (2) down the middle.

Low Ball Singles Drill

In this drill, start with one player on the junction of the service line and the centerline (the *T*) and the other player 1 yard behind the baseline in the middle of the court. Player A starts the drill by feeding the ball to player B's forehand or backhand. You, as player B, hit low balls at or away from player A, who remains on the service line for the entire drill. After you return the ball to player A at the service line, play out the point. This is an excellent drill because you work on some of the more pronounced changes between the 3.0 and 3.5 levels. First, you work on controlling the height of the ball on your groundstrokes by hitting low balls, an offensive shot at the 3.5 level. Second, at the net, you practice low volleys, wide volleys, and the midcourt game, which are problem areas at the 3.5 level. All four of these shots are part of the definition that distinguishes 3.5-level players from 3.0-level players. After you play 7 minutes at one position, switch and play the other position.

Defensive Lob Overhead Drill

In this variation of the Low Ball Singles Drill, you again start with one player on the *T* and the other 1 yard behind the baseline in the middle of the court. Player A feeds the ball away from the baseline player by hitting it closer to the corners of the court. You, as player B, run to the ball and hit a defensive lob deep into the court and recover to the middle (see figure 3.38). The best way to hit your lob deep is to aim above the windscreens and behind the service line. When you return the ball, player A practices her defensive and offensive overheads, depending on how deep the ball goes. Once the ball is in play, continue playing the point to its conclusion. To make the drill more interesting, use the 2-1 scoring system. If player B wins the point, she scores two points. Player A scores one point for every point she wins. The first one to score 11 points wins. From the baseline, this drill works on your defensive lobs in a match-type situation, which gives you more confidence in this shot during your matches. At the net, this drill works on improving your decision making on your overhead. It lets you experiment with hitting offensive and defensive overheads in a match-type situation, helping you find your limitations for each of these shots. If you're having problems hitting your overheads, refer to the Quick Tips section on overheads! After playing one game to 11 points, switch positions and play again.

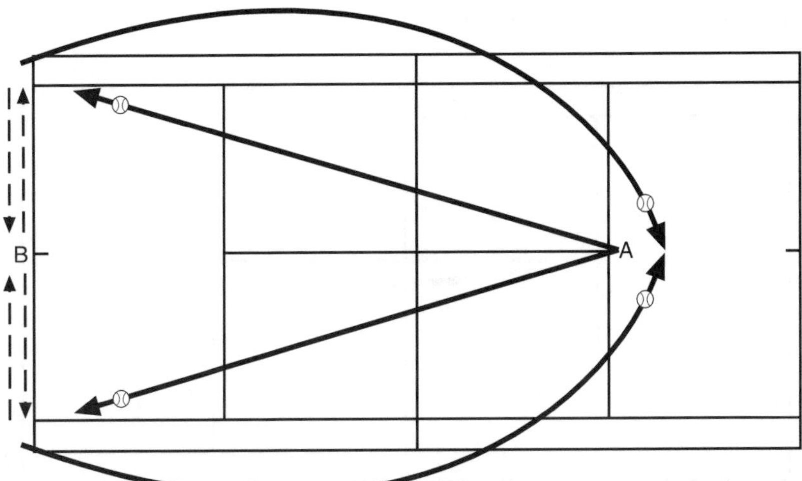

Figure 3.38 Defensive Lob Overhead Drill with player A feeding an offensive ball to either corner and player B hitting defensive lobs and recovering to the middle. After the lob, player A hits overheads.

Backspin Drill

This drill can be done with either two or four players. Both players start in the middle of the court on the service line (with four players, start on the service line in the middle of the service boxes). Player A hits the ball softly to player B and lands it in front of him. Player B slices the ball back to player A, who catches it (see figure 3.39). Each player does about 5 minutes at each position. Player B returns a line-drive slice softly so it skids or slides in front of player A. If the ball is staying low and moving forward on your return, you know that you're hitting a line-drive slice. If the ball is popping up and not moving forward, your racquet face is probably too open on contact or you're using your wrist to hit the shot. Remember, backspin is imparted to the ball by the downward motion of your racquet, not by slapping at the ball with your wrist. After you get the hang of the drill, slice the ball gently back to each other. To make it more challenging, hit five in a row over the net. As you get better, increase your goal to 10, and so on. Once you become proficient at this drill, move back to the middle of the backcourt (no-man's-land) between the service line and the baseline and try it from there. Your ultimate goal is to be able to slice consistently from baseline to baseline.

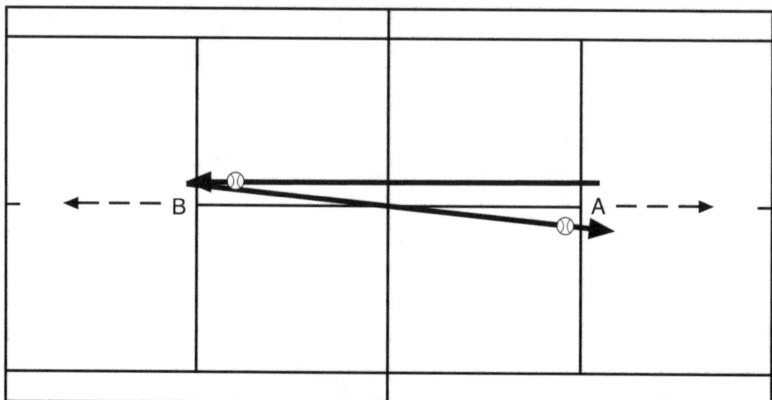

Figure 3.39 Backspin Drill with player A feeding the ball to player B and player B returning the ball with backspin. Both players move backward as they become more successful.

Other Drills That Still Apply

Chapter 2: High Ball Drill, Triangle Drill, Recovery Drills, Directional Movement Drill, and Approach Shot Drill

Doubles Drills

Doubles take on a different focus at the 3.5 level because you now have to think in terms of offense and defense when you play. Therefore, the doubles drills we prescribe point out all the offensive and defensive plays associated with the formations from which you'll start. Also, since doubles at the 3.5 level is a mixture of all the formations you've learned so far, plus the two-up formation, the drill section is extremely diverse.

Midcourt Drill

This drill can be done with two or four players, but you make more efficient use of your court time with four players. In this drill, each player starts on the service line in the middle of one of the service boxes. Your partner is the player in the opposite crosscourt box, and the two of you drill independently of the other two players. Thus, two balls are in play simultaneously, so there is constant action. Either you or your partner (it doesn't matter which) starts the rally, and you volley crosscourt from the service line with an emphasis on form and consistency. You don't move forward, because the sole purpose of this drill is for you to practice your midcourt game, which is the transition shot that gets you from the baseline to the net. This is a basic drill, but it works on the shot that is most important for the transition to the two-up formation, a good starting point for improving your offensive tennis at the 3.5 level. After 7 minutes, switch halves of the court and do the drill in the other direction.

Low Ball Doubles Drill

This variation of the Midcourt Drill can also be done with two or four people. In this drill, you start with two players on the service line in the middle of the service box and two players 1 yard behind the baseline in the middle of their halves of the court. Your partner is the player on the opposite half of the court (crosscourt), and you drill independently of the other two players; thus, two balls are in play simultaneously during the drill. Players A and B start the drill with a crosscourt feed. You, as players C and D, hit the ball crosscourt and low. Once the ball is returned crosscourt, play out the point crosscourt, with players A and B remaining on the service line for the entire point, hitting low and wide volleys (see figure 3.40). Your emphasis in this drill is on developing a consistent feel for hitting the ball low and crosscourt from the baseline and on your form on low and wide volleys at the net. Once you become proficient at these three shots, you're well on your way to the 4.0 level! After 7 minutes, switch sides of the court and practice the shots you haven't worked on yet. After you do the drill on one half of the court, switch and do the drill crosscourt to the other half.

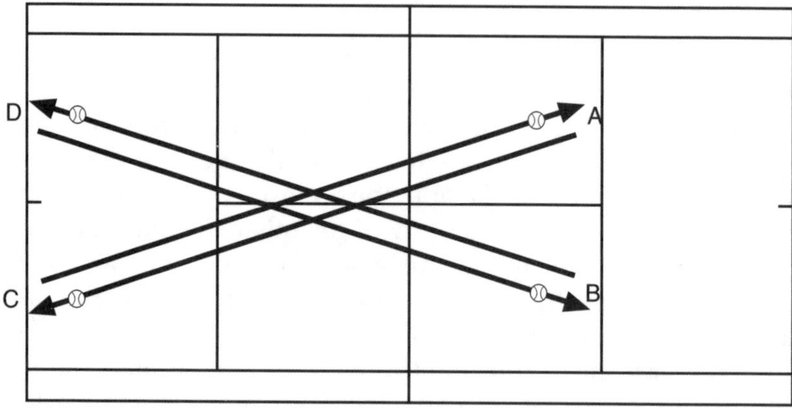

Figure 3.40 Low Ball Doubles Drill with players A and B feeding crosscourt shots to players C and D. Players C and D are working on low crosscourt groundstrokes while players A and B are working on low and wide volleys.

Middle Teamwork Drill

In this drill, you start in the same positions as for the Low Ball Doubles Drill, except players A and B start in the back third of the service box. Also, Doubles Drill, you put only one ball in play, because you want to focus more on teamwork than on form. To start the drill, player A or B feeds the ball to one of four areas: in the alley on the deuce court side, down the middle on the deuce court side, down the middle on the ad court side, or in the alley on the ad court side. You, as players C and D, try to hit the ball low and down the middle on every shot (see figure 3.41). This conditions you to attack the middle from all parts of the backcourt against opponents who play the two-up formation. It teaches you to communicate by helping you determine who should take which balls. When the ball is returned successfully to the middle, play out the point. Players A and B work on their communication in the two-up formation and on their volley down the middle to the baseline team. After you do this drill several times, you know who is responsible for the ball down the middle from every angle on the court, because it helps you get a better feel for each other as a team. Also, it conditions you to volley the ball down the middle against a two-back team, which helps you learn how to open up the court. After 7 minutes, switch ends of the court and try the other formation.

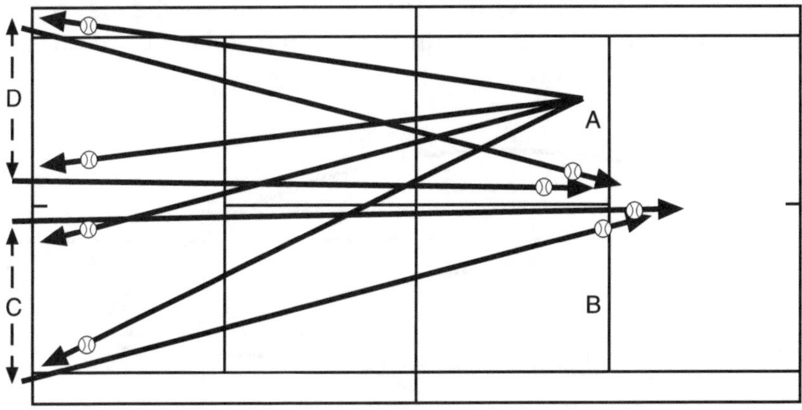

Figure 3.41 Middle Teamwork Drill with players A and B standing at the net and either one feeding balls to players C and D, who are both on the baseline. (The diagram shows player A feeding the balls.) Players C and D are both hitting all balls down the middle while players A and B are practicing volleying balls that come back to the middle.

Offensive-Defensive Overhead Drill

In this drill, you start in the same positions as for the Middle Teamwork Drill. To start the drill, player A or B feeds the ball anywhere she wants. You, as players C and D, have to hit a defensive lob deep into the court and continue to lob defensively on all balls that are returned to you. Remember, a good way to hit your defensive lobs deep is to aim above the windscreens and behind the service line. This drill helps you learn to play defensively in the two-back formation by giving you time to recover to the middle, so you're ready for the next shot.

Players A and B practice hitting offensive and defensive overheads. If you get a defensive overhead, land the ball behind the service line in the middle of your drilling partner's side of the court and recover back to the two-up formation. Doing this teaches you to not give up the two-up formation you work so hard to get into during the point (see figure 3.42a). If you get an offensive overhead, practice hitting the ball hard through the middle or taking pace off the ball to hit angles into the alleys (see figure 3.42b). This helps you determine what pace to use on the middle and angle overheads, which also develops consistency and increases your confidence in match play. If you're having problems hitting your overheads, refer to the Quick Tips section on overheads to help you fix them quickly. After 7 minutes, switch ends of the court and try the other formation.

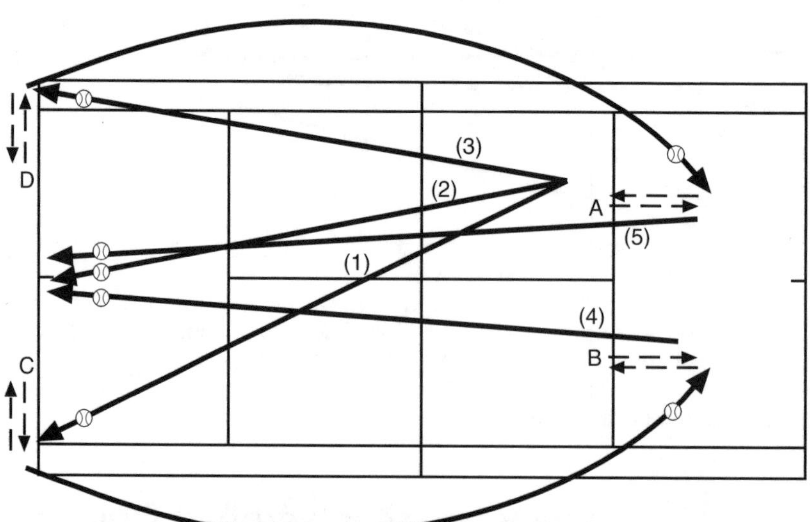

Figure 3.42a-b (a) Offensive-Defensive Overhead Drill with players A and B feeding balls (lines 1, 2, and 3) to players C and D, who are both on the baseline. (The diagram shows player A feeding the balls.) Players C and D are both hitting defensive lobs to return the balls. If the lobs are deep, players A and B hit defensive overheads down the middle.

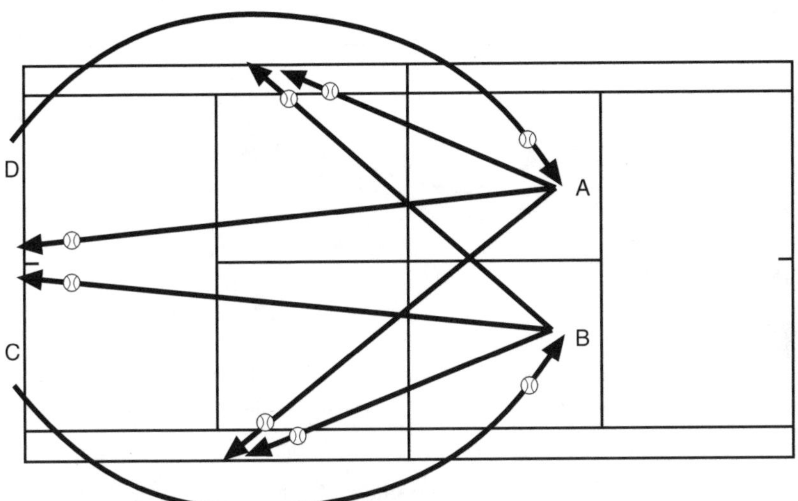

Figure 3.42a-b (b) Offensive-Defensive Overhead Drill with players A and B hitting offensive overheads (to the middle and the two angles) off short lobs from players C and D.

Kill Drill

In this drill, each of the four players starts on the service line in the middle of one of the service boxes. To start the drill, one team feeds the ball to the other team, and you play out the point with all four of you at the net. To be successful in this drill, you have to learn to hit the volley low over the net, because it often causes your drilling partners to pop the ball up. When you do hit the volley low, close in to the net (move forward a step or two) and look to put the high ball or pop-up away. This drill also sharpens your reflexes at the net, which comes in handy when all four players are at the net. At the 3.5 level, you'll find yourself in this situation numerous times during a match, so you need to become accustomed to it. You can score the game by playing the first team to score 11 points wins.

Volley Options Drill

In this drill, one team starts in the two-up formation with each player in the back third of the service box. The other team starts in the defensive one-up, one-back formation. Player A or B feeds the ball to

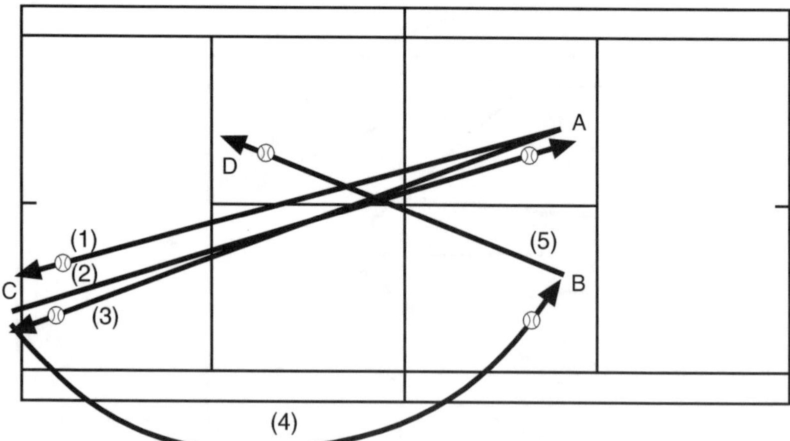

Figure 3.43 Volley Options Drill with player A feeding a ball to Player C (1); player C hitting a low ball back to player A (2); player A hitting a low volley back to player C (3) or player C hitting a high ball to player B (4), who hits an offensive volley through player D (5).

player C (shot 1). Player C practices driving the ball low at the feet of players A or B, preferably down the middle or crosscourt, because those are the shots you'll hit in your matches (see figure 3.43). When the ball comes over, you (as player A or B) play either an offensive or defensive shot, depending on the height of the ball. If the ball is low (shot 2), volley crosscourt to player C, which is a good defensive play (shot 3). In this case, you want to volley the low ball defensively because it's a higher percentage shot than hitting it through the net player. If the ball is returned high (shot 4), hit the volley through the net player (player D), which is a good offensive play (shot 5). You must learn to put away this shot at the 3.5 level. By disciplining yourself to hit low and high balls to these areas, you always play the highest percentage shot, which translates into more success in your matches. After 5 minutes, change halves of the court with your partner and try the other position on your side of the court. After you do that, both teams change sides and each player tries both positions on the other side of the court.

Lob Options Drill

Another drill with the same setup as the Volley Options Drill is to have player C hit a lob off the feed. When player C lobs, you and your partner (players A and B) determine whether to hit an offensive or defensive overhead. If you're at midcourt or closer and the ball is in front of you (shot 2), hit an offensive overhead through player D (shot 3). If you're in the backcourt or the ball is behind you (shot 5), hit a defensive overhead to player C (shot 6). This drill gives you practice at making decisions on when and where to hit offensive and defensive overheads (see figure 3.44).

On the other half of the court, if players A or B set up to hit an offensive overhead, you (as player D) retreat as far as you can on your side of the court until the other team starts to hit their overhead (line 4 in figure 3.44). Then you stop and play the point from wherever you are. If player A or B backs up to hit a defensive overhead, player C stays on the baseline and you (as player D) read the other team to determine what to do. If you think you can hold your own against the other team's defensive overhead, stay at the net. If you don't, back up to the baseline to a defensive position. This drill helps you practice the options you have against the lob. After 5 minutes, change halves of the court with your partner and try the other position on your side of the court. After you do that, both teams change sides of the court and each player tries both positions on the other side of the court.

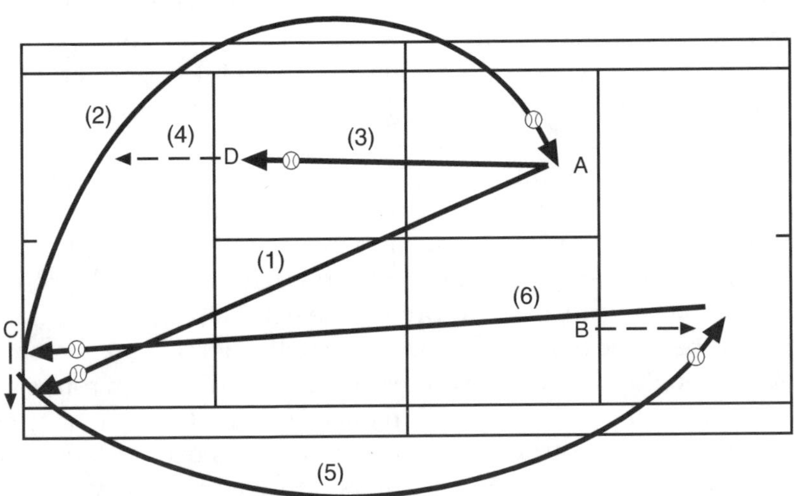

Figure 3.44 Lob Options Drill with player A feeding a ball to Player C (1); player C hitting a short lob back to player A (2); player A then hitting an offensive overhead through player D (3), who moves as far back as he can before player A hits the overhead (4). If player C hits a deep lob (5), player B moves back and hits a defensive overhead back to player C (6).

Four Play Drill

This is essentially the same drill you did in the first and second chapters, but with a few new twists. (At this point, go back to chapter 1 and reread how to perform this drill.) The changes occur mainly from the offensive perspective. First, when the baseline player starts the drill with a short ball crosscourt, you now hit an approach shot and go to the net, which puts you in the two-up formation. Your partner, who starts at the net, reacts accordingly by moving forward a step and following the direction of the ball. Then you play out the point.

Another change occurs when the baseline player starts the rally with a lob over the net player's head. At the 3.0 level, we instructed you, as the baseline player, to stay on the baseline; however, at the 3.5 level, we want you to go to the net. It's a very simple play that scores big results, because the return play from your opponents is usually predictable. Once you see the net person turn his back to run for the ball or switch to the other side of the court to let his partner take the ball, you approach the net. There's one difference in your approach, though. Since it's difficult for them to drive a high ball while running, your opponents will probably lob the ball. Therefore, you advance only to the service line and your partner backs up to the service line, so you're ready to hit your overhead. This is an underestimated way to get to the two-up formation and is used often at the 3.5 level.

The final change occurs when the baseline player starts the drill by hitting deep to the other baseline player. The change is that you play the ball deep to force your opponent to either miss, hit the ball to your partner at the net, or hit the ball short. If the other team hits the ball short, you approach the net. The last drill option, where the baseline player starts the rally to the net person, remains the same. Do this drill for 5 minutes at each position, then rotate so each person can play each position once. We don't comment as to why you do what you do on each option in this drill because we already did that in previous chapters. However, what you take away from this drill is better decision making in a game situation. You don't have to think about what to do in match play, because you're automatically programmed to respond to each situation as it unfolds.

Other Drills That Still Apply

Chapter 2: Recovery Drills, Volley Rally Drill, Doubles Approach Shot Drill, Standard Doubles Drill, Return Drill

These singles and doubles drills concentrate on the most important elements of the game at the 3.5 level and are all you need to help you improve. Understanding these drills and their situational applications helps you become not only a better tennis player, but also a smarter tennis player. The drills represent changes in strategy and focus from the 3.0 level. Therefore, it's imperative that you understand everything we covered in chapter 2, the 3.0 chapter, because those things are the fundamental prerequisites to being successful at the 3.5 level. Good luck!

The 4.0 Level

NTRP Guidelines

The verification guidelines for the 4.0-level player, as specified in the NTRP Guidebook, are as follows:

Groundstrokes—You have a dependable forehand and hit with depth and control on moderately paced shots. You may try to place the ball too well on a difficult shot. On your backhand, you direct the ball with consistency and depth on moderately paced shots.

Serve—You place both first and second serves and use spin. You frequently hit with power on your first serve.

Volleys—You're developing low and wide volleys on both sides of your body. You possess depth and control on the forehand side. On the backhand side, you direct your volley but usually lack depth.

Specialty Shots—You follow aggressive shots to the net and are beginning to finish off points. You hit to your opponent's weaknesses and have a dependable return of serve. You're able to lob defensively on difficult shots and offensively on setups. Also, you put away easy overheads, and you poach in doubles.

Generally, your groundstrokes are dependable, and you hit with directional intent and depth on moderately paced shots. However, you may still lose rallies due to impatience, and you're not yet playing high-percentage tennis. In doubles, your teamwork is evident, and you're becoming more comfortable at the net.

OBJECTIVES

The objectives at the 4.0 level have less to do with the strategic aspects of the game than they did at the 3.5 level. Rather, they deal more with the physical aspects of increasing your inventory of shots and refining the shots you already have, because the real difference between 3.5- and 4.0-level players is the ability to execute shots and strategies better.

Develop Consistency in All Areas of Your Game

Without developing consistency in all areas of your game, you're a mediocre 4.0-level player at best, because this level consists of a diverse group of players who can hit many different shots and play all the doubles formations. You may have a few flashes of brilliance by beating some players who are better than you, but over the long run, you also lose to a lot of players you should beat. In other words, your inconsistency on the court translates into inconsistency in your match results! Developing consistency at the 4.0 level also takes a different form in that you have to be more specific with it. For example, consistency at the 4.0 level doesn't mean that you can just hit every ball back into play. You have to do each specific thing we show you consistently, such as hitting the ball deep when you're on the baseline, keeping the ball low when someone approaches the net, and volleying the ball into the open court. If you're unable to do these specific things consistently, you limit your options during matches and put yourself at a strategic disadvantage.

Learn to Hit Topspin

Since the pace of the game increases at the 4.0 and subsequent levels, hitting topspin becomes more important because it provides you with a greater margin for error. If you hit the ball hard and flat, you have to hit it almost perfectly every time. This takes about three times more practice to master than topspin, and most 4.0-level players don't have the luxury of unlimited practice time. Therefore, by hitting topspin, you can hit the ball harder without having to be as precise in your stroke (or practice as much), which develops your consistency.

To hit topspin, you do three things. First, close your racquet face. This can be easy or difficult, depending on which grip you use. If you use a Continental grip, it's almost impossible to hit topspin consistently, because you start with the racquet face open (see figure 2.12). This makes hitting topspin (and high balls) more difficult, because you have to use too much wrist, which is why we don't recommend this grip. The best grip for hitting topspin is the semi-Western grip for the forehand and the Eastern or two-hand grip for the backhand, because you start your stroke with the racquet face closed (see figures 4.1, 4.2, and 4.3). This is essential for the third step of the topspin stroke, hitting over the ball, which we cover last. Second, start your forward swing lower than the ball (see figure 4.4a) so that you swing up at it. The upward motion of your swing and the closed racquet face combine to put overspin or topspin on the ball. Third, finish over the top of the ball as you follow through (see figure 4.4b). This keeps you from opening your racquet face in the middle of your stroke, ensuring proper completion of the topspin groundstroke.

Our Quick Tips section helps you identify problems when hitting topspin so you can correct them in practice and in matches.

Figure 4.1 Semi-Western forehand grip.

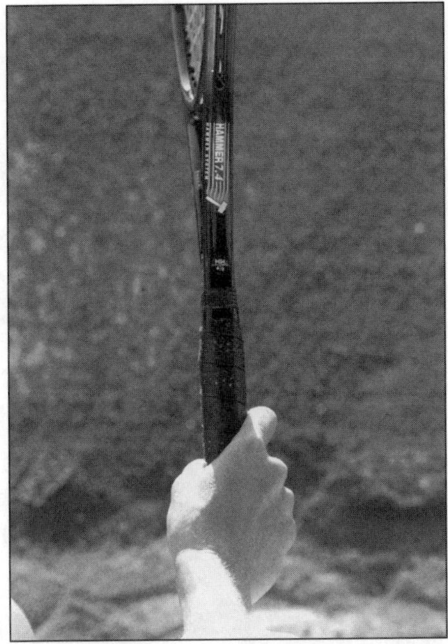

Figure 4.2 Eastern backhand grip.

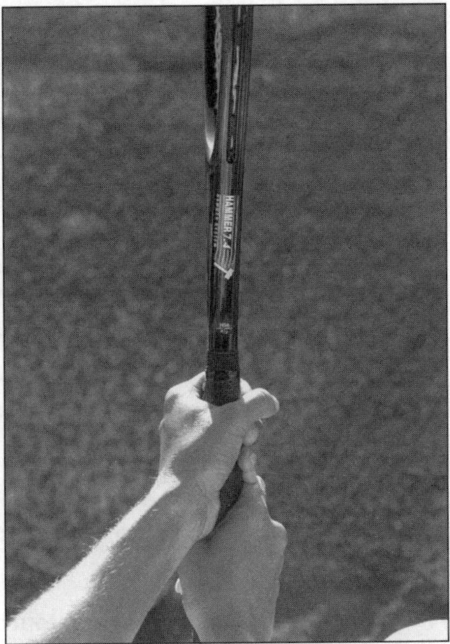

Figure 4.3 Two-hand backhand grip.

a

b

Figure 4.4a-b (a) Player starting her forward swing from below the ball with the racquet face slightly closed. (b) Player finishing her swing over the top of the ball as she follows through.

Quick Tips

Hitting Topspin

⊖ **Problem**—You're hitting your groundstrokes long.

⊕ **Solution 1**—You're making contact with the ball with your racquet face too open. In this case, check to see if you're using the correct grip (see figures 4.1, 4.2, and 4.3). If you aren't using one of the grips we recommend, you're probably making it too hard on yourself to hit topspin.

⊕ **Solution 2**—If solution 1 doesn't work, you probably aren't following through correctly. Make sure you finish your stroke over the top of the ball (see figure 4.4b). This ensures that your racquet face is closed on contact, which is proper for the topspin groundstroke.

• •

⊖ **Problem**—You're hitting the ball short or into the net.

⊕ **Solution 1**—You're probably making contact with the ball with your racquet face too closed. In this case, open your racquet face. This helps you hit the ball higher over the net.

⊕ **Solution 2**—If solution 1 doesn't work, you probably aren't swinging up on the ball enough. In this case, concentrate on starting your forward swing below the ball and hitting the ball from low to high (see figure 4.4a). The best way to do this is to aim higher over the net. Don't worry about hitting the ball long, because if you hit good topspin, the ball arcs back into the court.

If you find you're missing your topspin shots the same way repeatedly, try our quick tips to help you work through your problem. These tips are most helpful in match situations because they're easy solutions that can get you out of some tight spots.

Develop the Diversity of Your Serve

You have to further develop the diversity of your serve to shore up any weaknesses on your second serve and turn your first serve into an offensive shot. To do this, address three areas.

First, work on the depth of your second serve (getting the ball in the back third of the box). This is something you have to learn by feel, which essentially means you have to serve a lot of baskets of balls until you know what works for you. Serving deep is important at the 3.5 level and above because short second serves are weak shots that are taken advantage of at your expense. If you recall, you began working on taking advantage of weak second serves at the 3.5 level (see chapter 3), and you continue to do so at this level. Therefore, your 4.0-level opponents are already aware of what a weak second serve is and how to attack it.

Second, you have to be more precise with the placement of your serves, which makes your serve more offensive. When choosing where to place your serves, you have three options on each side (see figure 4.5). You can serve the ball wide to the forehand or backhand (option 1), into the body (option 2), or down the middle to the backhand or forehand (option 3). Each of these options gives you an advantage. When employing option 1, you pull your opponent off the court. When she returns the ball, you capitalize on this advantage by hitting the ball into the opening you create. When employing option 2, you usually "handcuff" your opponent, because she can't extend her arms to hit the ball and has to block it back, forcing her to hit a weak return. When this happens, use one of the three offensive options described in chapter 3 for weak or short balls: Drive the ball

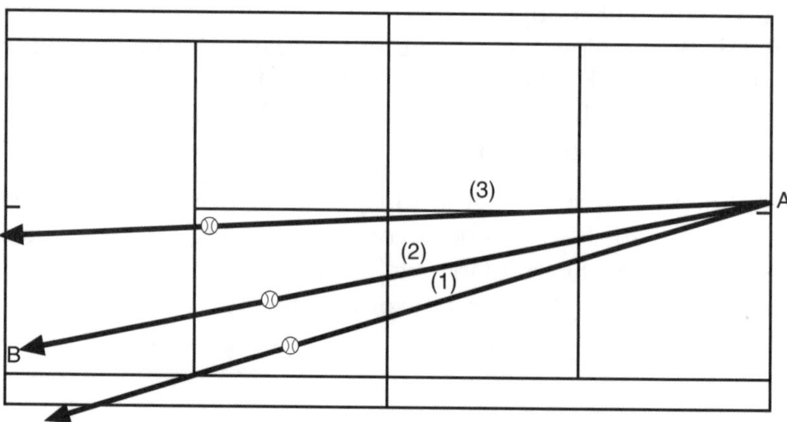

Figure 4.5 Player A hitting three options on the serve to the deuce court, pulling player B off the court (1), hitting into the body of player B (2), or hitting down the middle (centerline) (3). The same three options are used in serving to the ad court.

into one of the corners, hit an approach shot and go to the net, or hit a drop shot. When employing option 3, use it as an element of surprise or to exploit a weakness of your opponent. When you do this successfully, look for a weak return on which you can use one of the above three offensive options.

Hitting these serves requires only minor adjustments in your regular service motion. To hit the serve wide to the forehand in the deuce court or down the middle to the forehand in the ad court, gradually open your shoulders before you hit the serve. This causes the ball to go in the direction your shoulders are pointing, which puts the ball where you want it. To serve into the body of your opponent, hit your normal serve but aim the ball at her inside hip (her left hip in the deuce court and her right hip in the ad court). When you do this, the ball travels at an angle into your opponent's body, making it very difficult for her to get out of the way of the ball. This often handcuffs your opponent and produces the desired effect: a weak return. To hit the serve down the middle to the backhand in the deuce court or wide to the backhand in the ad court, keep your shoulders closed until you start to hit the ball; then open them through the serve. Again, this causes the ball to go in the direction your shoulders are pointing when you start the serve.

Third, you need to put more spin on your serves, because it makes your first serve more offensive and your second serve more consistent. In chapter 3, we showed you how to do this and told you to experiment with it, but now is when you need to start using it. First, you add offense to your first serve with option 1 (see figure 4.5) because you can spin the ball away from your opponent and with option 2 (see figure 4.5) because you can spin the ball into your opponent. The spin gives you a little something extra with which to hurt your opponent. Second, the extra spin allows you to swing harder at the ball and still get it into the service box. Since you no longer have to hit your second serve softly to ensure getting it into the service box, it is harder for your opponents to take advantage of your second serve. You also have more confidence on the big points and are less likely to choke. Choking often results from being afraid to hit a shot; you hit it so softly that you freeze in the middle of the shot and miss. When you spin the second serve, you're less likely to freeze up or choke because you're able to swing harder at the ball while maintaining your consistency. The result is more second serves in the box and fewer double faults.

As you can see, you probably have some work to do in diversifying your serve. Just remember that the serve is the hardest stroke in tennis, so it'll take time and lots of practice to achieve this objective.

Develop Different Types of Shots

This entails adding new shots to your repertoire and refining the shots you already have. In the remainder of the Objectives section, we specifically address the four new shots you need to learn: the half volley, the passing shot, the serve and volley, and the angle volley. In the Keys to Success section, we show you how to refine some of the shots you already know how to hit and tell you when to use these shots.

Learn the Half Volley

The half volley is defined as a ball that you have to play immediately after it bounces (usually in the midcourt area). This shot comes into play more often and is important for you to learn at the 4.0 level for two reasons. First, the fact that you play more aggressively by going to the net more often increases your chances of having to hit this shot, because you spend more time in the midcourt area. Second, when you go to the net at this level, the players can hit the low ball to your feet with greater precision and consistency, which forces you to hit more half volleys. But don't panic, because, as always, we're going to show you how to hit this shot.

First, quickly decide whether you want to volley the ball in the air or let it bounce and half volley it. The general rule in making this decision is to volley the ball if you can, but if you have to let it bounce, then half volley the ball. Second, bend your knees as you go down for the half volley (see figure 4.6). The common error is to bend at the waist. By bending at your knees, you keep your upper body above your lower body, which maintains your balance and allows you to use the proper form. Third, turn to the side and, keeping your racquet strings slightly closed, make an abbreviated take-back to your back foot on the same side from which you're going to hit the ball (about the same length as the take-back for your volley) (see figure 4.6). This movement is abbreviated more out of necessity than by design, because you don't have time for a full take-back. It also puts you in the proper position to finish your stroke. Fourth, keeping your wrist firm and your racquet strings square to the net at contact, swing easily toward your target as if guiding the ball to it (see figures 4.7 and 4.8). You might think keeping your racquet strings square to the net makes the ball go into the net, but it doesn't, because the ball is rebounding upward. It actually forces the ball upward and over the net, even though you're swinging toward your target. The common mistake here is to open your racquet face to help get the ball over the net. However, this causes the ball to go up even more, resulting in your hitting a pop-up or "sitter" for which your opponent will make you pay.

With these instructions and the right amount of practice, you can improve your half volley in a hurry, so get out there and get started!

Develop Your Passing Shots

A passing shot is one you hit past your opponent when he's at the net that he doesn't touch. In previous chapters, we showed you the two most important parts of hitting the passing shot. In chapter 2, we showed you how to control the direction of the ball, which is

Figure 4.6 Player bending his knees and turning to the side for a half volley.

Figure 4.7 Contact for the half volley with the strings square to the net.

Figure 4.8 The follow-through for a half volley.

necessary to hit the ball away from your opponent when he's at the net. In chapter 3, we made subtle references to the passing shot and taught you how to control the height of the ball, in particular, the low-ball shot, which makes the passing shot more difficult to return if you don't hit the ball past your opponent. Since you have working knowledge of how to hit these two shots, it's just a matter of putting them together. You've already done this at the 3.5 level, but not in this manner. At the 3.5 level, you learned to hit low balls down the middle in doubles and down the middle and to the outside in singles—the basis for the passing shot. All you have to do now is hit more aggressively by aiming the ball to the open court, where your opponent can't make a play on it. You have to hit more aggressively at the 4.0 level because the low balls you hit to your opponent come back. Therefore, you have to do a little more to stay ahead of your competition.

There are three things to remember when hitting the passing shot. First, don't attempt it if you're not balanced. This is an offensive shot and is used only when you're set to make a proper swing at the ball. If you're not set, play a defensive shot; otherwise, you'll have a low success rate with the passing shot. Second, train yourself to think that if you miss the shot, you want to miss it into the net (as opposed to missing the ball long). This helps you keep the ball low on your passing shots. Third, aim your passing shot 1 to 1.5 feet inside the singles lines. This increases your margin for error and results in a higher percentage of your passing shots being successful.

The passing shot isn't too hard to learn because you already have all the necessary tools to hit it. You just have to practice it!

Learn to Serve and Volley

By learning this shot combination, you give yourself an offensive option with which you can put immediate pressure on your opponent. However, the success of this shot depends on two variables. The first variable is your first serve. Since it's essentially your approach shot, you must hit a first serve that doesn't allow your opponent to hit an offensive return. If she does, it puts you at an immediate disadvantage. Any other type of return (neutral or defensive) gives you a chance to make an offensive volley into the open court. The second variable is your opponent's ability to return serve. If she returns serve poorly by hitting high balls or balls with no pace, it's easier for you to make the transition to the net and win the points. If your opponent returns serve well by hitting low balls at your feet or low balls away from you or past you, it's more difficult to make the transition to the net and win the points. As you can see, these two variables are related because they directly oppose each other. For example, if you hit a strong first serve, your opponent is more likely to hit a weak return. Thus, you have to weigh these two variables against each other in deciding whether or not to serve and volley.

At the 4.0 level, you're beginning to serve more offensively, but you aren't quite at the point where you want to serve and volley in singles, because the returner has more room in which to return the ball and her ability to return is far more developed than your ability to serve and volley. This makes for a losing recipe. However, in doubles you can serve and volley successfully because you have less court to cover and a partner at the net to help you intimidate your opponents. Furthermore, your goal in doubles is to get to the two-up formation, so the serve and volley can be a big offensive weapon if you learn to do it effectively.

Learning to serve and volley isn't too difficult because we've already covered most of the key points in earlier chapters. In its purest form, it's an extension of the approach shot in that you make the transition from the baseline to the net. The difference is that your approach shot is your serve! The key is to serve and then continue forward to the net. A lot of players can't serve and volley well because they toss the ball behind their heads, which forces them to regain their balance before they can go to the net (see figure 4.9, a-b). The proper form is to toss the ball in front of you so that you're already moving forward and can continue to the net after you swing (see figure 4.10, a-b). Once you do this, follow the rules for approaching the net that we've discussed in earlier chapters. Move forward until just before your opponent strikes the ball, then split-step to get ready for your volley. Even if you don't make it to the service line, start your split-step before your opponent hits the ball. If you do this, you're prepared to hit your first volley successfully.

You needn't look any further than Wimbledon for an excellent example of how to serve and volley. Since Wimbledon is played on grass, the fastest surface you can play on, most players serve and volley on every serve. And since the surface is so fast, the players can't make it all the way to the service line for their first volley. There-

a

b

Figure 4.9a-b (a) Toss behind player's head showing player's negative balance. (b) The ending position (incorrect form).

a

b

Figure 4.10a-b (a) Proper toss out in front of the player's body for positive balance into the court. (b) The ending position (correct form).

fore, they split-step behind the service line just before their opponent makes contact with the ball. The proof is on the grass. Picture the stadium court during "Breakfast at Wimbledon": There's a big brown spot 1 to 3 feet behind the service line where the players make their split-step. Yes, the pros are better than you, but you can do the same thing they do if you're prepared they way they are. So stop wherever you are in the court and split-step before you hit your first volley. After making your first volley, move forward to the net a few steps, following the flight of the ball, and split-step again. This puts you right where you want to be for the remainder of the point. It's no more complicated than that!

Learn to Hit the Angle Volley

This specialty shot is very valuable to have at the 4.0 level because it adds diversity to your arsenal of offensive shots. You use it in two ways. First, when your opponent is in the middle of the court, use it to open up the court. It works because you force your opponent to run forward and to the side at the same time, leaving more space in which to hit the ball. The second way you can use the angle volley is for putting away the ball. You do this by angling the ball away from your opponent when he's out of position. This is effective because the ball is bouncing away from him, making it especially hard to retrieve.

To hit the angle volley, you must be choosy about when to do so for two reasons. First, it's harder to hit an angle volley from the middle of the court than from the outside of the court (alleys), because there is less court in which to land the ball. Thus, you'll make more errors in attempting it. Second, the farther from the net you are, the harder it is to hit an angle volley, because the ball doesn't angle away from the middle of the court as much as it does when hit from close to the net. This makes it easier for your opponent to run down the ball.

The form for the angle volley is the same as for your regular volley except that you make contact with the ball earlier. Essentially, you hit the ball so early that you contact the side of it. A good way to remember to do this is to keep your arm between your body and the net (see figure 4.11). This forces you to hit the side of the ball, producing the desired effect—an angle volley. We prescribe some drills that help you practice this specialty shot in the Practice Drills section at the end of the chapter. It doesn't take long for you to hit this shot with ease, but you have to practice it.

Figure 4.11 Player contacting the side of the ball with his arm between his body and the net.

KEYS TO SUCCESS

The keys to success at the 4.0 level are essentially the same as at the 3.5 level with one general exception: You have to execute better in all areas of your game. In chapter 3, you were introduced to thinking offensively and defensively during a point, taught the differences between offensive and defensive tennis, and taught the basic shots associated with each type. As you progressed through the 3.5 level, you became more comfortable with this new approach. By the time you reach the 4.0 level, you internalize all this and are able to do two things in each situation that arises. First, you immediately are able to recognize all the options associated with your situation. You don't have to think about what your options are. For example, if both you and your opponents are in the one-up, one-back formation and they approach the net, you know immediately that your two options are (1) to play the ball back low to the middle or to the person approaching the net, or (2) to lob the ball over the head of the person who is playing up in the one-up, one-back formation. Second, you are able to hit the basic shots associated with each of those options (i.e., the low ball in the former option and the lob in the latter). If you have problems in either of these areas, you'll probably have trouble competing at the 4.0 level, because everyone pretty much knows all the different strategies, formations, and shots. The way you differentiate yourself is by playing better offensive and defensive tennis, hitting your shots with more confidence, and feeling more comfortable in all the doubles formations. These are all components of better execution and help make the strategies you employ more successful.

Hit With Consistent Depth on All Your Shots

At the 3.5 level, the definition of depth was expanded to include all areas of the game, not just groundstrokes, and this holds true at the 4.0 level as well. By now, you've had plenty of time to work on and get comfortable with hitting the ball consistently deep in all areas of your game. The problem is that most players at the 4.0 level have done the same, plus they've improved their offensive and defensive skills. Since your competitors are better in all these areas, hitting the ball consistently deep on all your shots becomes more essential to your basic match strategy, because it keeps your opponent from attacking you and sets you up to attack.

Increase the Pace of Your Game

The 4.0 level is the jumping-off point for players who want to speed up their games. Many players hit the ball harder, which is what the game calls for at this level. However, don't get lured into overpowering your opponents, because this comes at the expense of consistency. You simply want to increase the speed of your shots while staying within your power range (hitting the ball as hard as you can while still being able to hit it consistently). The key is in your footwork. As the game gets faster, you have to work harder to set up for the ball. If you get to the ball quicker, the harder balls that your opponents are hitting look just like the balls they were hitting when the pace was slower. This allows you enough time to control the ball and hit it with a little more pace. So make up your mind that you're going to move those feet!

Become Comfortable at the Net

There are two reasons for becoming comfortable at playing the net. First and foremost, you have to play more aggressively to be successful at the 4.0 level. The best way to do this is to play the net, because it's easier to force your opponent when you're in the frontcourt than when you're in the backcourt. Also, playing aggressively from behind the baseline is beyond the reach of most 4.0-level players. Second, if you're not already comfortable at the net, obviously you've made it to this level on the strength of your groundstrokes, which leaves the net as the final frontier in improving your game. If you fit this profile, you need to become more comfortable at the net, because most players at the 4.0 level can use a variety of strategies and play multiple formations. This calls for you to play a multidimensional game, which means you have to play the net.

Playing the net effectively provides you with several ways to beat your opponent. For example, if you're strictly a baseline singles player and your opponent is an excellent defensive player who runs down every ball, you're going to have trouble ending points. If you become more comfortable with your volleys, you add the option of advancing to the net to end the point. The only problem is that not everyone feels comfortable at the net. Some people are naturally more comfortable at the net than others, because some people are naturally more aggressive and volley better than others. For those of you who aren't comfortable at the net, the way to become comfortable is to gain confidence in your ability to play the net and to overcome any fear you might have of being hit by the ball. The only way to do this is through perfecting your form and playing the net in practice and in matches!

Improve Your Offensive and Defensive Skills

Improving your offensive and defensive skills helps you better execute the strategies you learned at the 3.5 level. At the 4.0 level, your basic match strategy is the same as it was at the 3.5 level—to hit the ball consistently deep on your groundstrokes and look for a ball you can hit offensively. However, at the 4.0 level, you have to make your opponent pay for hitting weak shots by converting a higher percentage of them into points for you. You do this by playing more aggressively than you did at the 3.5 level. Don't panic, because this doesn't necessarily mean you have to charge the net all the time! However, it does mean that you have to improve your offensive skills by playing more aggressively within your game and by sharpening your offensive skills through better execution.

First, you have to play more aggressively within your game. At the 4.0 level, you know what your strengths are and have started to build your game around them. Now it's time to add more aggressiveness to these strengths, which can come in many forms. In singles, playing more aggressively is dictated by the type of game you play. For example, if you're a baseliner, you play more aggressively by hitting your groundstrokes harder and with more spin and by driving short balls into the corners with more pace and spin. On the other hand, if you like to play the net, you approach using more spin or mix the serve and volley in your game plan to keep your opponent off balance. In doubles, most players at the 4.0 level charge the net, so to play more aggressively, you either have to beat the other team to the net or play a defensive strategy more aggressively. Whatever type of game you play—baseline, net, or all-court—you have to play it more aggressively to convert your opponents' weak shots into points won for you.

Second, to play more aggressively, you must sharpen your offensive skills by hitting your shots with more pace, control, and spin. We discussed the importance of pace earlier in this chapter, so here we concentrate on control and spin. The advantage of hitting the ball with more control is that you can capitalize on your opponents' mistakes more readily by exposing yourself to less risk. For example, if your singles opponent hits the ball short and moves to slightly inside the baseline, you're able to play the ball aggressively into one of the corners by simply controlling the depth and direction of the shot, because you can get the ball behind her with a good, deep corner shot. This by itself is enough to send your opponent scrambling. You don't have to take the added risk of hitting the ball with more pace. Essentially, you're dissecting your opponent's poor positioning with accuracy. You can also play more aggressively by adding spin to your game. The addition of spin immediately forces your opponent to adjust her strokes to combat the spin and also helps you better execute the same strategies you used at the 3.5 level. When you play aggressively from the baseline, use topspin on your groundstrokes because it gives your opponent a different look. It also helps you to be more consistent by enabling you to control the ball better at faster paces. Thus, you execute better when you hit more aggressive shots. You can also use backspin, which, as you learned in chapter 3, is used more in conjunction with your net game (i.e., the approach shot and the volley). Using backspin on these shots keeps the ball low and forces your opponent to swing upward more, resulting in higher, easier volleys that you can hit offensively. Essentially, the backspin in this part of your game doesn't help you play more aggressively by helping you end the point; rather, it helps you play more aggressively by helping you set up the point better. Furthermore, when you hit backspin, the ball travels slower, giving you more time to get to the net and more time to recover when you're at the net.

The other half of the aggressiveness equation is defense. Since your opponents have improved offensive skills, you obviously have to improve your defensive skills. The way to do this is to hit your defensive shots with more control and spin. These are two of the ways we showed you to improve your offensive skills, however, they now apply in a different context.

First, you must have more control on your defensive shots than on your offensive shots, due to your situation. When you're in a position where you have to hit a defensive shot, your opponent has basically forced you into hitting a very precise shot because you're at some kind of disadvantage. For example, in both singles and doubles, if you hit a short ball and your opponent hits an approach shot and goes to the net, you have two choices: (1) hit an offensive shot if you're set up properly; (2) hit a defensive shot if you're not. If you hit an offensive shot, you are set up properly and aren't at a disadvantage. If you hit a defensive shot, you aren't set up and are at a disadvantage. Now that we've established that you're at a disadvantage when you hit a defensive shot, let's continue the example. You now have two choices for your defensive shot: (1) hit a defensive lob; (2) play the ball low to your opponent's feet. Both these shots, if they aren't hit with precision, cause you to lose the point. If you hit the lob short, your opponent puts the ball away. If you hit the low-ball shot too high, your opponent volleys the ball into the open court or through your partner at the net for a winner. Either way, you lose the point. The precision with which your aggressive opponent forces you to hit the ball is the increased control you need to combat aggressive players at the 4.0 level.

Second, you can play better defensive tennis if you add more spin to your defensive groundstrokes, because it improves your accuracy, recovery, and efficiency. It improves these three areas of your game because it helps counter the increased pace and pressure you play against at the 4.0 level. For example, when your opponent has a hard serve that you're having trouble returning and he's staying on the baseline, you can use backspin to "block" the ball back deep. To hit this shot, you shorten your backswing and make a long follow-through with the backspin stroke (see figure 4.12, a-b). Using backspin against a hard serve gives you more time than hitting a regular groundstroke because it's a more efficient shot. This is just one example of how to use spin to improve your defensive skills. In the following sections, we give you more examples of the types of spin to use in specific situations for both singles and doubles.

a

(continued)

Figure 4.12a-b (a) Short backspin backswing for the block shot with the racquet face open.

b

Figure 4.12a-b *(continued)* (b) Long, slightly downward follow-through.

Modify Your Strategy

The final key to success is to modify your singles and doubles strategies by improving your offensive and defensive skills.

Singles Strategy

Your main goal for singles at the 4.0 level is better execution of the strategies we introduced you to at the 3.5 level through improved offensive and defensive skills. Since improving your execution involves many skills that are intertwined, we show you specifically how and where you can improve your offensive and defensive skills within the strategic framework we laid out for you in chapter 3. At this point, we recommend that you reread the Keys to Success section on singles strategy in chapter 3.

Playing Your Offensive Shots More Aggressively. Your basic goal from the baseline is still the same—hit the ball consistently deep to force your opponent into hitting a short ball that you can play offensively. To accomplish this at the 4.0 level, you have to hit with more pace and move your opponent around the court by controlling the ball better. This allows you to exploit any stroking or movement weaknesses of your opponent. When you force your opponent to hit a short ball, you have the same three offensive options we showed you in chapter 3: drive the ball into one of the corners, hit an approach shot and go to the net, or hit a drop shot.

To drive the ball into one of the corners more aggressively, you can do two things. First, you can drive the ball with more pace, which, if executed properly, impairs your opponent's ability to play defense. The problem is that it's more difficult to hit the ball consistently when you hit it harder. Therefore, add topspin to this shot to help you overcome this problem, because it provides you with a greater margin for error and translates into a higher percentage of shots made. Furthermore, it puts more action on the ball, making it harder for your opponent to control the ball. For these reasons, hitting the ball with topspin translates into more points won for you. Second, you can hit the ball deeper into the court. If you're having problems with your accuracy because you're not getting the ball deep into the corners, more control is probably a better solution than more pace. Again, the answer is to hit this shot with topspin, because it provides greater margin for error. This is important when hitting the ball deeper, because it minimizes the risk involved.

To hit your approach shot more aggressively, you can do two things. First, you can hit it with backspin to help set up the point better. At the 3.5 level, you concentrated on hitting the approach shot deep without regard for how high the ball bounced. Much of the time, you could get by with an approach shot that bounced waist high because the 3.5-level players were just learning how to hit the ball low to your feet. At the 4.0 level, you can't get by with an approach shot that bounces waist high because the good players consistently hit the ball from above the level of the net to your feet, which forces you to hit difficult low volleys and half volleys. However, if you hit your approach shot with backspin, you keep the ball low, forcing your opponent to hit the ball higher, resulting in easier volleys that you can hit more aggressively. There are three reasons for this. First, you force your opponent to hit the ball from below the level of the net, which makes it harder for him to land the ball below the level of the net (at your feet). Second, you make your opponent alter his swing to adjust to the different bounce of the ball, which decreases his ball control. Third, the ball travels slower, which gives you more time to get into position for your first volley.

The other way to hit your approach shot more aggressively is to drive it deep into the court when your opponent is at a disadvantage.

The key to this play is knowing that you can force your opponent to hit a defensive shot, because this more than likely sets you up to hit an offensive shot on your first volley. For example, if you pull your opponent to one side of the court and he hits a short ball, you know that you can force him to hit a weak reply by driving the ball to the other side (into the open court). In this situation, use your regular groundstroke on your approach shot to set up your first volley. This play makes sense because you're anticipating that you're going to force your opponent to hit a defensive shot.

To hit your drop shot more aggressively, narrow its definition to a ball that bounces twice before it reaches the service line. To accomplish this task, you must do two things. First, arc the ball a little higher over the net, because it causes the ball to bounce vertically. If you hit the ball low over the net, it usually bounces horizontally through the court (i.e., toward your opponent). Second, hit the ball with backspin, because it causes the ball to bounce vertically (or back toward the net) and not as high. If you don't hit the drop shot with backspin, the ball bounces horizontally through the court and higher, giving your opponent a better chance to retrieve it.

Your other three offensive options at the 3.5 level were for use against someone who attacked you when they hit a poor approach shot: the low ball, the passing shot, and the offensive lob.

The first option, the low ball, isn't as effective an offensive shot as at the 3.5 level, because 4.0-level players are more proficient on their low and wide volleys. Therefore, you don't win many points by just hitting the ball low. You have to hit the low ball more aggressively to force your opponents to hit weak replies that you can take advantage of. To hit the low ball more aggressively, hit the ball at its highest point (but no higher than your shoulders, because you have to alter your stroke when you hit the ball from higher than this). The reasons are simple. First, the higher you make contact with the ball, the easier it is to hit the ball to your opponent's feet. For example, if your opponent is at the net and hits you a ball that bounces chest high, it's already above the level of the net, which means you can swing level or down at the ball to hit it to your opponent's feet. If you let the ball drop to knee height, you have to hit the ball from below the level of the net, forcing you into the more difficult task of swinging up to the ball to get it back to net level and then to your opponent's feet. Second, you give your opponent less time to prepare for his next shot. The extra time you give your opponent by letting the ball drop is equal to the time it takes for the ball to drop from the level at which you should hit it to the level at which you actually hit it. For example, if your opponent hits an approach that bounces chest high and goes to the net, the play that gives him the least amount of time to advance is for you to hit the ball from chest height. However, if you let the ball drop to knee height, the time it takes for the ball to drop from your chest to your knees gives your opponent an extra few steps toward the net, which could make the difference between his being in an offensive or defensive position to hit the first volley. At the 4.0 level, this could mean the difference between winning and losing! Third, it's easier to hit angle shots when the ball is above your waist, as opposed to below your knees, because you're landing the ball closer to the net than to the baseline. By hitting the ball at its highest point, you make it easier to hit the ball to your opponent's feet, give him less time to advance to the net, and create better angles.

To play the second option more aggressively, you have to go for more on your passing shots. At the 3.5 level, your main goal on passing shots was to hit the ball low and away from your opponent. Now you must hit them so your opponent can't reach the ball. To learn to do this, refer back to the Objectives section that covers passing shots.

To play the third option more aggressively, you have to hit a topspin lob, which we don't recommend at the 4.0 level. Rather, you stick with what you were doing at the 3.5 level and hit the ball over your opponent's head with a lower trajectory than you do for a defensive lob. This is more effective than the topspin lob, because you make fewer mistakes and get the same results. *Note:* If you feel you're ready to hit a topspin lob, refer to the Objectives section of chapter 5 to learn how to hit this shot.

Improving Your Defensive Shots. Now that we've covered how to play all the offensive options we showed you at the 3.5 level more aggressively, let's go over all the defensive options and how to improve on them. We start with the baseline. When you're rallying from the baseline and your opponent forces you out of the center of the court so that you don't have sufficient time to recover, you have two defensive options.

The first option is to lob the ball deep. At the 3.5 level, we told you to aim above the windscreens and behind the service line to get the defensive lob deep. At the 4.0 level, you have to hit it above the windscreens and into the back half of the backcourt, because 4.0 players have improved offensive skills. In particular, they have better overheads with which they can force you to hit a weak shot, so you don't want to give them anything they can hit aggressively.

Your second option against an offensive shot when playing at the baseline is to hit a high groundstroke over the net into the middle of the court or crosscourt. To improve on this shot, you have several choices involving the use of topspin and backspin to help you buy time to recover to the middle. However, how you want to play the defensive shot determines which type of spin to use. First, when you choose to hit a high, loopy groundstroke to recover, hit topspin, because it's a type of spin that is hit higher over the net and gives you a high margin for error. Thus, topspin is tailor-made for this shot, because it provides you with ample time to recover to the middle! Second, when you're on the run and can barely reach the ball, it's difficult to hit a high topspin shot. In this case, use backspin to play the ball back deep, because it's a simpler shot than the topspin shot. With backspin, the ball travels more slowly, so you don't have to hit the ball high over the net to give yourself time to recover. You simply hit your regular backspin shot. You'll use this option more and more as you climb the NTRP Ladder.

The last defensive shot we showed you was the defensive overhead. This shot doesn't come into play as much as it did at the 3.5 level, because 4.0 players are faster and have more offensive skills (i.e., better overheads). Therefore, the overhead is hit offensively more often than defensively at this level. When you do hit the defensive overhead, your main goal is still to hit the ball back deep into the court so you can return to the net or retreat to the baseline. The form for the defensive overhead remains the same.

At the 4.0 level, we include the low ball as a defensive shot. It's one of the offensive shots we showed you how to play more aggressively earlier in this section; however, it's an offensive shot only if your opponent hits a poor approach shot. If your opponent hits a strong enough serve, approach shot, or volley that you don't have time to hit your strokes, you must have the low ball as a defensive option, because any balls you hit high at the 4.0 level are put away. To improve on this shot, use your volley stroke to hit backspin. For example, if your opponent is serving and volleying and you're having trouble returning the ball with a full swing, use backspin to "chip" the ball to the server's feet. To hit this shot, shorten your backswing and your follow-through and use the high volley motion with emphasis on the correct footwork (cross-stepping) (see figure 4.13, a-b). As a result, the ball doesn't go as far in the court, and thus lands

a

b

Figure 4.13a-b (a) Shortened backspin backswing for the chip shot with the racquet face open. (b) Short, low follow-through.

at the volleyer's feet. Essentially, you're using the pace of the serve to return the ball to the server's feet. This makes it an excellent defensive play, because you don't have to generate your own power, you have more control with a shorter backswing, and it doesn't take much time to execute. The chip shot is a great way to use spin to improve your defensive skills and can be used in tight spots against good approach shots as well as hard volleys.

Approaching the Match. Now that we've covered the new and improved offensive and defensive options, we address your approach to the match. As stated earlier, play more aggressively when you have the opportunity. However, in formulating your strategy, don't take more risk than needed to win the match. Therefore, you start the match by hitting the ball deep and by identifying your opponent's weaknesses, rather than attacking from the outset. This is harder to do at the 4.0 level because the players cover up their weaknesses better than 3.5-level players. For example, a 4.0-level player who has weak groundstrokes but is strong at the net may attack the net more often and on shots that aren't high-percentage plays. She does this so she can play to her net strength and cover up her baseline weaknesses. Once you figure out what your opponent's weaknesses are, you decide how to play based on your own strengths.

If you play from the baseline and at the net equally well, then play the ball deep and mix up your three offensive options off the short balls. This confuses your opponent and causes her to guess at which defensive shot to hit when you attack. This translates into easy points for you. For example, if you drive the ball into one of the corners the first time your opponent hits it short, the next time she'll probably play a high defensive shot to the middle of the court, because she thinks you're going to stay back. If you approach the net in this situation, you'll surprise your opponent and have an easy high volley to put away. By mixing your offensive options this way, you're essentially staying one step ahead of your opponent. As recommended earlier in this chapter, play your three options more aggressively.

If you play well from the baseline and not at the net, play the ball deep and drive it into the corners or hit a drop shot off any short ball hit by your opponent. Once again, when you get a short ball, play your options more aggressively. However, with this style of play, play your options even more aggressively than with any of the others, because it's easier to defend. For example, most players who play this style don't come to the net when they drive the ball into one of the corners. Since they remain on the baseline, their opponent only has to hit the ball back high over the net to recover to the middle and overcome her mistake. However, if they play more aggressively on the short balls, they're able to put the ball away or force their opponent into a weak reply. *Note:* If you're this type of player, don't discount approaching the net as one of your options, because it is effective for the same reasons it is for those who play the baseline and the net equally well.

If you don't play well from the baseline and play well at the net, play the ball deep and go to the net on all short balls. Once again, when you get a short ball, hit your approach shot more aggressively. The success of this strategy boils down to how well your opponent hits passing shots, low balls, and lobs, and how well you volley and hit overheads. By hitting your approach shots more aggressively, you can negatively affect your opponent's ability to hit low balls, passing shots, and lobs, which positively affects your ability to volley, hit overheads, and win points. Also, you can serve and volley with this strategy, but we don't recommend doing this in singles at this level, because most players' returns are more developed than their serves (i.e., the returners win most of the points).

Depending on your strengths and weaknesses, employ one of these three basic offensive strategies in your matches. However, tennis isn't a game where you can expect everything to work perfectly, which is why we also covered the defensive options you use against these strategies earlier in this chapter. As in the last chapter, there is no section on defensive strategy, because you have to be extremely good at it to be successful! Therefore, you want to play defense when the situation arises rather than to use it as a strategy.

Doubles Strategy

In doubles at the 4.0 level, you use the same formations and have the same offensive options as you did at the 3.5 level. Again, your main goal is to better execute these formations and options through improving your offensive and defensive skills. Since improving your execution involves many skills that are intertwined, we show you specifically how and where you can improve your offensive and defensive skills within the framework we laid out for you in chapter 3. At this point, we recommend that you reread the Keys to Success section on doubles strategy in chapter 3.

One-Up, One-Back Versus One-Up, One-Back. Offensively, the improvements you need to make revolve around playing more aggressively. In the first doubles scenario, the one-up, one-back versus the one-up, one-back formation, there are several things you can do more aggressively to set up your attack. First, as the baseline player, you can increase the pace of your groundstrokes. By doing so, you force your opponents to improve their footwork and racquet preparation. If they don't, they fall behind the pace of the game. This causes them to lose some control on their strokes and translates into short balls and balls hit to your partner at the net, which effectively accomplishes your goal as the baseline player.

Second, you can change the spin on your groundstrokes to keep your opponent off balance. For example, during a baseline rally, hit the ball deep with backspin and, on the next shot, hit the ball deep with topspin. By changing the spin on your groundstrokes, you don't give your opponents the same look on every ball. This keeps them from getting into a groove on their strokes, because they have to prepare differently for each shot, which causes them to do what you want—hit the ball short or to your doubles partner at the net.

Third, as the server in the one-up, one-back formation, you can increase the pace and/or spin of your serve to set up the point. By adding these extras to your serve, you turn it into an offensive shot instead of just a necessary evil with which you start the point. When you succeed at this by forcing your opponents to hit the ball short or to your partner, you follow the strategies we formulated for you in chapter 3 and the modified strategies we've just shown you.

Aside from these three offensive additions to the strategy for the one-up, one-back versus the one-up, one-back formation, all your other offensive strategic goals remain the same.

From the defensive perspective, some skills need to be modified. First, you have to change your goal on your defensive lobs. At the 3.5 level, your goal was to hit the ball above the windscreens and behind the service line. However, at the 4.0 level, your goal is to hit your defensive lobs above the windscreens and into the back half of the backcourt, because players at this level hit their overheads more offensively in the midcourt area. Therefore, by hitting the ball deeper, you nullify this improvement.

Second, you have to work on your reflex volleys, which you're forced to hit when your opponents hit the ball at you from close range. Your main goal on the reflex volley is to get the ball back into play. If your opponents make a mistake by hitting you a ball that you can volley offensively, take advantage of their generosity and volley the ball back to their net player. Otherwise, just get the ball into play! The key to executing the reflex volley is to be as efficient as possible, because you have less time to react to the ball than on a normal volley. To do this, it's imperative that you always set up in the ready position (knees bent and racquet out in front of you) when you're at the net. It's also important that you not get scared at the net, because you're more apt to abandon the ready position—your main defense against the ball hitting you! Stay calm and focus on the ball, and you'll return a lot of balls.

Third, when your partner hits a short lob, you, as the net player, have to retreat and focus on two things. First, back up with your shoulders square to the net to help maintain your balance. Don't turn to the side, as you do when backing up for an overhead, because you don't yet know to which side the ball is coming. Second, back up as far as you can until your opponents start their swing, then split-step. It doesn't matter where you are in the court when you split-step, because you're simply giving yourself more time to react to the overhead. Plus, you're only going to stay there for one shot. Once your opponents hit their overhead, read the shot to determine what to do next. If your opponents hit a short overhead to you with little pace, play the ball back to their feet and return to the net. This is an offensive play out of a defensive position. If your opponents hit a hard, deep overhead to you, hit a defensive lob and continue moving backward to the baseline. This is a defensive play out of a defensive position. The only other possibility is if your return of the overhead goes over your opponents' heads and they have to retreat to get the ball. In this case, both you and your partner go to the net. This is an offensive play out of a defensive position. These are your options when your opponents have a short overhead and you're forced to retreat to a defensive position. Other than these three defensive improvements, there are no other modifications to the one-up, one-back versus the one-up, one-back formation that weren't already covered in chapter 3.

Transition From One-Up, One-Back to Two-Up. In the second doubles scenario, the transition from the one-up, one-back to the two-up formation, there are two ways to play more aggressively. First, add backspin to your approach shots. You do this for the same three reasons we discussed in the Singles Strategy section. First, it forces your opponents to swing up at the ball from below the level of the net, which results in higher, easier volleys for you. Second, it forces your opponents to adjust their groundstrokes to counter the effects of the backspin, which causes them to have control problems. Third, it gives you more time to get to the net, because the ball travels slower when you hit backspin.

The other way you can play more aggressively in this scenario is to serve and volley. We don't recommend this play in singles, because the returners are usually more advanced than the servers and the servers have too much court to cover. However, although your opponents' returns are still more advanced than your serve, it's a play we feel you can execute successfully in doubles, because you force your opponents to hit the ball more precisely and right to you. If you position yourselves correctly by following the flight of the ball, you cover the alley and force your opponents to hit the ball right to you by leaving only half the court in which to hit the ball. This puts more pressure on your opponents' returns. For example, if you serve and volley wide to the deuce court and your partner moves toward the alley, you leave your opponents only two options on the return: (1) hit a good, low return crosscourt, or (2) lob over the net person's head. If they hit any other shots, they're at a grave disadvantage, because you have the offensive skills to make them pay for their errant shots. The key to executing this play successfully is to serve and volley on a good first serve, because you set up the point well. If you hit a weak serve and advance to the net, your opponents are able to hit an aggressive low ball to your feet or lob over your partner's head, which puts you at a disadvantage from the beginning of the point. So make sure you hit a good first serve when you choose to serve and volley! Once you make your transition and advance to the net, use the same positioning rules and shots we showed you in the two-up section of chapter 3.

Other than these two ways to play more aggressively, you make the transition from one-up, one-back to two-up the same way as we showed you in chapter 3. *Note:* We cover how to play more aggressively and how to play defensively against the transition from one-up, one-back to two-up in the Two-Up Versus One-Up, One-Back section because they're exactly the same.

Two-Up Versus One-Up, One-Back. Now we look at how to play the two-up formation more aggressively against the one-up, one-back formation. The differences occur when your opponents hit a ball high or a lob at the net. At the 3.5 level, you put these shots away through the net person. At the 4.0 level, you have to convert these opportunities in one of five ways.

First, because your opponents volley better and have better defensive skills, you must volley and hit overheads with more pace, giving them less time to react. This results in more points won for you. A word of warning: You don't have to hit harder or swing at the ball to increase the pace of your volleys. The key is to improve your form by stepping to the ball and making contact with it in front of your body. This helps you use your body weight to increase the pace.

Second, you have to volley and hit overheads more precisely. When there's a hole in the other team's positioning, you must be able to volley the ball or hit your overhead into the opening to win the point. If you can't, you make it very tough on yourself, because players at the 4.0 level have improved defensive skills and are able to nullify your advantage. Also, since players at this level volley better, you have to volley the ball to the net person's feet as opposed to higher in his hitting zone. For example, if you have a high volley and hit it waist high to the net person, chances are the ball will come back, which can be costly, depending on what kind of shot your opponents hit. If they return the volley for a winner, you lose the point, which is the worst-case scenario. If they return the volley high, you have a second chance to put the ball away, which is the best-case scenario. If they return the ball low, you have to volley the ball defensively, putting you in a worse position than the one from which you started, because you didn't convert the opportunity you had on the high ball. Therefore, you're forced to make at least one more volley to win the point, which brings us to the third way to end the point.

After you volley the ball to the opposing net player's feet, expect the ball to come back and close to the net by advancing a couple of steps. In this case, don't worry about your opponents lobbing over your head, because they're hitting a reflex volley and more than likely won't be able to control it. What's important is that you're closer to the net for your next volley, which makes it harder for your opponents to hit the ball to your feet and easier for you to put the ball away. If the ball comes back after you close to the net, it'll probably be a high ball. In this case, volley to the retreating net person's feet again and continue to do so until the point ends.

The fourth way to play more aggressively is to angle the high volleys and lobs away from the baseline player, because it gives you more ways to set up and end the point. These shots are mostly used by the net player on the opposite half of the court from the baseline player, because he has room in which to angle the ball (player A in figure 4.14). You use these shots in two different situations. First, when you're having trouble creating an opening, use these shots to set up the point. By angling the ball into the alley, you pull the baseline player forward and to the other side, creating a large gap into which both you and your partner can put the ball away. Second, when you're having trouble winning points by hitting these shots through your opponents' net player, angle the high volleys and overheads away from the baseline player (see figure 4.14). Depending on how fast the baseline player is, you can win a lot of points with these shots. If you don't put the ball away, at least you create an opening for your next shot. Just remember that the closer to the middle and the farther back you are, the harder it is to angle the ball effectively.

The fifth way to play more aggressively is to expand the range in which you hit offensive overheads. At the 3.5 level, lobs that are behind the service line are usually hit defensively. At the 4.0 level, lobs in the midcourt area have to be hit offensively, a natural progression for the faster, more agile players at this level. This shouldn't pose a problem for you. You just have to be aware of this new goal on the overhead and work on it.

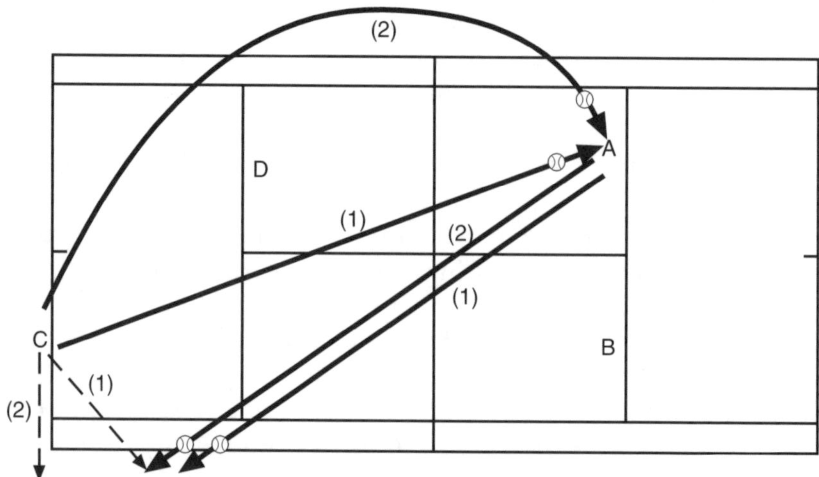

Figure 4.14 Player A angling off a high groundstroke (1) or a lob to the open court hit by player C (2). In both cases, player C is pulled off the court.

Defensively, you actually have the same two options you had at the 3.5 level. You volley the low balls back to the baseline player, and those overheads that you can't hit offensively you hit defensively. The reason you still only have two defensive options from this formation is that it's a predominantly offensive formation.

Now let's look at it from the one-up, one-back perspective. The only way to play more aggressively against the two-up formation or a team in transition is to hit the low-ball shot more offensively. If you recall, we already wrote extensively about how to hit this shot more offensively in the Singles Strategy section under your three offensive options against someone who attacks you. All the same principles apply here; however, the difference is in how you take advantage of the weak volley or approach shot. When you force your opponents to hit a weak volley, you play offensively by making the transition from the one-up, one-back to the two-up formation. The other two offensive options mentioned in the Singles Strategy section can't be played more aggressively. First, the passing shot isn't really a doubles shot, because a team that positions themselves properly seldom gets passed. Second, to hit an offensive lob more aggressively, you have to hit a topspin lob, a shot we don't recommend at the 4.0 level. Therefore, your options for playing more offensively against this formation are extremely limited.

The ways that you can improve your defense against the two-up formation are identical to those we showed you for improving your defense against the one-up, one-back formation, except for one addition. When your opponents hit a shot you don't have much time to prepare for, use the backspin chip shot we showed you earlier in the Singles Strategy section. It works well against approach shots that pull you out of position, hard volleys, and serve and volleyers who serve hard.

Two-Up Versus Two-Back. The next situation we cover is the two-up versus the two-back formation. The only way to play the two-up formation more aggressively is to use the angle shot we described in the Objectives section. Remember that you have the advantage when you and your partner are at the net. Therefore, you hit the ball to the middle until your opponents give you a shot that you can play offensively. In chapter 3, we defined that as a high volley or a short lob. Here, we're adding balls hit to the outside of the court (not in the middle) to that definition, because you can hit the angle shot off them. This is an important offensive shot against the two-back formation, because you can use it to set up or end a point. For example, if your opponent hits the ball from the middle of the court to the outside, you can angle the ball crosscourt. If they don't retrieve the ball, it's obviously a winner. If they do hit the ball back, you've created an opening you can exploit by hitting the ball deep into it (both players) or by hitting another angle shot to the other half of the court (the player on the same half of the court to which the angle shot was hit) (see figure 4.15). If you choose the option of angling the ball twice, you use both of the angle volleys we just showed you. You open up the court with the first angle volley, then put the ball away with the second angle volley. This example shows how useful the angle shot is in your quest to play this formation more aggressively.

Defensively, you have the same options you had at the 3.5 level. You hit the low balls deep down the middle, and those overheads you can't hit offensively, you hit defensively.

On the other side of the court, the two-back formation is basically a defensive formation. Usually when you play this formation, you're not looking to play more aggressively, although it is possible. The only way to play it more aggressively is to drive the ball from its highest point, because it's easier to get it to your opponents' feet, giving them less time to recover at the net. This results in some weak volleys on which you move forward and continue to hit low balls with your groundstrokes; or you go to the net as a team, which takes

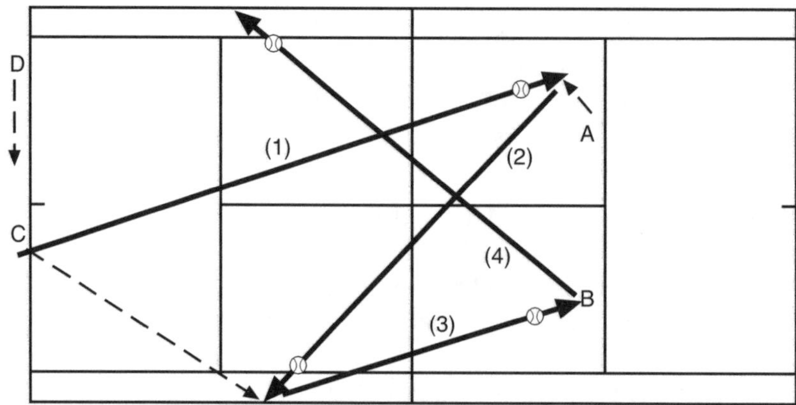

Figure 4.15 Player C hitting to the outside of player A (1). Player A angling a volley wide in front of player C (2). Player C hitting the ball to player B (3). Player B hitting an angle in front of player D, who has moved to the middle to cover the open court (4).

you out of the two-back formation. Other than this addition, you play this formation the same way you did at the 3.5 level.

Defensively, you have the same strategic goals as you did at the 3.5 level. The defensive improvements you can make are to chip the balls you can't drive and hit your defensive lobs deeper into the court.

Two-Up Versus Two-Up. The last situation you may encounter, the two-up versus the two-up formation, is one we haven't covered yet. The strategy here is simple: Volley the ball down the middle to your opponents' feet and close the net. By volleying the ball to the middle, you create confusion between your opponents, which results in your winning more points. Furthermore, if you're able to keep the ball low, you create an advantage, because the other team is more apt to "pop" the ball up (hit a high, easy ball), resulting in easy put-aways for you when you close to the net. Being closer to the net gives you better angles with which to put the ball away and gives your opponents less time to react. In general, the team that keeps the ball low usually wins most of these exchanges.

Approaching the Match. Now that we've covered all the doubles situations you can find yourself in, let's cover your strategic approach to a doubles match. As always, you have to know your strengths and weaknesses, because they dictate your approach to the match.

If both you and your partner play the net and move fairly well, you definitely want to get to the two-up formation as often as possible, because you can play most aggressively from this formation. With this strategic approach, look to get to the two-up formation at every opportunity, attacking short balls, weak serves, lobs over your opponents' heads, deep high balls, and on your good first serves. Remember to use all the new offensive skills we showed you earlier in this chapter. Once you get to the two-up formation, play percentage tennis the way we showed you in the sections on the two-up versus one-up, one-back; two-back; and two-up formations. If you're successfully making the transition to the two-up formation and you're losing badly, analyze the situation. Ask yourself if you're playing the formation properly, or if you're not executing properly. It might help you remember a tactic or shot that makes a difference in the match. If you're not executing properly because your opponents are playing well, change your strategy and switch to the one-up, one-back formation, where at least one of you can still play offensively. This provides more stability to your game by giving you a chance to get some kind of rhythm started from the baseline.

If both you and your partner play the net reasonably well but are more confident from the baseline, play the one-up, one-back formation, because you can still play it offensively against the one-up, one-back and two-back formations. However, if your opponents attack the net and get to the two-up formation, you must play this formation defensively. At the 4.0 level, you encounter a problem in this formation, because most teams are looking to advance to the two-up formation, and the teams that play more aggressively usually win. As always, if you're playing this formation and losing badly, analyze the situation. Ask yourself if you're playing the formation properly, or if you're just not executing. If you're not executing properly because your opponents are forcing you to make mistakes, change your strategy and switch to the two-up or the two-back formation. In choosing one of these strategies, analyze what your opponents do well. For example, if they play the two-up formation well, you might not want to concede the net by playing the two-back formation. You might want to take it away by playing the two-up formation, forcing your opponents to play another formation with which they might not be comfortable. By doing this, you just might happen upon something that helps you win the match! Whichever formation you choose to play, make sure that you feel comfortable playing it, and play it the way we showed you!

If both you and your partner are uncomfortable at the net and like to play the baseline, you still start in the one-up, one-back formation, because you have a chance to play more offensively with one player at the net. If you start losing badly, switch to the two-back formation. Basically, the point here is not to give up your chance to play offensively unless you must, because your opponents, with their more aggressive style of play, will more easily take advantage of your two-back defensive style of play. On the other hand, this can be a successful strategy, but it becomes harder to execute as you climb the USTA Ladder, because you have to play with a great deal of precision and patience. If the two-back formation doesn't work, your only other option is to play the two-up formation, which is difficult because you aren't playing to your strengths.

These are the optimal approaches to use based on your strengths and weaknesses. However, this isn't a perfect assessment of how to play. Rather, these are guidelines to follow to help you with your basic strategy until you find what works for you!

PRACTICE DRILLS

At the 4.0 level, you have to focus on improving your offensive and defensive skills on your various options and know how and when to hit the new shots we've shown you. The following singles and doubles drills help you accomplish these tasks.

Singles Drills

In the following section, we put together a set of singles situation drills that help you with all the offensive and defensive shot and strategy modifications we've suggested.

Topspin-Backspin Drill

In this drill, both players start on opposite ends at the center mark, 1 yard behind the baseline, and each player is responsible for hitting either topspin or backspin on every shot. For example, you, as player A, choose topspin. You start the drill with a feed down the middle, and on every ball after that, you have to hit topspin. Meanwhile, player B has to hit backspin on every shot. This form drill helps you develop both topspin and backspin to add diversity to your shot selection, which is one of your objectives. During the drill, when the ball is short, hit a backspin approach shot if you're hitting backspin and a topspin drive into one of the corners if you're hitting topspin. This gives you more specific practice on your short ball options. To make it more interesting, use the 2-1 scoring system. The person hitting backspin scores two points for every point she wins. The person hitting topspin only scores one point for every point she wins, because it's easier to hit topspin. Play to 11 points, then switch and hit the other type of spin. This may seem like an easy drill, but it takes some time to get used to it.

Passing Shot Drill

In this drill, player A starts at the junction of the centerline and the service line, or the *T*, and player B starts 1 yard behind the baseline in the middle of the court. Player A starts the drill by feeding the ball to one of three spots: the forehand side, the backhand side, or right at player B (see figure 4.16). Player B has to hit the ball past player A, aiming for the targets shown in figure 4.16. There's no lobbing. As player B, remember to aim the ball about 1 to 1.5 feet inside the singles lines, giving yourself some room to err. Also, if you miss, remember to miss the passing shot into the net, because it ensures that you're aiming the ball low over the net. As player A, you're working on your low and wide volleys and on putting the ball away if your drilling partner hits it high. Score this drill with the 2-1 scoring system. If you hit a clean passing shot or volley winner (an untouched ball), you score two points. If you win the point in any other manner, you score one point. Play to 11 points, then switch positions.

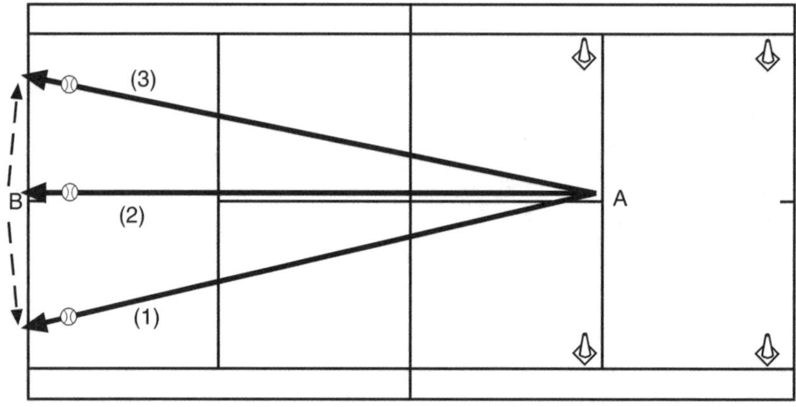

Figure 4.16 Passing Shot Drill with player A feeding a ball to the forehand side of player B (1), the backhand side of player B (3), or right at player B (2). Player B hits down-the-line or crosscourt passing shots. The targets near the service line are for the crosscourt shots; the targets near the baseline are for the down-the-line shots.

Attack the Second Serve Drill

You were introduced to this drill at the 3.5 level. At the 4.0 level, it's basically the same, except you now have a more specific focus on some of the options. When you approach down the line off your return (option 2), you have to hit the ball closer to the singles lines than to the center mark. To help you accomplish this, pretend there's a semicircle extending 3 yards to either side of the center mark (if you play on clay courts, you can lightly draw this semicircle on the court). Also, hit your approach shots with backspin. When you hit a drop shot off your return (option 3), your goal is to make the ball bounce twice before it gets to the service line. This helps you keep the ball from going too far into the court and giving your opponent an easy setup. When you drive your return into one of the corners (option 1), your goal remains the same as at the 3.5 level.

Two Approach Drill

In this drill, both players start on opposite ends of the court at the center mark, 1 yard behind the baseline. One of you starts the drill with a feed down the middle, and you play out the point. The key to this drill is the 3-2-1 scoring system, because it makes it advantageous to go to the net. The scoring is as follows: If you hit an approach shot, come to the net, and put the ball away, you score three points. If you hit an approach shot, come to the net, and your drilling partner misses the ball, you score two points. If you win the point from the baseline, you score one point. In this drill, remember to approach on two types of balls. As always, you approach on short balls; however, when you come in on the short balls, use backspin to force your drilling partner to hit high balls over the net, which results in easy, high volleys for you. You also approach on high, deep balls that you feel force your drilling partner to hit defensive shots. Remember, the definition of a good approach shot is any approach shot that gets a defensive response. If you learn to use this type of approach shot effectively, it gives you another way to approach the net besides off a short ball. Play two out of three games to 15 points.

Deep Volley Drill

In this drill, player A starts at the junction of the centerline and the service line, or the *T*, and player B starts 1 yard behind the baseline in the center of the court. Player B starts the rally by feeding the ball to player A. You, as player A, have to volley the ball past the service line to begin the point. If you fail to do this, the point is annulled and you start over. Once you successfully volley the ball past the service line, play out the point. If at any time during the point your volley lands in front of the service line, you lose the point. Otherwise, anything goes. This drill gives you work on your low and wide volleys (your midcourt game) and helps you learn to hit all your volleys deep. As player B, you work on hitting low balls, passing shots, and lobs, depending on your situation. This gives you a chance to hone your decision-making skills against an attacking opponent in a game-type situation. Play to 11 points, then switch positions.

Short Ball-Lob Approach Drill

In this drill, both players start on opposite ends of the court at the center mark, 1 yard behind the baseline. To start the drill, player A alternates between two options: feeding a short ball or lobbing the ball into one of the corners. If player A chooses the first option, you, as player B, hit an approach shot and go to the net (remember to stay to the side of the centerline to which you approach) (see figure 4.17). This drill gives you important work on your backspin approach shot and midcourt volleys. As player A, you work on your offensive and defensive skills, depending on the shot your drilling partner hits. Again, this gives you a chance to hone your decision-making skills against an attacking opponent in a game-type situation.

If you, as player A, choose the second option, follow your lob in to the net and advance to the back two-thirds of the service box (remem-

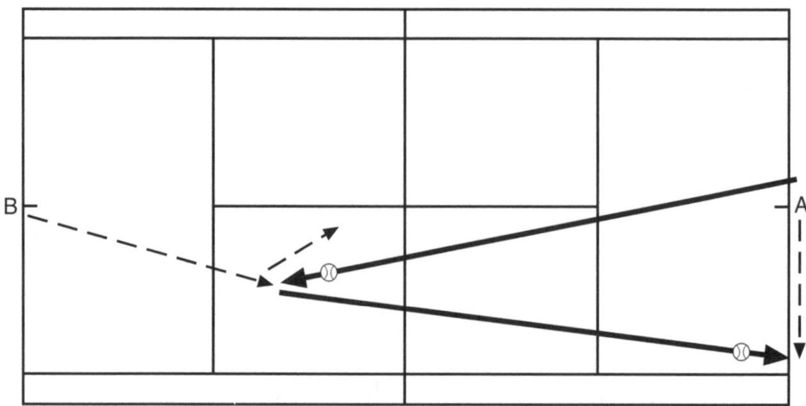

Figure 4.17 Short Ball-Lob Approach Drill showing option 1 with player A feeding a short ball to player B, who hits an approach shot and moves up to play the net.

ber to stay to the side of the centerline to which you approach) (see figure 4.18). This positioning affords you a chance to make a good play against either a lob or a low-ball drive by player B. This second option gives you practice approaching the net in a different manner (i.e., off a lob). As player B, you get practice hitting deep lobs and low balls against deep lobs. After 7 minutes, switch and try the other position.

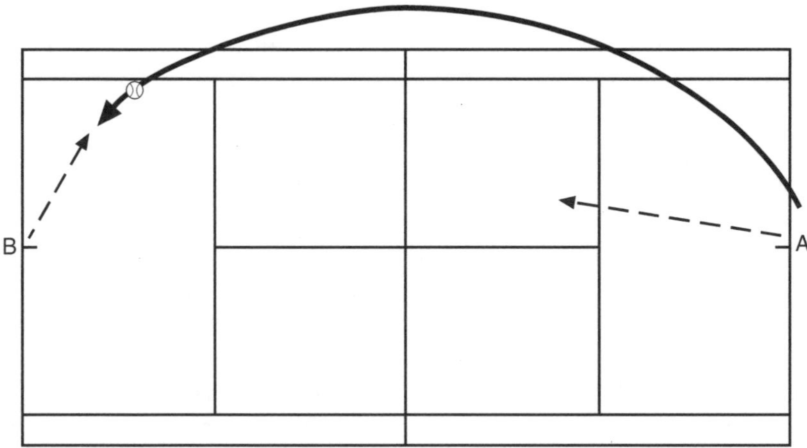

Figure 4.18 Short Ball-Lob Approach Drill showing option 2, with player A feeding a lob to player B's backhand corner and following up the lob to the midcourt area. Player B returns the shot and the point is played out.

Note: Since we don't condone serving and volleying in singles at the 4.0 level, we don't include any serve-and-volley drills in this section. If you want to practice your serve and volley, refer to the Serve-Volley, Serve-Return Drill in the Doubles Drills section or the Singles Serve-Volley, Serve-Return Drill in the 4.5-level Singles Drills section (chapter 5).

Other Drills That Still Apply

Chapter 2: High Ball Drill, Recovery Drills, Directional Movement Drill, Approach Shot Drill

Chapter 3: Approach Shot Combination Drill, Defensive Baseline Drill, Low Ball Singles Drill, Defensive Lob Overhead Drill

Doubles Drills

The following doubles drills show you how and when to employ your new offensive and defensive skills, so you'll feel comfortable with any situation you encounter during a match.

Serve-Volley, Serve-Return Drill

In this drill, one player starts from the standard doubles serving position (halfway between the center mark and the doubles line) and the other starts in the standard doubles return position (back far enough in the court that you can keep the ball in front of you). You serve and play out the point crosscourt, but with a twist. On first serves, you have to serve and volley. Don't panic! We've already shown you that serving and volleying is exactly like approaching the net, except the serve is your approach shot; so you come to the net exactly the same way as for a regular approach. Remember, the key is to toss the ball in front of you so your weight continues into the court after you serve, which gets you to the net faster. The returner in this drill concentrates on driving the ball back low to the server's feet. Remember to cut off the ball on an angle and take it as high in the air as you can. This gives you the best chance of returning the ball to the server's feet. Play out the points crosscourt, with the doubles line and the centerline extended to the baseline as your boundaries.

If you miss your first serve, play a second serve. On the second serve, the returner has to return crosscourt and approach the net. When he approaches the net, the returner hits the approach shot deep to put the server on the defensive. After split-stepping and making his midcourt shot, he continues to the net.

When your drilling partner attacks after you serve, take a step back behind the baseline to give yourself more time and room to keep the ball in front of you for your next shot. Then play the first ball to the attacker's feet, because there's plenty of room in which to hit the ball when your opponent is approaching. When this happens, you have a greater margin for error because your opponent doesn't advance very far into the midcourt area. Thus, you don't have to hit a perfect low shot on the first try. For example, if the first ball you hit to an attacker is waist high (instead of at his feet), he's at the service line and will probably play the ball back to the baseliner (the returner). In this case, no harm is done, because the volleyer didn't hit the ball through the net player. (However, you aren't right back where you started. The attacking team now has the advantage, because they have control of the net, and your next shot has to be more precise.) In this drill, play out the points crosscourt, with the doubles line and the centerline extended to the baseline as your boundaries. Play and score this drill as you would a Ping-Pong match by alternating servers every five points, with the first team to 21 points winning. Since you're just learning to serve and volley, you'll make some errors in the beginning, but you'll get better as you do the drill more. *Note:* Pay close attention to how well you do when you're being attacked on second serves and when you're attacking second serves, because these two plays are critical at the 4.0 level.

Angle Volley Drill

This drill can be done with two or four players, but you make more efficient use of your court time if you use four. In this drill, all four players start halfway between the service line and the net, 1 yard from the singles line. Your partner is the player in the opposite crosscourt box, and your drill is independent of the other two people drilling. To start, one of you feeds a ball toward the alley (the outside of the court), which is a forehand volley in the deuce court and a backhand volley in the ad court (for right-handed players). You continue to volley the ball crosscourt toward the alley, which forces you to hit angle volleys (see figure 4.19). This is simply a form drill to sharpen your angle

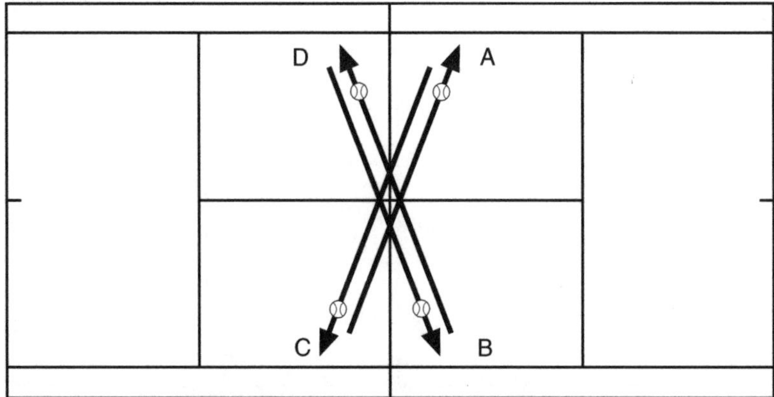

Figure 4.19 Angle Volley Drill with players A and B feeding balls to the diagonal positions (A to C and B to D). Players A and C are hitting crosscourt forehand angles and players B and D are hitting crosscourt backhand angles.

volleying skills and to get you more comfortable with hitting angle volleys. Remember that you want to hit the side of the ball by keeping your arm between your body and the net. After you do 7 minutes to one half of the court, switch and practice your angle volley the other way.

Doubles Deep Volley Drill

This is the doubles variation of the Deep Volley Drill we showed you in the Singles Drills section. In this drill, one team starts in a two-up formation and the other starts in a one-up, one-back defensive formation (as if lining up to return serve). Player A starts the drill from the baseline by feeding a low ball to the feet of either of the net players (players C and D). Player C or D has to hit her first volley behind the service line to player A (see figure 4.20). If she fails to do so, the point is annulled and you start over. If player C or D is successful, continue the drill by playing out the point. This is an excellent drill for getting you into the habit of hitting low volleys defensively to the baseline player against a one-up, one-back formation—the correct shot in this situation. It also gives you practice in both the two-up versus one-up, one-back formation and the one-up, one-back versus two-up formation. If you want to score the drill, use the 2-1 scoring system, with the one-up, one-back team scoring two points for every point won and the two-up team scoring one point for every point won. After playing to 11 points, switch formations.

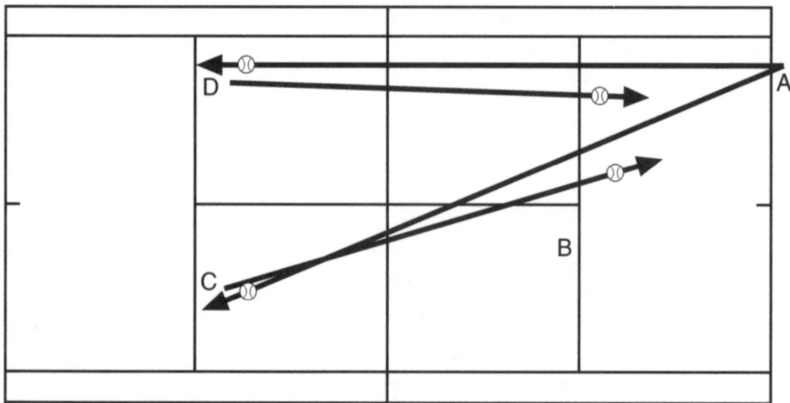

Figure 4.20 Doubles Deep Volley Drill with player A starting the drill by feeding a low ball to player C or D, who must hit the first volley past the service line to begin the drill.

Three-Look Approach Drill

This drill gets its name because it gives you practice approaching the net against the three different formations.

In the first "look," start with both teams in a one-up, one-back formation. Player A, whose team isn't allowed to lob, starts the drill with a short feed crosscourt to player C. You, as player C, hit a deep approach shot (preferably with backspin) to player A and go to the net. Player D moves even with player C in the back third of the service box (see figure 4.21). Remember to follow the direction of the ball so your team is in proper position. When player A makes the return, your team chooses one of the two options you have in this situation. If the ball is returned low, volley the ball back deep to player A (a defensive play) (see figure 4.22). At the 4.0 level, there is no need to try to create an offensive opportunity that isn't there. Since you volley well enough to hold the net, you can wait until your opponents hit you a high ball you can put away. This leads us to your second option. If the ball is returned high by player A, you (as players C and D) volley the ball into the gap or through the net person (see figure 4.22). The key that differentiates you from the 3.5-level player is that you have to put this shot away. When your opponents make a mistake like this, you can't give them another chance to return the ball. Play to 11 points using the 2-1 scoring system, with the team being attacked scoring two points for every point they

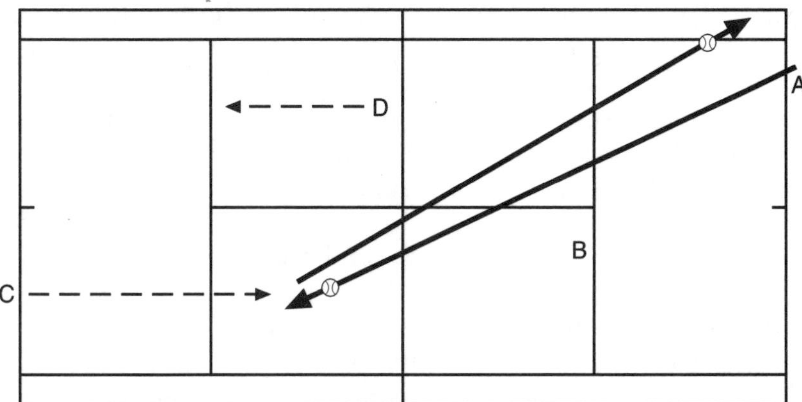

Figure 4.21 Three-Look Approach Drill showing look 1 with player A feeding a short ball to player C, who hits a crosscourt approach shot back to player A. Player D moves back to the back third of the service box to join player C. Player A hits only groundstrokes back to players C and D (no lobs).

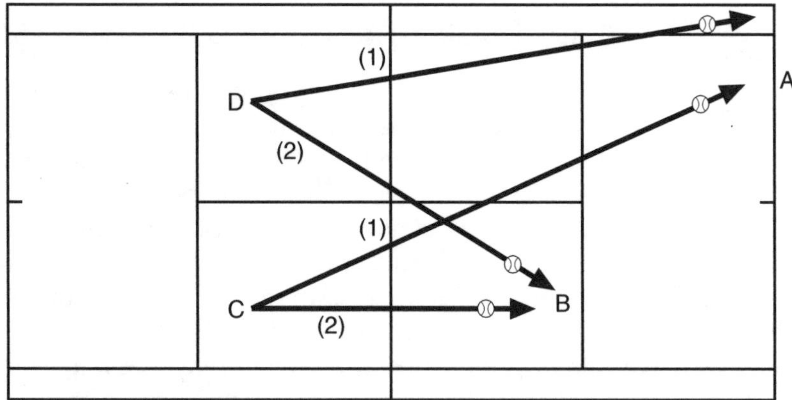

Figure 4.22 Three-Look Approach Drill showing a continuation of look 1 with players C and D volleying low balls back to player A (1) or volleying high balls through player B (2).

win and the team attacking scoring one point for every point they win. After each game to 11 points, rotate clockwise one position (player A goes to player B's position, player B goes to player C's position, etc.) until you've each drilled at all four positions.

In the second "look," start with one team in the two-back formation and the other team in the one-up, one-back formation. Player A or B, whose team isn't allowed to lob, starts the drill with a short feed to player C. You, as player C, hit an approach shot (preferably with backspin) down the middle or into one of the alleys and go to the net. Player D moves even with player C in the back third of the service box (see figure 4.23). Remember to adjust your positioning with the direction of the ball. When player A's team makes the return, your team uses one of your three options in this situation. First, if player A's team returns the ball low, volley the ball back deep down the middle (a defensive play) to keep your advantage at the net (see figure 4.24). This allows you to wait for another ball that you can volley more aggressively. Second, if they return the ball high, volley the ball aggressively down the middle, the largest part of the court, to cause confusion and/or open up the outsides of the court (see figure 4.24). Your other option off a high ball is to angle the volley into one of the alleys (see figure 4.24). This enables you to put the ball away or to open up the middle and/or the other alley. Since you've just learned the angle volley, this is a new option that takes a little time to master; however, it shouldn't take long, because it's

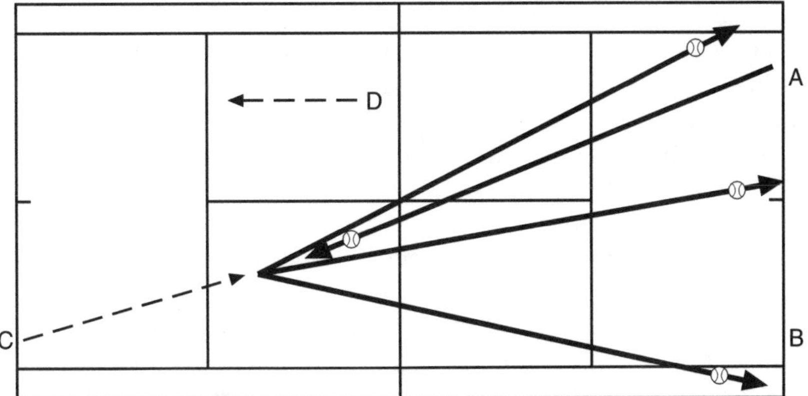

Figure 4.23 Three-Look Approach Drill showing look 2 with player C hitting the three possible approaches against the two-back formation and player D stepping back to join player C in the back third of the service box.

one of the easier shots to learn. As stated in the Keys to Success section, you win most of the points when your opponents hit the ball high to you at the net, because that's one of the main skills that separates you from 3.5-level players. Play to 11 points using the 2-1 scoring system, with the two-back team scoring two points for every point they win and the one-up, one-back team (the attacking team) scoring one point for every point they win. After each game

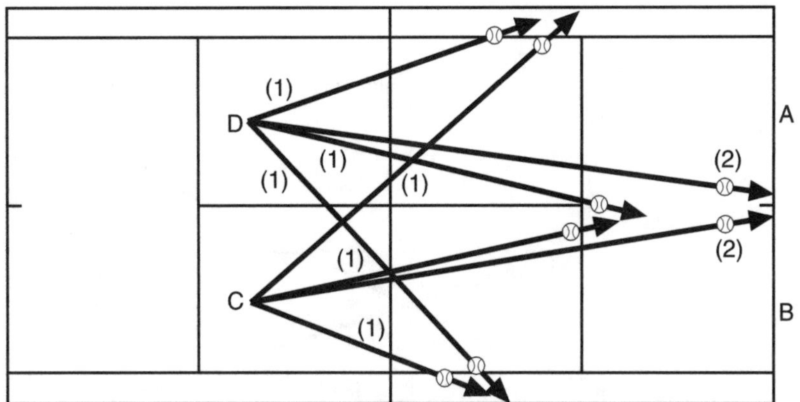

Figure 4.24 Three-Look Approach Drill showing a continuation of look 2 with players C and D hitting the offensive options off high balls, the two angles, and the middle (1), or the defensive option, hitting deep down the middle off a low ball (2).

to 11 points, rotate clockwise one position (player A replaces player B, player B replaces player C, etc.) until you've all drilled at each position. *Note:* When attacking the two-back formation, an effective play is to approach to the ad court alley, because you attack your opponents' baseline weakness (the backhand for right-handers) and put your strength (the forehand volley for right-handers) in a position to cover the middle (see figure 4.25).

In the third "look," start with one team in the two-up formation, with both players on the service line, and the other team in the one-up, one-back formation. Player A or B starts the drill with a short feed to player C. As player C, you hit an approach shot low to the other team's feet and continue to the net (see figure 4.26). You haven't seen this play yet, but you'll see more and more of it as you move up through the levels, because more teams play the two-up formation. The key to executing this play successfully is to hit the approach shot low, because if you hit it high, the point will be over on the next shot. Players at the 4.0 level are too good to let you get away with hitting a high ball in this situation. However, if you hit your approach shot low, you have the advantage, because it's hard for your opponents to volley the ball low to your feet; thus, you're more than likely the one getting the high ball to put away! Play to 11 points using the 2-1 scoring system, with the team approaching the net scoring two points for every point they win and the team starting in the two-up formation scoring one point for every point they win.

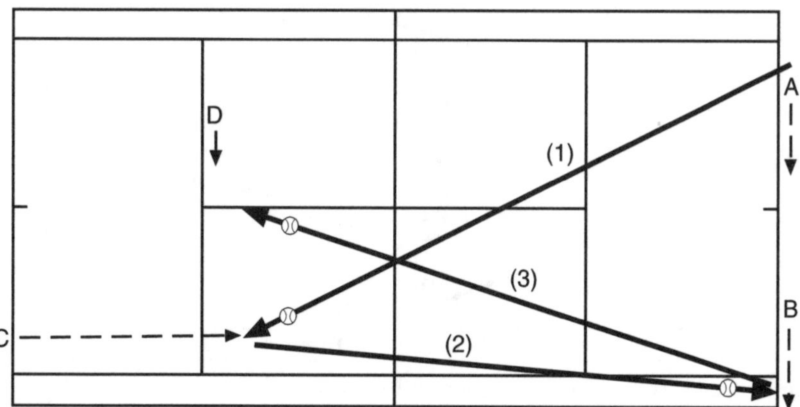

Figure 4.25 Player A hitting a short ball (1). Player C attacking the backhand side of player B with the approach shot (2), putting player D in the middle with a good chance of hitting a forehand volley (3).

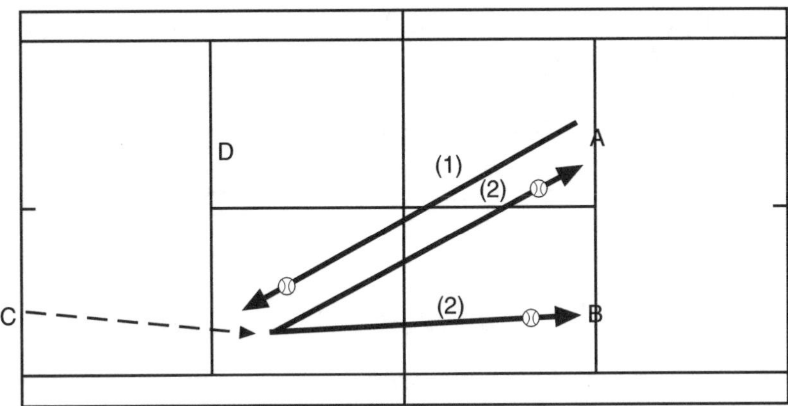

Figure 4.26 Three-Look Approach Drill showing look 3 with player A feeding a short ball to player C (1), who hits a low approach shot to the feet of players A and B (2).

After each 11-point game, rotate clockwise one position (player A replaces player B, player B replaces player C, etc.) until you've all drilled at each position. *Note:* The best places to play the approach are to the backhand volley in the middle or the backhand volley to the outside (for right-handers), because player D is set up to make the middle volley with his strength, the forehand volley (for right-handers) (see figure 4.27).

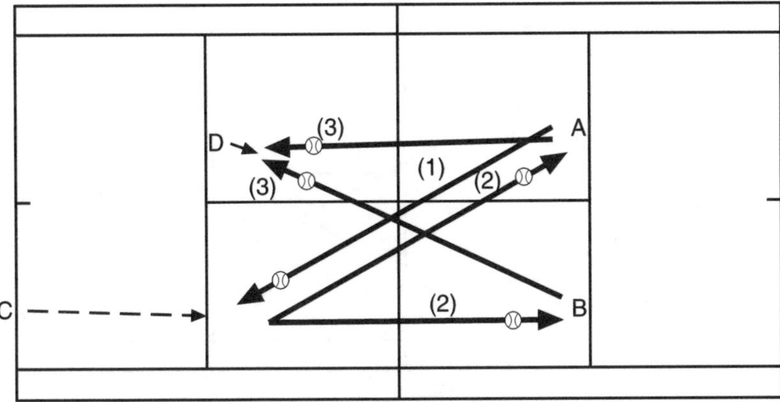

Figure 4.27 Player A feeding a short ball to player C (1). Player C approaching to the outside of player B or the inside of player A (2). Player A or B hitting a forehand volley (3). *Note:* Player C approaches to the outside of player B (backhand) or to the inside of player A (backhand, middle).

The purpose of the Three-Look Drill is to practice against the three different situations you encounter when you approach the net, the last of which we haven't covered yet. The common keys to executing all these drills successfully are hitting the good approach, which gives you and not your opponent an advantage, and putting the ball away when you have the opportunity. These are important things to learn, because they are two of the keys to success at the 4.0 level!

Attack One-Up, One-Back Drill

In this drill, you start with one team in the two-up formation and one in the one-up, one-back formation. Player A starts the drill by feeding a high groundstroke or a short lob to either player on the two-up team. Players C and D on the two-up team have to put the ball away by hitting it through player B and closing behind the shot in case the ball comes back (see figure 4.28). The emphasis for the two-up team is on putting the ball away, because to compete at this level, you have to do this consistently.

If player A starts the drill with a high ball, you, as player B, work on your reflex volleys. Remember to keep your racquet up in the ready position and not get scared. If player A starts the drill with a

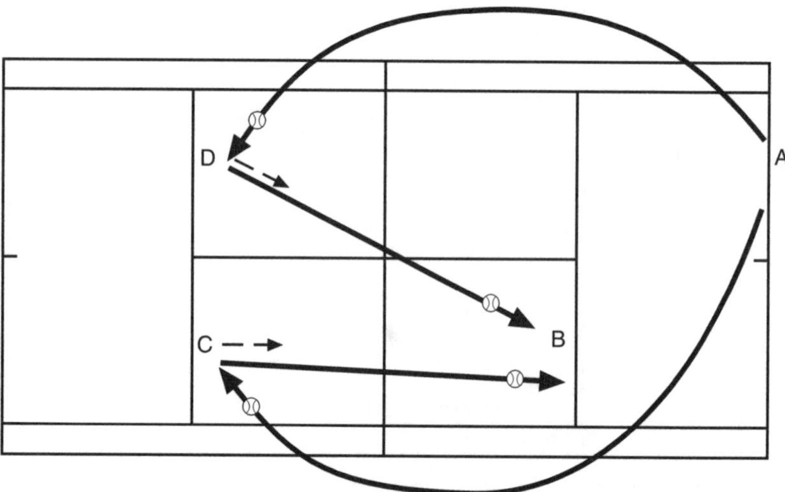

Figure 4.28 Attack One-Up, One-Back Drill with player A feeding a high groundstroke or a short lob to players C and D, who hit through player B's side of the court and close in toward the net.

short lob, your team works on defensive positioning. In this situation, you align yourselves as a team to best cover the overhead. We covered this in chapter 3 when we showed you how to put away short lobs. Remember to align yourselves to cut off the crosscourt angle overhead. If you're player B, retreat to the opposite half of the court from which the ball lands. Player A does the same. For example, if the ball is hit short to player D, player B retreats toward the ad court alley and player A moves toward the middle to help plug the hole created when player B retreats toward the alley. This gives you maximum court coverage (see figure 4.29). Drill for 5 minutes at one position, then rotate clockwise until you've each drilled at all four positions. This is a valuable drill because it helps you with your offensive and defensive skills in the two-up versus the one-up, one-back formation and vice versa.

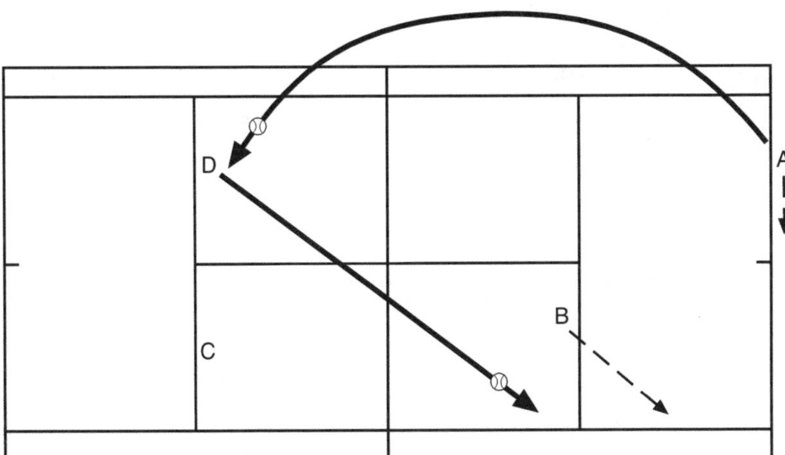

Figure 4.29 Attack One-Up, One-Back Drill showing the defensive movement for players A and B, with player A feeding a short lob to player D, who hits an overhead toward player B. Player B is backing up toward the alley and player A is moving closer to the center mark.

Attack Two-Back Drill

In this drill, you start with one team in the two-up formation and the other in the two-back formation. Player A starts the drill with a high ball or a short lob to player D. If the feed is a high ball, player D volleys down the middle or angles the ball to player B's half of the court. If the feed is a lob, player D hits the overhead down the middle or angles it crosscourt (see figure 4.30). As player D, you're encouraged to use variety in your shot selection. This drill helps improve your decision-making skills and also gives you practice setting up and ending points using the angles. As players A and B, you work on court positioning. If player D angles her high volley, player B runs forward toward the alley and player A shifts to the middle to help cover the hole (see figure 4.30). In this situation, pay attention to how far player B recovers. The farther she recovers into the court, the farther you (player A) move back to your original side of the court, giving you better court coverage. If player D has a short lob, move toward the opposite half of the court to the angle of the ball, as we showed you in chapter 3. This gives you maximum court coverage. When player D goes to hit the overhead, practice breaking on the ball, which helps you anticipate where she's going to hit her shot. Do this drill for 5 minutes, then rotate clockwise to the next position. After you've completed the rotation four times, change by having player B start the drill to player C and do another four rotations.

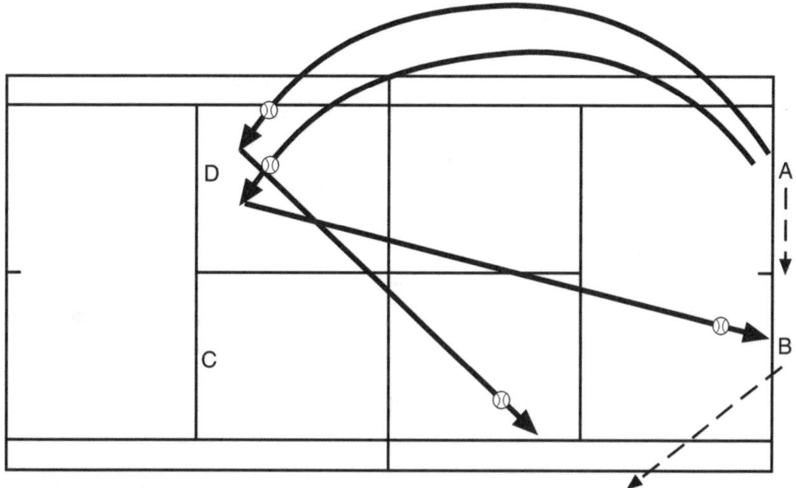

Figure 4.30 Attack Two-Back Drill with player A feeding a lob or a high ball to player D, who hits a crosscourt angle or to the middle. Players A and B are moving to the opposite side to cover the holes (to the left, where the ball is hit by player D). If the ball is fed to player C, the drill is the opposite.

Middle Drill

This drill is the same as the Middle Drill in chapter 3, except you keep score. Use a standard one-point scoring system and play to 11 points. Even though the two-up team has the advantage, you'll be surprised at how close the baseline team comes to winning. The main difference in this drill between the 4.0 and 3.5 levels is that you're able to perform it better. It's also more pertinent to your keys to success in this chapter, because it improves your offensive and defensive skills.

Other Drills That Still Apply

Chapter 2: Recovery Drills, Doubles Approach Shot Drill, Standard Doubles Drill

Chapter 3: Midcourt Drill, Low Ball Doubles Drill, Offensive-Defensive Overhead Drill, Kill Drill, Lob Options Drill, Four Play Drill

These are the singles and doubles drills we feel are most important to your development at the 4.0 level. Each drill adds something to the way you played a certain shot or situation at the 3.5 level. This helps you identify the differences between the levels and improve upon them. So what are you waiting for? Get out there and practice!

The 4.5 Level

NTRP Guidelines

The verification guidelines for the 4.5-level player, as specified in the NTRP Guidebook, are as follows:

Groundstrokes—On the forehand side, you use speed and spin effectively and control depth well, but you tend to overhit on difficult shots. You're very dependable and are offensive on moderately paced shots. On the backhand side, you control the direction and depth of your shots but may break down under pressure. Furthermore, you hit with power on moderately paced shots.

Serve—You use power and spin. You're developing offense and serve aggressively with limited double faults. You frequently hit with good depth and placement on your second serve.

Volleys—You handle a mixed sequence of volleys, but your most common error is still overhitting. You have good footwork and are developing touch. On the backhand, you have depth and directional control.

Specialty Shots—You hit approach shots with good depth and control. You consistently hit volleys and overheads to end the point. Also, you frequently hit service returns aggressively.

Generally, you're hitting with more pace and have more intentional variety in your game. You're beginning to vary your tactics according to your opponent, and you cover up your weaknesses well. You also have good anticipation and are beginning to handle pace. In doubles, your teamwork is evident, and you're becoming more comfortable with the two-up formation.

OBJECTIVES

All but one of the 4.5-level objectives are merely extensions of those at the 4.0 level. The sole exception is a mental objective. This is important because you must play multidimensionally at the 4.5 level in order to win. The way to do this is to have as many ways as possible to beat your opponent.

Develop Consistency in Your Ability to Compete

This is a mental objective because it addresses your ability to assess and deal with all the various things happening in a match at one time. It becomes more important at the 4.5 level and above because there are so many ways to win a match. Players who have the determination it takes to find ways to win matches are usually the most successful. For example, there are thousands of players at the professional level who have beautiful strokes and can hit all the shots; however, only the best competitors end up in the Top 100. Competitiveness involves many factors. A positive attitude, a calm demeanor, good anticipation of shots, hustle, strategic insight, opponent assessment, and big-point toughness, are but a few of the traits a good competitor might have. If you want to make it through the 4.5 and subsequent levels, ask yourself if you compete well. If you don't, look at the previous examples and see if there's any area where you can improve. If none of those seems lacking, look at any other intangibles you might be having trouble with that fit into this category. If you're losing close matches against players at your level or higher and don't know why, this could be the solution!

Learn to Put Good Backspin on Your Volleys

Having good backspin on your volleys becomes increasingly important at the 4.5 level because the players hit low balls and passing shots better. If you put good backspin on your volleys, the ball stays lower to the ground because it slides through the court. Your opponent has a tougher shot because he's forced to hit up to the ball from the most difficult position possible in this situation. This translates into more easy, high volleys for you. To put good backspin on your volleys, you have to use the proper form. At this point, refer to the second key to success in chapter 2 to review the proper form for volleys. In addition to proper form, there are three keys to hitting the ball low on your volleys. First, keep the head of the racquet above the level of your wrist at all times. This prevents your racquet head from coming up to the ball, which keeps the ball from floating or popping up. Second, make sure you punch downward on high volleys. This makes the ball come straight off your strings to your target, causing it to slide through the court. Third, make sure you have a level "punch" on low volleys. This makes the ball come up off your strings enough to get it over the net, but not enough to make it float. If you check your overall form and concentrate on these three keys to keeping the volley low, you will improve the backspin on your volleys.

Learn the Inside-Out Forehand

This shot is used against players who have a mediocre to poor backhand groundstroke. To hit the inside-out forehand effectively, you have to move fairly well, which isn't a problem for singles players at the 4.5 level. In its simplest form, it's nothing more than running around your backhand to hit a forehand. The difference is that you always hit the ball to the ad court corner, gaining the advantage by pitting your forehand groundstroke against your opponent's weaker backhand stroke. This pins your opponent in the ad court corner and forces him to play defensively, because it makes it difficult for him to change the direction of the ball (i.e., hit the ball down the line). Thus, you can continue to hit the ball in the same direction (crosscourt) until he makes an error or hits a short ball that you can play more offensively by using one of your three offensive options for short balls. If you develop it properly, this shot can turn into a lethal weapon for you!

Learn the Topspin Serve

This serve is called the topspin serve because, after the ball clears the net, it dives into the service box and bounces high like a topspin groundstroke. It is a very valuable serve to have at the 4.5 level for three reasons. First, it's the most consistent serve there is, because it can clear the net by several inches or several feet and still land in the service box, depending on how you hit it. This greater margin for error and the increased consistency it provides are why the topspin serve is used mainly on second serves. Second, because the topspin makes the ball bounce deep into the court, it prevents your opponent from attacking you. Thus, she's forced to start the point from behind the baseline with a nonaggressive shot. Third, the topspin serve takes longer to reach your opponent because the ball goes higher over the net. This gives you more time to come to the net when you serve and volley. *Note:* You usually use this shot to serve and volley in doubles because your opponents have to play the ball right to you. However, it can be effective in singles against someone who has trouble with high balls.

To hit the topspin serve, you prepare the same way as for a regular serve, but you make two changes. First, change the culmination of your service motion. Instead of snapping over the top of the ball with your wrist, as you do on a flat or slice serve, snap up to the ball with your wrist to lift it over the net. The key to keeping the ball from flying over the fence is to close your racquet face on contact as you do for a topspin groundstroke (see figures 5.1 and 5.2, a-b). This gives the ball the same action it has for a topspin groundstroke, making it come back down into the service box and

Figure 5.1 Flat serve with the wrist snapping down at the ball after contact.

a

b

Figure 5.2a-b (a) Topspin serve with the wrist and racquet coming up to the ball at contact. (b) Closed racquet face on contact for topspin serve.

bounce high. Second, toss the ball at 12 o'clock instead of 1 o'clock (see figure 5.3, a-b). This puts the ball in a better position to swing up at it, making it easier to perform the topspin service motion. Since this serve is difficult to learn, we suggest you serve slowly at first until you get the feel of it, then speed up after you become more comfortable with the motion. This serve takes a lot of practice to perfect, so be patient.

Learn the Topspin Lob

This specialty shot is an extension of the topspin groundstroke we've already shown you. The difference is that you hit the ball higher in the air because you want it to go over your opponent's head and land behind him. To accomplish this, you do two things. First, you only hit the topspin lob on balls that bounce waist to chest high. This makes it easier to use your body to get the ball into the air and over your opponent's head. If the ball bounces below your waist, this shot is much more difficult to execute because you have to lift and spin the ball to get it over your opponent's head. Second, when

a

(continued)

Figure 5.3a-b (a) Toss at 12 o'clock.

b

Figure 5.3a-b *(continued)* (b) Toss at 1 o'clock.

you start your swing toward the ball, you swing upward at a sharper angle. On the groundstroke, you drive through the ball by accelerating the racquet at a 45-degree angle. On the topspin lob, you brush upward on the back of the ball by accelerating the racquet at almost a 90-degree angle (see figure 5.4, a-b). This causes the ball to arc higher than the regular topspin forehand and gives it enough room to go over your opponent's head.

It's also important to know when to hit the topspin lob. You hit this shot when your opponent is playing too close to the net. This is from the starting position or if your opponent is getting too close to the net on the approach. In either case, you'll have plenty of room in which to land the ball. This gives you a greater margin for error, which is important in hitting such a precise shot.

Now let's compare the topspin lob to the defensive lob. The difference between the topspin lob and the defensive lob is twofold. First, there's a difference in the ball's speed of ascent and descent. The topspin on the ball causes it to reach its peak and fall to the ground faster than the defensive lob. Second, there's a difference in the bounce of the ball. The topspin causes the ball to bounce away

Figure 5.4a-b (a) Topspin groundstroke follow-through. (b) Topspin lob follow-through.

from your opponent, as opposed to straight in the air, as with the defensive lob. Thus, there are advantages to hitting a topspin lob, but there's also a drawback. It is an all-or-nothing shot that is difficult to execute, because it requires a great deal of precision. If you don't hit the ball over your opponent's head, he usually wins the point with an easy overhead smash. On the other hand, when you do get the ball over your opponent's head, you usually win the point, because it goes over his head so quickly and bounces away from him. Therefore, to execute this risky shot properly, you must know how and when to hit it.

KEYS TO SUCCESS

The keys to success at the 4.5 level are much the same as at the 4.0 level in that you have to execute better in all areas of your game. More specifically, you have to add more aggressive shots to your repertoire. Also, you have to shore up and better disguise your weaknesses, because your opponents are better able to take advantage of them. In brief, you're eliminating your weaknesses and adding to your strengths.

Gain Confidence in Executing All the Shots You Learned at the 4.0 Level

Since these are the last of the basic shots that you need to learn, it's important to develop confidence in them because they help you round out your game. We didn't show you these shots at lower levels because they all pertain to how to play more aggressively, something you don't need to know at the lower levels. However, you do need these shots at the 4.5 level, because playing aggressively is a necessity. Once you have confidence in these shots, tennis really gets fun, because it becomes a matter of who can outthink whom.

Develop a Weapon

A weapon is the part of your game that is the strongest and that you feel most confident using. It's important to have something to go to in the clutch that gives you an edge on your opponent. This bolsters your mental toughness by helping you stay confident in important situations!

At this point, we suggest that you do an inventory of your game. If you don't already know what your weapon is, write down on a scale of 1 to 10 how strong you are at the following: forehand, backhand, serve, volleys, consistency, aggressiveness, and competitiveness. Now look at the numbers. Which are the highest? The areas with the highest numbers are the strongest part or parts of your game, those in which you have the most confidence. Therefore, you only need to polish these strengths to make them your weapons.

Notice that you can have two numbers that are high, but they usually go hand in hand. For example, in the case of a serve and volleyer, a good serve is usually accompanied by strong volleys. In the case of a player whose weapon is consistency, a good forehand and backhand are usually prerequisites. However, you don't have to combine two of the numbers to have a weapon. For example, you can simply have an excellent forehand that allows you to control a match. Steffi Graf is the prototypical example of this. She has a great forehand (her weapon), but she also doesn't have any weaknesses. Her lack of weaknesses is what keeps her in points until she gets a chance to use her weapon. Now let's regard Steffi Graf in a different light. Do you think that she would be one of the greatest women's players ever if she didn't have a great forehand? Our answer to that question is a definite no! She would be above average at best. That's why we say that, although you still need the fundamentals to eliminate your weaknesses, you must have a weapon.

If, after rating the parts of your game, you don't feel you have a weapon, work on developing one that is consistent with your strengths and is best for your situation. For example, if you like to play aggressively and play mostly doubles, work on your volleys to make them your weapons. If you like to play the baseline and play mostly singles, work on your groundstrokes to make them your weapons. There are plenty of options for developing a weapon, but remember that it should be best suited to your style of play and your situation, because you need to have confidence in it!

Improve Your Weaknesses

This is a preventive measure and is preferable to the fourth key to success—to cover up your weaknesses. At this level, it is fairly easy to identify your weaknesses, because you're good enough to analyze which part or parts of your game are causing you to lose matches. If you already know your weaknesses, begin to work on improving them. If you don't, do a quick inventory of your game, concentrating on four areas: (1) which strokes break down in your matches; (2) which shots give you the most trouble; (3) which styles of play give you the most trouble; and (4) problems with the fundamentals of strategy, such as hitting the ball deep. Once you identify your weaknesses, work on improving them.

Cover Up Your Weaknesses

If you haven't sufficiently improved your weaknesses, you have to cover them up. At the 4.5 level, players are smarter and can quickly figure out what your weaknesses are. Once they do, you're in for a long day, because they're going to play to them until you figure out a way to cover them up. When this happens, you often play your opponent's game and not yours, because you're forced to do things you don't normally do. In this situation, you have two options for reversing the trend of the match.

First, play to your opponent's weaknesses. This takes the pressure off you, because you keep the ball away from your opponent's strengths. It also gives you an opportunity to get back on the offensive, because you can attack your opponent's weak shots. When you do this successfully, you turn the match around and put the pressure back on your opponent.

Second, take away your opponent's strengths. This may or may not take pressure off you, depending on how you do it. For example, if your opponent volleys well and you're hitting weak passing shots when she attacks, beat her to the net. In this case, you keep the ball deep and attack the net on short balls and marginal balls (balls on which you might not normally go to the net). You might even consider serving and volleying to take away her attacking strength and put pressure on her passing shots. Your goal is to change the momentum of the match. If your opponent feels she can no longer win the match on the strength of her net game, the burden of winning shifts to the weaker part of her game. This takes the pressure off you if you play the net fairly well. If not, you've switched the pressure of the match from your passing shots to your net game, but it's still a positive change, because you're forcing your opponent to beat you in another way. And who knows? She might have been covering up her baseline weaknesses by coming to the net!

Use Your First Serve to Set Up the Point

How often have you watched a match on television where the players' first serve percentages are shown after each set? The reason for this is that it usually provides good insight into why one player is beating another. At the professional level, the first serve is an offensive shot and is used to set up points. Therefore, when you see a graphic that shows a player hitting 67 percent of his first serves into play, this means that he's immediately in control of two-thirds of the points he starts. And when a professional starts a point in control, he usually wins the point. That's why professionals hold serve so often and why holding serve is so important.

At the 4.5 level, your first serve must also be good enough that you control the point from the outset. At the 4.0 level, the objective was to improve your first serve by controlling and adding spin to it. At the 4.5 level, there are two differences. First, if you don't serve hard enough, increase the pace of your first serve. If you're using spin and hitting the three spots we showed you in chapter 4, but the ball is still being returned offensively, you fall into this category. Therefore, add pace, which turns those offensive service returns into defensive ones! Second, mix up your serve more. Since 4.5-level players have fewer weaknesses than 4.0-level players, you can't serve the ball to the same spot at the same pace with the same spin every time. You have to mix up your first serves so your opponent has to guess where you're going to serve. This rattles his confidence, because he can't get into a groove or rhythm on his returns. You're able to control the point better, because your opponent hits weaker service returns that you can play offensively.

Perfect the Strategies You Learned at Levels 3.5 and 4.0

In the two previous levels, we showed you in depth everything you need to know about the various strategies. The most important thing now is to use them wisely and execute them well, because you can ill afford to make strategic errors at the 4.5 level. If you do, your opponents will make you pay for them.

However, there's one strategic adjustment you can make, and that's in how you approach a match. At the 4.5 level, the tennis is more diverse and the players are smarter; therefore, you must analyze your opponent's game more quickly. You need to find out what weapons she has and discover her weaknesses and tendencies as soon as possible. This helps you formulate a game plan for each match early in the first set. If you don't do this, you'll often find yourself far behind before you figure out what to do. To better analyze your opponent's game, there are two things you can do.

First, assess your opponent's weapons, weaknesses, and tendencies by studying her during the warm-up. You do this by paying attention to her strokes. Check to see if she has a stroking strength or weakness. This gives you an immediate indication of which stroke to hit to and which stroke to stay away from. Also, check to see how well she plays the net. This gives you an indication of how she'll play during the match. If she volleys well, she's probably an all-out attacker or a player who attacks to mix up the points. If she doesn't volley very well, that's probably a weakness. Check to see if she likes to hit topspin or backspin. This gives you a clue as to whether your opponent likes to attack or stay back. Baseliners usually hit topspin, and attackers usually use backspin to attack.

Second, once the match starts, pay attention to your opponent's strategy. This is the same strategic approach we showed you in chapter 4; however, to help you recognize these tendencies more quickly, we put them in our quick tips format.

Quick Tips

Analyzing Your Opponent's Game

SINGLES

⊖ **Problem**—Your opponent is very aggressive and is winning points from you at the net.

⊕ **Solution 1**—Hit the ball deep on your groundstrokes. This keeps him back at the baseline and makes it harder for him to approach.

⊕ **Solution 2**—If solution 1 doesn't work (maybe your opponent is a serve and volleyer), hit your returns and passing shots lower over the net. This makes him hit more difficult volleys because he has to volley up from below the level of the net.

⊕ **Solution 3**—If solution 2 doesn't work, take the pace off the ball. This forces your opponent to hit a different kind of ball, one he may not be accustomed to, because he has to generate the pace. This challenges his ability to maintain his patience and form.

⊕ **Solution 4**—If solutions 1, 2, and 3 don't work, get to the net before your opponent. This takes away your opponent's strength and forces him to play a game he may not be comfortable with.

• •

⊖ **Problem**—Your opponent is a human backboard and is winning points from you at the baseline.

⊕ **Solution 1**—Don't try to do too much with the ball, because human backboards don't have much offense. This helps you cut down on your unforced errors, the weapon human backboards beat you with.

⊕ **Solution 2**—Be patient and wait until you have a good ball to hit offensively. This ensures that when you attack, you have a good chance of winning the point, because you set it up properly.

⊕ **Solution 3**—If solutions 1 and 2 don't work, attack the net. This puts pressure on your opponent, because he has to play very precisely to pass you, hit at your feet, or lob over you.

• •

DOUBLES

⊖ **Problem**—Your opponents are very aggressive and are winning points from you in the two-up formation.

⊕ **Solution 1**—Hit the ball deep on your groundstrokes. This keeps them on the baseline and makes it more difficult for them to get to the net.

⊕ **Solution 2**—Go to the net before your opponents do. This takes away their strength and forces them to play a different game that they may not be comfortable with. It also gives you the edge, because you're in a position to play more aggressively.

⊕ **Solution 3**—If solutions 1 and 2 don't provide you any relief, hit your returns and low-ball shots lower over the net and to the middle. This forces your opponents to play the ball from below the level of the net and to hit the difficult shot in the middle.

⊕ **Solution 4**—If solution 3 doesn't work, lob the ball deep to get your opponents off the net. This gives you a better chance of hitting the ball low to their feet (if they return to the net after hitting the shot) or attacking them by advancing to the two-up formation (if they don't).

• •

⊖ **Problem**—Your opponents are winning points from you in the one-up, one-back formation.

⊕ **Solution 1**—Go to the net. This takes away your opponents' offense and forces them to play defense from a less than optimum position.

⊕ **Solution 2**—If solution 1 doesn't work, play the one-up, one-back formation with your baseline player focusing on hitting the ball deep to set you up at the net. This gives you a chance to play offense, because you can poach and fake at the net.

⊕ **Solution 3**—If solutions 1 and 2 don't work, play the two-back formation. This gives you a way to defend against your opponents' successful execution of the one-up, one-back formation.

• •

⊖ **Problem**—Your opponents are human backboards and are winning points from you in the two-back formation.

⊕ **Solution 1**—Be patient against the two-back formation, which includes all the formations from which you play. This ensures that you wait for the right shot to play offensively and takes away their biggest weapon—waiting for you to miss.

⊕ **Solution 2**—Go to the net. This puts you in the most aggressive formation you can play against the two-back formation.

⊕ **Solution 3**—Play the ball to the middle. This opens up the outsides of the court for you to attack from the net or the baseline.

⊕ **Solution 4**—If solution 2 doesn't work, play the one-up, one-back formation. This leaves you with one player at the net in an offensive position.

These quick tips help you quickly assess your opponent's strategy and zero in on what strategy to employ to play successfully against them!

PRACTICE DRILLS

At the 4.5 level, you must continue to focus on improving your offensive skills. You must add new shots and improve the shots you already have. The following singles and doubles drills help you accomplish these goals.

Singles Drills

The following singles drills focus on improvement of your offensive and / or defensive shots in specific areas of your game.

Inside-Out Forehand Drill

In this drill, both players start in the middle of the court, 1 yard behind the baseline. The drill is be done between two right-handers or two left-handers, not between a right-hander and a left-hander, because you don't want to run around your backhand to hit the ball to your opponent's forehand. Player A hits the ball down the middle to start the drill. Player B then hits the ball to player A's ad court (backhand side for right-handers). When player B hits the ball crosscourt, you, as player A, have two options. The first (and preferred) option is to run around your backhand and hit a forehand to player B's backhand. The alternative option is to hit a backhand to player B's backhand. If you're successful in performing your first option, cheat over to the backhand side so you hit the next return with a forehand to player B's backhand. Continue to hit forehands until the point ends. If you're forced to use the second option, both players continue to hit the ball crosscourt until one of you is successful at the first option. Then you hit forehands for the remainder of the point. In the beginning, this drill takes patience, because you're trying a new shot. It also takes a while to learn when to hit an inside-out forehand and when to hit a backhand. But once you get the hang of it, it's a cinch! Do this drill for 10 minutes.

Topspin Lob Drill

In this drill, one player starts in the back third of the service box in the middle of the court and the other 1 yard behind the baseline at the center mark. Player A starts the drill with a feed to either of the corners, and player B retrieves the ball and hits a topspin lob over player A's head (see figure 5.5). After player B hits the topspin lob, play out the point. As player A, you practice your overheads and running down balls that are hit over your head. As player B, you get a feel for hitting topspin lobs and a chance to practice hitting them in a game-type situation. Remember, this shot isn't effective if you don't get it over your opponent's head. So if you make an error, make sure you err on the deep side. After 5 minutes, switch places and drill for 5 more minutes.

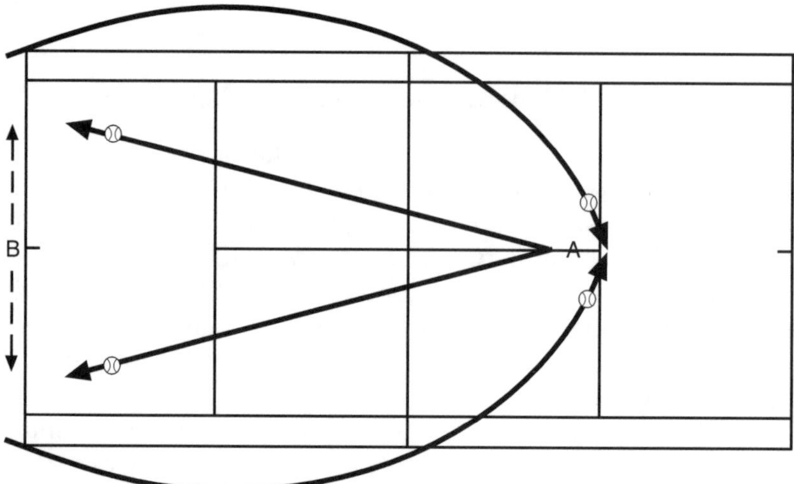

Figure 5.5 Topspin Lob Drill with player A feeding a ball in either corner to player B, who returns it with a topspin lob.

Singles Serve-Volley, Serve-Return Drill

In this drill, one person starts in the singles serving position and the other starts in the standard return position. Player A, the server, starts the drill and has to serve and volley on first serves. As player A, you practice three things. First, when your opponent starts to hit the ball, practice split-stepping. This gives you the balance you need to shift either way with the return. Second, after you make your first volley, practice following the ball. This helps you position yourself properly for the next shot. Third, practice volleying the ball into the open court. This gives you practice moving your opponent and taking advantage of your opportunities. As player B, you practice returning the ball at your drilling partner's feet and hitting passing shots, your only options against a serve-and-volley player.

If player A misses her first serve, she stays back, and player B must attack her second serve. When you attack player A's second serve, you have the same options and do the same things you did in the Attack the Second Serve Drill in chapter 4. After 7 minutes at one position, switch and play the other position.

Alley Drill

In this drill, both players start on the same side of the same alley on opposite sides of the net, 1 yard behind the baseline. Player A starts the drill by hitting a forehand straight into the alley, and player B returns a backhand the same way (see figure 5.6). You continue to rally until someone hits the ball outside the alley. After drilling for 5 minutes on one stroke, switch alleys and practice the other stroke. This is an excellent drill for the down-the-line shot, because it narrows your focus.

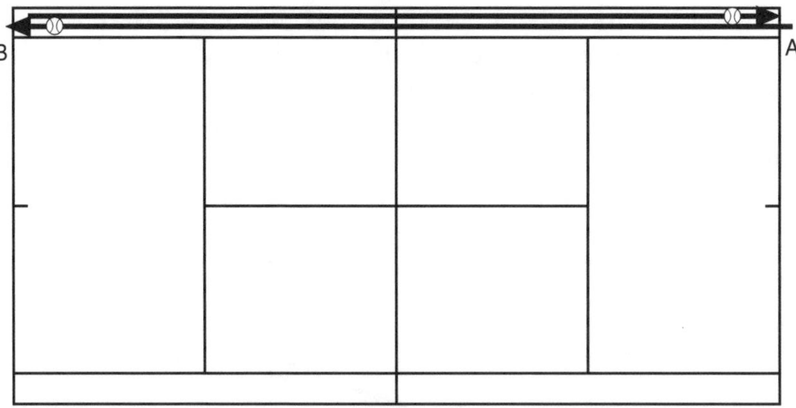

Figure 5.6 Alley Drill with player A feeding a forehand down the alley to player B's backhand, after which they rally the ball in the alley using the same strokes. The drill is the opposite for the other alley.

Other Drills That Still Apply

Chapter 2: High Ball Drill, Recovery Drills, Directional Movement Drill, Approach Shot Drill

Chapter 3: Approach Shot Combination Drill, Defensive Baseline Drill, Low Ball Singles Drill, Defensive Lob Overhead Drill

Chapter 4: Topspin-Backspin Drill, Passing Shot Drill, Two Approach Drill, Deep Volley Drill

Doubles Drills

In doubles at the 4.5 level, you have to continue improving your offensive and defensive skills and strategy. The following drills will help you accomplish this by working you in these areas in match-type situations.

Return-Chip Drill

In this drill, one player starts in the doubles returning position and the other on the opposite half of the court, on the service line halfway between the centerline and the doubles line. Player A starts the drill by serving the ball into the opposite box. Player B has to return the serve by driving or chipping the ball, depending on how hard player A hits it. Once player B returns the ball crosscourt, play out the point, using the doubles line and the extended centerline as boundaries (see figure 5.7).

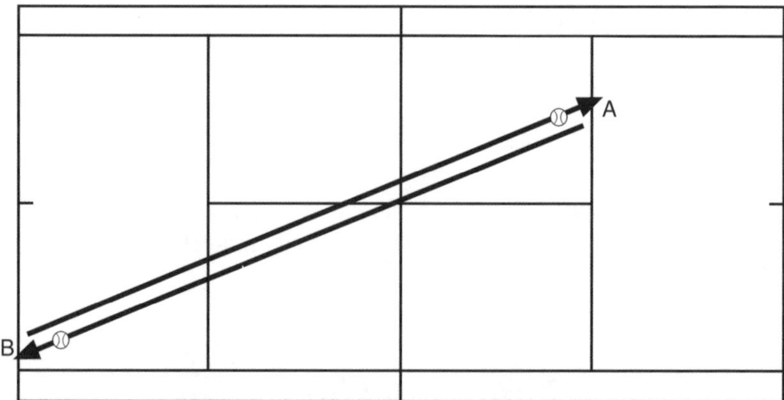

Figure 5.7 Return-Chip Drill with player A serving from the middle of the service line to player B, who either drives or chips the return back to the feet of player A (depending on the speed of the serve).

As player A, work on hitting over the ball on the feed, which helps improve your serves and overheads. Also, when player B returns the ball, work on your first volley, a key shot at this level. As player B, work on deciding whether to drive or chip the return, a critical decision that you must make against a serve-and-volley player. Also, work on keeping the returns low. After 7 minutes, switch and try the other position.

Poach, Fake, and Pass Drill

In this drill, both teams start in an offensive one-up, one-back formation and remain in the offensive position throughout the drill. One baseline player starts the drill with a crosscourt feed to the other. Once the ball is in play, they have two options. They can return the ball crosscourt or hit a passing shot down the alley; but they can't lob the ball. The net players also have two options. They can either fake that they're going to poach or they can poach, but they can't just stand around waiting for something to happen.
As the baseline players, work on keeping the ball away from the net person by hitting the ball crosscourt and by hitting the passing shot down the alley when the net players are out of position. As the net players, work on faking to get the baseline players to hit you the ball and timing your poaches so they don't pass you. To make this drill more interesting, use the 3-2-1 scoring system. If you win the point with a clean winner (volley or groundstroke), you score three points. If you poach and force your opponent to miss, you score two points. And if you win the point from the baseline or from an error, you score one point. After one game to 21 points, the baseline and net players switch, and you play another.

Take the Net Drill

In this drill, one team starts in the two-back formation and the other in the two-up formation. The two-back team starts the drill with a feed to the two-up team, which then volleys the ball back. After this exchange, play out the point with an emphasis on the two-back team taking the net from the two-up team. As the two-back team, concentrate on taking the net away from the two-up team by approaching as a team on short volleys or on lobs hit over the two-up team's heads. As the two-up team, concentrate on keeping the net by volleying the ball deep and hitting offensive overheads. Play to 11 points using the 2-1 scoring system. The two-back team scores two points every time they take the net and win the point, with all other points won scoring one point. After one game to 11 points, switch positions and play another.

Defensive Block Lob Drill

In this drill, one team starts in the two-back formation and the other in the two-up formation. Team A, players A and B, starts the drill with a short lob to team B, players C and D, one of whom then smashes the overhead at or near one of the players on team A. The players on team A lob the ball by blocking it (shortened backswing with a long follow-through) (see figure 5.8, a-b). After team A lobs the ball back, continue in the same sequence of shots (see figure 5.9). As team A, work on blocking the lob to get one more ball back into play. This a shot you need at the 4.5 level because 4.5 players

a

Figure 5.8a-b (a) Short backswing for the block lob.

b 

Figure 5.8a-b (b) Long, high follow-through.

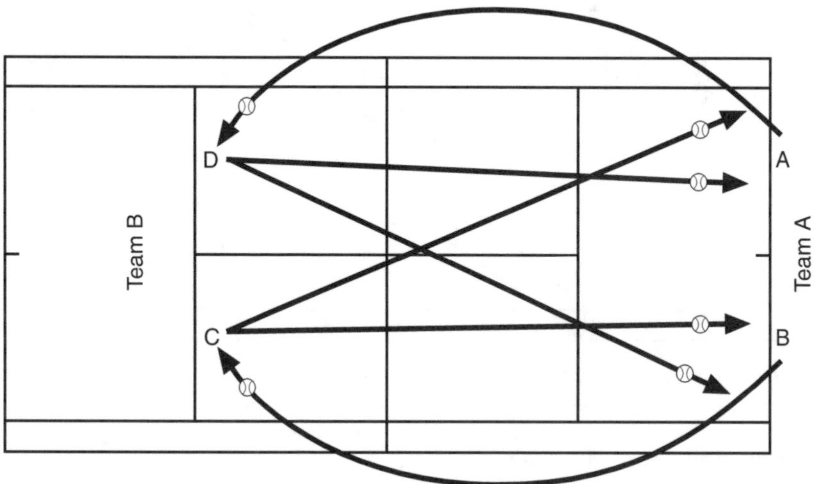

Figure 5.9 Defensive Block Lob Drill with team A (players A and B) feeding a short lob to team B (players C and D), which hits overheads at or near team A. Team A is practicing block lobs.

hit their overheads harder, giving you less time to prepare. As team B, work on placing your overheads. After 5 minutes on one side, switch and try the other side.

Groundstroke Angle Drill

This drill can be done with two or four players, but you make better use of your court time with four. In this drill, both players start with their right foot on the singles line of the deuce court, halfway between the baseline and the service line. Player A starts the drill with a short feed into the deuce court alley. Player B returns the forehand crosscourt and short into the deuce court alley. Then both of you continue to hit the ball crosscourt and short into the alleys (see figure 5.10). This drill works your angle groundstrokes, which give you another way to attack your opponent at the 4.5 level. After 5 minutes to one side, switch and try it to the other. Remember to hit the side of the ball with your arm between you and the net, just as we showed you for the angle volley.

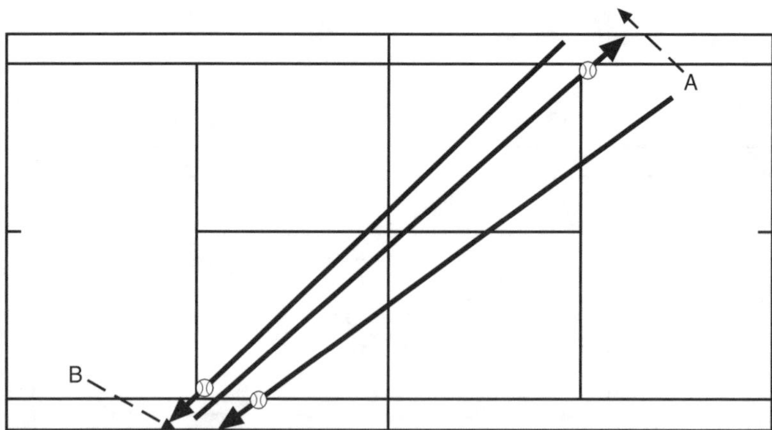

Figure 5.10 Groundstroke Angle Drill with player A feeding a short, wide groundstroke to the deuce court alley of player B, who hits a groundstroke short into the deuce court alley of player A. They continue to rally forehand crosscourt angles until someone misses.

Other Drills That Still Apply

Chapter 2: Recovery Drills, Standard Doubles Drill

Chapter 3: Midcourt Drill, Low Ball Doubles Drill, Offensive-Defensive Overhead Drill, Kill Drill, Lob Options Drill, Four Play Drill

Chapter 4: Serve-Volley, Serve-Return Drill; Angle Volley Drill; Doubles Deep Volley Drill; Three-Look Approach Drill; Attack One-Up, One-Back Drill; Attack Two-Back Drill; Middle Drill

These are the singles and doubles drills we feel are most important to your development at the 4.5 level. Each new drill helps you build on what you've already learned in earlier chapters by directing your focus to the new areas that need attention. This makes for more efficient use of your practice time because it gets right to the point. So what are you waiting for? Get out there and improve that tennis game!

The 5.0 Level and Beyond

© Ron Angle

NTRP Guidelines

The verification guidelines for the 5.0-level player, as specified in the NTRP Guidebook, are as follows:

Groundstrokes—Your forehand is a strong shot that features control, depth, and spin. You use the forehand to set up offensive situations, have developed good touch, and are consistent on your passing shots.

Serve—You have a large variety of serves on which to rely. You place your serve effectively with the intent of hitting to your opponent's weaknesses or creating an offensive situation. You force weak returns or set up your next shot by using good depth, spin, and placement on your second serve.

Volleys—You hit most volleys with depth, placement, and direction and play difficult shots with depth. When given the opportunity, you hit volleys for winners.

Specialty Shots—You hit approach shots and passing shots with pace and a high degree of effectiveness. You lob offensively and hit overheads from any position. You hit midcourt volleys with consistency and mix aggressive and off-paced service returns.

Generally, you're "match wise," play percentage tennis, and "beat" yourself less than the 4.5-level player. You vary your game plan according to your opponent and frequently have an outstanding shot or attribute around which your game is built. In doubles, you have solid teamwork.

As you can see from the previous description, for the most part you have all the shots at the 5.0 level. You might not be great at all of them, but you have them all. This is where the three main differences between 4.5- and 5.0-level players lie. First, at the 5.0 level, you have more shots with which to beat your opponent. This obviously gives you more and better ways to play offense and defense. Second, you execute the shots and strategies better than at the 4.5 level. This makes your game more diverse because you play all areas of the game. Third, you're a better mental player because you're "match wise," an important trait because the first two differences make the 5.0 level more involved. It's no longer who has the best shots; it's who can figure out how to win. It's who can figure out

how to exploit their opponent's weakness or weaknesses. It's who can play to their strengths and cover up their weaknesses the best. These are the three main differences between the 4.5 and 5.0 levels.

Generally, at the 5.5 level you hit dependable shots and serves in stressful situations and have developed good anticipation. You can pick up cues from such things as your opponent's toss, body position, backswing, and preparation. You analyze and exploit your opponent's weaknesses and have developed power and / or consistency as a major weapon. Furthermore, you vary your strategies and style of play in competitive situations.

This is the level at which good teaching professionals play. At this level, it usually comes down to who has the bigger game, who is more confident, and / or who is the smarter player.

From the 6.0 to the 7.0 level, you're competing among players who don't need NTRP ratings because their rankings or past rankings speak for themselves. At the 6.0 level, you've typically had intensive training for national competition at the junior and collegiate levels and have obtained a national and / or sectional ranking. At the 6.5 level, you have extensive satellite tournament experience (semiprofessional) and have a reasonable chance of succeeding at the 7.0 level. At the 7.0 level, you're a world-class player who is committed to tournament competition on the international level and whose major source of income is tournament prize winnings.

About the Authors

Chris Dazet (left) and Brett Schwartz (right).

Brett Schwartz and **Chris Dazet** are experts on the USTA's NTRP rating system, having more than 12 years experience as USTA certified verifiers between them. They've worked with or coached teams that have played at every level of the USTA league, sending teams to the district and sectional playoffs.

Schwartz is the assistant men's tennis coach at Louisiana State University. He is the former director of tennis at Tops'l Beach and Racquet Club in Destin, Florida.

When not involved in tennis, Schwartz enjoys golfing, fishing, reading, and writing.

Dazet is the director of tennis at Bocage Racquet Club in Baton Rouge, Louisiana. He has verified or rated more than 8,000 players through rating clinics and local and state tournaments.

When he's away from tennis, Dazet likes to fish and travel.

More tennis titles from Human Kinetics

Reaching peak fitness for competition

USTA's Complete Conditioning for Tennis
(25-minute videotape)
United States Tennis Association
1997 • Item MUST0918 • ISBN 0-88011-918-7
$24.95 ($37.50 Canadian)

Practical, cutting-edge advice to help your team excel

Coaching Tennis Successfully
United States Tennis Association
Foreword by Stan Smith
1995 • Paper • 200 pp • Item PUST0461
ISBN 0-87322-461-2 • $19.95 ($29.95 Canadian)

Strengthen yourself, strengthen your game

Power Tennis Training
Donald A. Chu, PhD
Foreword by Todd Martin
1995 • Paper • 176 pp • Item PCHU0616
ISBN 0-87322-616-X • $14.95 ($19.95 Canadian)

To request more information or to place your order, U.S. customers call
TOLL FREE 1-800-747-4457.
Customers outside the U.S. place your order using the appropriate telephone/address shown in the front of this book.

HUMAN KINETICS
The Information Leader in Physical Activity
http: // www.humankinetics.com /